Teacher/Student Responsibility
in Foreign Language Learning

PETER LANG
New York • Washington, D.C./Baltimore • Bern
Frankfurt am Main • Berlin • Brussels • Vienna • Oxford

Beverly-Anne Carter

Teacher/Student Responsibility *in* Foreign Language Learning

PETER LANG
New York • Washington, D.C./Baltimore • Bern
Frankfurt am Main • Berlin • Brussels • Vienna • Oxford

Library of Congress Cataloging-in-Publication Data

Carter, Beverly-Anne.
Teacher/student responsibility in foreign language learning / Beverly-Anne Carter.
p. cm.
Includes bibliographical references and index.
1. French language—Study and teaching—Foreign speakers.
2. Languages, Modern—Study and teaching. I. Title.
PC2066.C37   448'.071—dc22   2005017860
ISBN 0-8204-8131-9

Bibliographic information published by **Die Deutsche Bibliothek**.
Die Deutsche Bibliothek lists this publication in the "Deutsche
Nationalbibliografie"; detailed bibliographic data is available
on the Internet at http://dnb.ddb.de/.

© 2006 Peter Lang Publishing, Inc., New York
29 Broadway, New York, NY 10006
www.peterlang.com

Printed in Germany

To my family: my husband Bill, my sons Marc, Gérard, Chris, and Peter, my mother Barbara L. Francis and my aunt Jean L. Providence, with thanks for their love, inspiration and unfailing support.

Table of Contents

Preface

This book is the published version of my Ph.D. dissertation completed in 2001. Although the references have been updated to include some recent work on learner autonomy, the text of that dissertation remains basically unchanged.

Publication of this book was made possible with a grant from the Campus Research and Publication Fund Committee, University of the West Indies, St. Augustine, Trinidad and Tobago.

I wish to thank Dr. Elaine K. Horwitz for permission to use an adapted version of the Beliefs About Language Learning Inventory (BALLI) in this book.

I am indebted to a number of people who helped either with the original dissertation or with this book. My colleagues in the Faculty of Humanities and Education have been very supportive. I thank them for this. My particular gratitude is due to my dissertation supervisor and mentor, Dr. Ian E. Robertson, whose vision of the possibilities often far exceeded mine. I would like to express my appreciation for the encouragement, support, and friendship of Kathi Bailey, Leni Dam, Jeanette Morris and Zena Moore. I would like to thank my students who have helped me to become the teacher that I am. My present or former students, Vanessa Williams, Sujin Huggins, Shanti Liverpool, and Daniela Jodhan made important contributions to editorial work on this manuscript. Marsha Pearce is due my particular thanks for her patience and care in typesetting the manuscript. Finally, special thanks to the acquisition and production staff of Peter Lang Publishing, in particular, Sophie Appel, who enabled a dissertation written far from the centres of power to be turned into a book in the public space.

Chapter One

UNDERSTANDING AND ANALYZING THE UWI FRENCH LANGUAGE STUDENT

What follow are the results of a naturalistic/interpretive study on learner autonomy conducted among a group of first-year undergraduates who were advanced learners of French.

1.1 Background to the Research

What skills do language students need for the 21st century? The question of appropriate curriculum is uppermost in my mind as I try to meet students' French language needs during their three years in the undergraduate program. Ten to fifteen years ago, many of the students who wished to study foreign languages at the University of the West Indies, St. Augustine, entered with a solid command of grammar and an appreciation of French literature. The majority of these students were bound for a traditional language career.

Many of the assumptions about the traditional language student no longer hold. A change in the curricular focus at secondary level, from grammar in the lower levels and literature at higher levels, to communicative competence as the primary goal of all language learning, has had a major impact on the skills and competencies of today's language students. In an age of satellite television and the Internet, students relate to foreign languages and cultures differently from the time when images of the target language and its culture were conveyed chiefly by textbooks and literary works. The question remains, how do university level teachers of French equip their students with skills to meet their language learning needs in an era characterized by unpredictability and constant change?

There is no current research that documents whether the shift in curricular goals or the environmental factors referred to above have in fact given rise to a new kind of language student. But my colleagues and I, who have taught successive generations of students, note that today's language students are likely to be more fluent, but less accurate; and while they may have more experiential knowledge of French and Francophone culture, they possess less mastery of critical literary skills.

The goals of today's foreign language students are also likely to be different from those of their peers of an earlier generation. While some foreign language students still aspire to traditional language careers—as interpreters, translators, or foreign language teachers—many do not. Like their peers in other countries, as John (1990) notes, the majority of students in our classes conceive of their first degree in languages as a stepping-stone to a postgraduate degree in a non-language field. These students wish to work as foreign-service officers, public-relations practitioners, or specialists in tourism or marketing. In addition to the traditional-age students (the 18-21 year olds who enter university shortly after secondary school), mature students with different backgrounds and different goals add a new note of diversity and complexity to the population of first-year students.

What first motivated me to begin this research was a need to gain a better understanding of incoming French language students. Who are the first-year language students? Why have they decided to continue foreign language study beyond the secondary level? What do they hope to accomplish during their undergraduate language career and, above all, how could I best support their foreign language learning?

Issues of content and methodology are often the starting point for research in classroom-based acquisition. However, in the case of the learners in this study, neither the prism of content nor methodology seemed the most appropriate route to explore their foreign language learning. In addition, while both behavioral and mentalist accounts of acquisition have yielded rich insights into the phenomena of language and second language acquisition (SLA), relying chiefly on either of these strands of linguistic research has meant that the social and cultural dimensions of language acquisition have been given somewhat short shrift. Indeed, neither behaviorist nor cognitive perspectives seemed to have sufficient explanatory power for how these advanced learners were proceeding with their acquisition of French as a foreign language after seven years of classroom exposure.

My decision to use new techniques and new concepts to investigate factors that might be significant to the students' acquisition seemed in keeping with a current thrust in linguistic research. According to Davis (1995, 432), current research interest in SLA seems to be moving beyond the perspective of acquisition as a "mental individualistic process" and seeking to include an analysis of the larger socio-cultural context in which acquisition takes place. This research stance seemed appropriate as I tried to make sense of the phenomenon that I encountered in exploring students' attitudes to their language learning.

My experience as a teacher in the French program since 1991 and the insights gained from reading several semesters' pre- and post-course questionnaires meant that I was not starting the research completely unaware of what I might discover. I had some knowledge of the kinds of problems, linguistic and non-linguistic, with which students grappled. Of particular concern to me was the fact that many students, particularly the traditional-age students, had difficulty in making the transition from a fairly structured school environment to the relative freedom of university. I was also concerned that many students seemed to have no clear short-term or long-term goals for their language learning. Many had come to university because it was what their parents or teachers expected, rather than because of any intrinsic motivation to continue their learning. They therefore needed to be coaxed into taking charge of their learning.

Some students reacted differently to higher education. For them, their time spent at university was the final hurdle before real life could begin. They tried to complete their course of study as quickly as possible, anxious to embark upon the after-university, post-learning, real world. Neither set of students seemed to have a "qualitative involvement" (Tudor 1996, 18) in their learning. They seldom wanted to take the initiative in their learning, being content to do only what was necessary to meet course objectives. I was convinced that these attitudes were detrimental to students' growth as advanced language learners. It was the prevalence of such attitudes that convinced me of the need to conduct research among first-year French language students.

In coming to the problem addressed by this study, the question of teacher and student responsibility in language learning, I grew to realize that the difficulties that incoming students faced could not be defined solely in linguistic terms. Although the poor grammar mastery and inadequate writing skills of some of these advanced learners were a cause for concern, similar to what Bushell (1995) has noted in the British context, even those students who possessed a higher degree of proficiency, judging from their Cambridge General Certificate of Education (GCE) Advanced Level results, were not immune to some of the non-linguistic problems identified above. It became evident that the way to meet students' needs did not lie solely in giving them more content information or more language practice to meet their perceived deficiencies. Indeed, the students' linguistic difficulties were compounded by what appeared to be difficulties in learning. Many advanced learners of French seemed unable to function as truly advanced learners.

My involvement in a teacher-training program for trainee teachers of English as a Second Language forced me to reexamine some of my assumptions about the role of teachers. I began to reflect on the need to support my students' learning, for I began to understand that my view of my role and responsibility had perhaps prevented me from developing a better understanding of the problem.

Although such attitudes are now changing, I think that many university lecturers[1] see their primary responsibility as supplying content information. I often heard colleagues making complaints that reflected my concerns about the students—surface learning, no critical thinking skills, too passive, too teacher-dependent—yet few of us recognized the need to include in our content-specific information, information on learning how to learn. I think that, as university lecturers, we cling to two assumptions: the first connected to our perceptions of our role; the other linked to the students' role. Thus, although we recognize our students' learning deficiencies, we often do not see it as part of our responsibility to help them learn how to learn. Furthermore, we sometimes operate on the mistaken belief that by *withdrawing* support, we can nudge our students into being more autonomous (see Dam 2003, for a good discussion of the teacher's responsibility in autonomy). Mainly though, I think, we assume that students who have "made it" to higher education, have, by so doing, demonstrated their fitness as students: they know how to learn. The paradox is that many "good" students are in fact poor learners. They may be cue-oriented and may have learned test-taking skills, but they are fundamentally ill equipped to manage their own learning.

In reassessing my role as a lecturer in French, I realized that my responsibility to improve my students' proficiency fulfilled only part of my responsibility to them. I had an equal responsibility to improve their learning. I needed to reflect on the implications of this new responsibility. I had always seen my role in terms of providing language support for my students until they were capable of assuming that role for themselves. I am not sure at what point in my teaching career I developed this attitude, although it certainly dates back to the twelve-year period during which I taught French at the secondary level. I remember an article[2] written by a former student, a participant in a student exchange to Martinique over twenty years ago. This article began with an account of our arrival in Martinique and highlighted my behavior as the students entered the target language culture for the first time. According to this student's account, I deliberately stood back and encouraged them to negotiate on their own, the immigration procedures, and therefore, their first experiential contact with French language and culture. My presence gave them the confidence to try to negotiate the language for themselves but I made it clear that the onus was on them.

Coming across this article many years later, I was struck by this student's account of her first contact with the French language and the role I played in it. I was somewhat surprised at this student's story, because I had not realized that I had been a proponent of learner autonomy that far back. But reflecting on this article led me to consider the kind of supportive role that I needed to adopt toward my students' learning. Unless I gave my present students an appropriate level of scaffolding and supported their *learning* skills as I have traditionally supported students' *language* skills, I could not expect them to have the confidence to assume responsibility for their learning, nor be prepared to negotiate their learning independently of me.

My need to explore more fully this new insight about my responsibility for my students' learning led me to the literature on learner autonomy, particularly contributions by Holec (1981, 1987, 1997); Boud (1988); and Little (1991, 1996, 1999). According to the literature, autonomous learners have the capacity to assume responsibility for their learning. This was what I desired in my French students—the capacity and a willingness to accept ownership of their learning, without needing to be coerced or cajoled into doing it *for* or *because of* me. I wanted them to develop a "qualitative involvement" in their learning.

But autonomy, I discovered in the literature, had twin focuses: students' learning autonomy and their linguistic autonomy. In teaching for autonomy, one is expected to attend to students' learning autonomy alongside their linguistic autonomy. I had found empirical support for my intuition about the need to shore up my students' learning. It seemed that students' learning autonomy was an important part of their overall autonomy as language learners. Thus, not only was it advisable to integrate a focus on learning into my focus on language learning but it was essential that I do so.

From my present vantage point, it seems naïve that I needed the authorization of the literature on autonomy to confirm my teacher's instincts that my students required more learning support. At the time I simply felt a sense of liberation that I was not neglecting my primary responsibility as a teacher of language, in seeking to improve my students' learning.

My hesitation in making a focus on students' learning explicit in my teaching is not surprising given my earlier statement that language teaching has traditionally been preoccupied with appropriate methodology and the transmission of linguistic content. Whether the teacher viewed her teaching as art, or science, her major responsibility was to be an efficient instructor. However, linguistic research has pushed back the boundaries to reveal a more dynamic mix of factors affecting the teaching and learning of foreign languages. Coming to grips with language learning as a phenomenon dependent on biological, cognitive, and social variables has challenged researchers and teachers to address students' learning differently. As contributions to Freed (1991) document, researchers have been striving for a better understanding of the variety of factors that promote or hinder language learning in order to uncover what goes on inside the "black box" (Long 1980, 3) of the language classroom. A more holistic view of the multitude of factors that can promote or impede classroom-based acquisition can only enhance our understanding of second or foreign language (L2) acquisition. It is this holistic view of language learning that this study embraces.

The final issue that I wish to address as I present the background to this study is the impact of contextual factors on students' (language) learning. The students in this study share a common educational background as products of the same educational system. Moreover, like all entering students in French, they have been exposed to a minimum of seven years of classroom-based acquisition. In a study that sets out to explore students' attitudes and beliefs, and more precisely to explore how these attitudes and beliefs relate to their conceptions of teacher and student responsibility in (language) learning, I think it is necessary to highlight some contextual factors that may have shaped these attitudes and beliefs.

I believe that the students' perceptions of themselves as (language) learners are to some extent linked to their previous educational experience. Linguists such as Stern (1983), and more recently van Lier (1996), and Robertson (1996), who are proponents of educational linguistics, emphasize that language learning cannot be divorced from the wider educational context in which languages are acquired. Support for embedding acquisition in the socio-cultural context in which it occurs (Davis 1995) also comes from educational researchers such as Erickson (1986). Both these perspectives provide compelling reasons to examine the context of students' foreign language learning.

1.2 Some Contextual Factors that Frame
the Teaching and Learning of French

1.2.1 The Role of Public Examinations
The students in this study have been schooled in an educational system that sets great store by public examinations. They have had their learning formally assessed at three stages (at 11+, at 16+, and at 18+) by centrally controlled public examinations. One consequence of this is teachers', students', and the wider public's preoccupation with achievement as measured by examination success, often to the detriment of broader educational goals. The focus on examination success is exacerbated by the

fact that these examinations are used as placement examinations, leading to a phenomenon of "high-stakes testing" (Parris 1998, 189). Although, high-stakes testing is not confined to Western contexts, Pierson (1996), for example, explores the issue in Hong Kong, Greaney and Kellaghan (1995) argue convincingly that high-stakes testing is a common feature of public examinations in developing countries. Trinidad and Tobago, the site of this study, is a developing country. The authors explain the complex wash-back effect on the educational system when priority is given to high-stakes testing. Greaney and Kellaghan maintain that not only is achievement defined by examinations, but they see a far more detrimental narrowing of the curriculum to lower-order cognitive skills—at the expense of higher-order skills and practical skills—and a reduction of the learning content, even in pre-examination classes, to what is likely to be tested in the examination.

It is not difficult to imagine that in such a scenario, learning is seldom associated with the development of analysis, evaluation, and the acceptance of personal responsibility for learning, the kind of higher level learning skills deemed so important in higher education. But there is another negative outcome of the phenomenon of high-stakes testing and that is an over-reliance on the teacher as authority. What will be valued in a system premised on high-stakes testing are instructional approaches that place the responsibility for learning firmly within the hands of experts, be they teachers, private tutors, or even textbook publishers. It is almost as though learning were too important a responsibility to be confided to mere learners. As a result, students come to rely heavily on the guidance of the subject teacher or private tutor to steer them to success.

Furthermore, notwithstanding the attempts by some teachers to free students from the fixation with public examinations and to encourage more student-centered approaches, students and their parents often prefer very didactic, teacher-directed approaches, which they feel are more likely to result in examination success. A system such as the one described above will quite likely under-value student autonomy. The implications of this, for teaching and learning in all subject areas and at all levels, from primary to higher education, cannot be disregarded.

Yet the importance attached to high-stakes testing in this educational system provides, I believe, only a partial explanation of the attitudes and behaviors demonstrated by tertiary level French language students. Equally salient to understanding the student of French in this educational context is the socio-cultural context in which language learning, in general, and French language learning, in particular, are grounded. Thus, the second factor which merits some discussion as an important environmental factor that impinges on the attitudes, beliefs and behaviors of students, is the role of French as second foreign language in the curriculum.

1.2.2 The Role of French as Second Foreign Language

French is the second foreign language (L3) offered at the secondary level of education in this country. Historically, French played an important role in the linguistic background of Trinidad. Its status as a language of colonization assured it a preeminent role in the legislative, cultural, and religious life of the colony (Carrington, Borely, and Knight 1974). Even more recently, the popularity of French-lexicon Creole, the lingua franca in Trinidad[3] up to the early part of the 20th century, meant a continuing sensitivity to the lexifier European language. French-Creole, called *patois* locally, survives intact in small pockets even up to today, and though the *patois*-speaking population has shrunk considerably, the English-based Creole spoken in Trinidad is strongly influenced in a number of areas, including its lexicon, phonology, and syntax, by *patois* (Solomon 1993).

These factors may seem to suggest a natural place for French as a heritage language and the first foreign language in the curriculum. However, this is not so. Spanish, by virtue of Trinidad's proximity (fifteen kilometers) to Venezuela, and because of trade and social links between this country and its Spanish-speaking neighbors is the official first foreign language. Other factors, for example, the decision to make Spanish the compulsory foreign language in state-owned secondary schools; the psychological and geographical distance between Trinidad and Tobago and the French Caribbean islands; and the perceived difficulty of French as compared to Spanish have all led to French being relegated to second foreign language.

Yet, for all the official and public neglect, French has managed to survive and flourish[4] in the schools[5] where it continues to be taught. French teachers continue to stress the importance of French language learning and continue to communicate their love of the language to their students. French teachers seem to bring to their task, a zeal and a level of devotion that make French a popular subject in those schools where it is part of the curriculum. Data from diaries which students kept during this study revealed that the students' affective response to French is very strong.

Another factor that has supported the learning of French has been the role played by the French Embassy, through its many outreach activities, for over thirty years. The Embassy has provided a range of human and material resources that have made a positive impact on French language learning. These resources have contributed to keeping French alive and making it a viable alternative in foreign language education. Both the Embassy's efforts and the secondary school teachers' approach to wooing students to French have underscored the humanistic dimension of language learning, particularly in the emphasis on feelings, including personal emotions, and aesthetic appreciation (Stevick 1990).

The peculiar circumstances that surround French language teaching and learning have resulted, somewhat unfortunately, to my mind, in French language learning, being viewed in a restricted sense, more as a bridge to the target culture and less as a competency for a future career. Although, historically, this was what ensured the survival of French in the educational system, I think that to continue to cling to the received wisdom that Spanish is necessary and French, something of an indulgence, is detrimental to foreign language learning in this country. This study's exploration of the attitudes and beliefs of French language students will perhaps force stakeholders to address the issue of language learning, holistically, to ensure that, in the future, foreign language education does not take place *à deux vitesses*. New attitudes need to be cultivated to transcend the two-tier system of language learning that now obtains.

1.2.3 The Role of Technology
This brief analysis has drawn attention to two factors linked to the students' previous educational experience that are contributory to the attitudes and beliefs which students bring to their tertiary level study. The last factor is unconnected to students' previous educational experience, but, I think that its potential for framing the kind of language learning to which students will be exposed implies that it will be intimately linked to their future as language learners. That factor is the role of technology in students' language learning.

Many possibilities now exist for students to improve their proficiency via activities like tandem learning. E-mail and the Internet signal new ways of closing the gap between foreign language learners and target language communities. Increasingly, though, it is becoming clear that the promise of new technologies stems not only from the fact that they enable new tasks and promote new approaches to language learning, but also from the fact that they engender new ways of learning.

Given that this study explores how teachers and students assume responsibility for learning in the foreign language classroom, it is important to consider the integration of new technologies into language learning in contexts such as this one. It is likewise important to reflect on the potential of new technologies to change the teacher-student dynamic in language learning.

I feel that students who experience difficulty in making the transition from a very teacher-directed learning environment, to one where self-directed learning is valued, will be even more hard-pressed to function in a technology-supported learning environment. Indeed, a point that is often

stressed in the literature on educational technology is that new technologies
are premised on the active participation of learners in their learning. Barbot
(1997) defines this conceptual shift in the following terms:

> L'apprenant s'implique dans son apprentissage et investit en fonction de la
> rentabilité de son projet ... L'irruption de l'apprenant comme acteur de la formation
> ... modifie les relations humaines dans le système éducatif. (57)

> [The learner (in a technology-supported environment) becomes more involved in
> her learning and commits herself to the learning task based on the expected
> outcomes ... When the learner becomes an active participant in her learning the
> nature of human relationships in the education system is profoundly changed.]

It is because of my belief that technology will provide the backdrop
against which foreign language learning will be played out in the coming
decades, that this study, which looks at learner autonomy in foreign language
learning, assigns a significant role to technology. I agree with those (e.g.
Gaspar 1998) who contend that human society is on the cusp of a new age.
We are entering a transitional period that will eventually see the demise of
the factory-model classroom, partly as a result of the forceful entry of
technology into learning. Teachers will need to adopt new perspectives and
find new ways of being in a technology-supported learning environment. It
will no longer be enough to teach new things, it will become imperative to
teach in new ways.

As teachers, we must also reflect on Gardner's (1993) thesis that the
pace of change and the exponential growth of knowledge now make it
impossible to acquire all the world's extant knowledge. This argument, I
think, has special significance for language teachers. In the pre-
communicative competence era, there was the certainty that language
teachers could provide complete coverage of the foreign language in our
teaching. Communicative competence put paid to that illusion. The futility of
attempting to do the impossible has led to a more realistic outlook on what
language teachers can and cannot accomplish in their teaching. Technology
promises to push us farther down the road of relinquishing more of the
responsibility for learning to our students. Boud (1988b, 25) suggests that it
is the dynamic nature of present society, requiring learners to adapt to
frequent change and requiring them "to learn new forms of knowledge and
how to use that knowledge" that makes autonomous approaches so
necessary. Many commentators posit that education in an era of
technological change must be grounded in different premises. It seems that
students who can take away from our teaching a better understanding of how
they learn will have the tools to help them navigate the vast store of
knowledge that modern technology puts at our fingertips. Technology can, in

a best-case scenario, democratize knowledge. Teachers can no longer be knowledge brokers and gatekeepers in an open-market knowledge economy. Teachers need to position themselves elsewhere, in the knowledge equation. They need to be "re-placed" in teaching (Wolfe 1993, 179).

A change in the teacher's role and responsibility prefigures a change in students' role and responsibilities, according to Wright (1987). Students would need to adopt some of the responsibilities that would have traditionally been the teacher's in instructional approaches premised on teacher management of learning. If students have fairly traditional expectations both of the teacher's responsibility in their learning and of their own responsibility in learning, the shift from teacher-directed language learning to self-directed language learning would need to be the object of special focus in classroom practice.

This study, which relied on a qualitative/interpretative methodology, focused on how students conceptualized the role of the teacher and learner in foreign language learning, in order to discover whether students would be prepared to accept more responsibility for their learning. An important aspect of the study was exploring whether students had any beliefs that might affect their willingness to become autonomous.

This study sought to answer several research questions in order to explore the concept of learner autonomy. These questions addressed the concept of autonomy by exploring students' attitudes to the assumption of responsibility for learning. The questions posed were the following:

- What are the students' conceptions about responsibility in language learning?
- What do they think are the teacher's responsibilities?
- What are students' responsibilities?
- What in students' view is the nature of language learning and how is their view of language learning related to the role they are prepared to assume in learning?
- What does it mean to be an autonomous learner?
- How do the students interpret their role in language learning after the intervention to promote learner autonomy?

This study drew on data elicited from first-year students of French as a foreign language during the 1997/98 academic year. It was the major component of a Learner Autonomy Project (appendix A), which formed my doctoral research. The Learner Autonomy Project (LAP) engaged students in a number of activities intended to promote learner autonomy. The activities were of two types:

A. Projects such the production of a students' guide for French-speaking students enrolled in the English as a Second Language program at the University of the West Indies, St. Augustine and a grammar work-book for the students' own immediate use, but which could be used by their peers in subsequent years. These data were not included in the study;

B. Activities to encourage students to reflect on their learning and to clarify the meaning of autonomy, for example, learner diaries and a beliefs inventory. The data analyzed were drawn mainly from the diaries and the beliefs inventory.

There are two limitations to the research that need to be addressed here. The first concerns the use of technology. When I began this research, I had hoped to integrate computers into my French writing and grammar classes. This would have allowed me to explore the relationship between technology and autonomy within the context of my teaching. The students' guide and the grammar workbook, referred to above, were to have been produced in class on networked computers.

Unfortunately, a number of problems arose which made it impossible to integrate computers into my teaching, in the way that I had planned. At the time, this innovation was not yet a part of our teaching/learning practice and my efforts to document its introduction and integration were stymied by a number of insurmountable problems linked to the availability and security of the small number of computers that were available for language teaching and learning. This also meant that I was unable to collect observational data on students' learning with computers, as had been my intention. Nonetheless, I think that although only out-of-class learning[6] with technology was possible, the data that I collected were still valuable in helping me explore the link between technology and autonomy.

A second limitation of this research relates to the use of the qualitative paradigm. As the research is qualitative and interpretative, other researchers may interpret the findings in different ways. It is also possible that the use of a software package for qualitative data analysis may have produced different results from those obtained with manual sorting of the data. However, I have included what I hope are sufficient quantities of qualitative data to enable readers to judge whether the data support the interpretations that I make.

I think that the research is significant for a number of reasons, despite these limitations and others that will be discussed, at greater length, in chapter 3. It is significant because it enabled students to be participants in research about their own learning and to develop a greater understanding of themselves as learners. This I believe is a good thing, because it underscores the need for learners to be active participants, to develop that qualitative involvement in their own learning.

The primary aim of the research was, as I stated earlier, to help me gain a better understanding of advanced French language learners in this institutional context. This too must be seen as significant given the paucity of research on L2 acquisition in tertiary level language learners in Trinidad and Tobago.

This research can also inform subsequent research on environmental variables that affect advanced learners of French, as well as allow for comparisons between advanced learners of French and advanced learners of Spanish. There is also a clear need for studies of this kind in view of the thrust in foreign language instruction for non-specialist[7] language learners at the campus where I teach. Ideally, there must be a body of empirical research to help us devise the most appropriate methodology (Holliday 1994) for specialist and non-specialist learners in this social context.

Finally, the major significance of the research reported here must be in its contribution to the sub-field of learner autonomy. Like many proponents of learner autonomy, I think that learner autonomy is a good thing. However, much more research is needed to add to our knowledge of learner autonomy and autonomous language learning in different contexts. I hope that this study can make such a contribution. This study will, I hope, provide an understanding of learner autonomy in this social context and inform the wider debate on autonomy, by adding a Caribbean dimension to what is known about promoting learner autonomy among language learners.

NOTES

1. Lecturer is the generic term used here to refer to all teachers in higher education as in the UK.

2. Kathryn Birchwood, "Martinique, je t'aime." St. Joseph's Convent, San Fernando, School Magazine 1982: 14.

3. Solomon explains that socio-linguistically Tobago did not present the same picture.

4. Statistics from the Caribbean Examinations Council (CXC), the Regional Examinations body, indicate a steady increase in the number of Trinidad and Tobago candidates registering for French in the first ten years (1986-1995) of the examination. Figures for 1999, the latest available at the time of the study show that, in that year, 37% more candidates wrote the examination than in 1986.

5. French is taught mainly in "assisted" schools. Assisted schools are faith-based schools that receive two thirds of their funding from the state. These schools are nonetheless public schools open to students of all/no religious persuasion. French is taught to a lesser extent in fully state-owned/state-funded schools.

6. Some students had personal computers or used the computers in the campus's main library.

7. A Centre for Language Learning caters for the language learning needs of non-specialist language students.

Chapter Two

A REVIEW OF THE LITERATURE PERTAINING TO LEARNER AUTONOMY

The review of the literature begins with a brief overview of General Linguistics as the discipline within which this study is located. Next, the literature review discusses Learner Autonomy, which is the specific sub-field within Applied Linguistics that allows me to contextualize the discussion on teacher and student roles and responsibilities. The central concept of responsibility guided this study and shaped the research questions. Much of the literature review is therefore devoted to exploring the concept of responsibility, as it is discussed in the literature on Learner Autonomy.

But, responsibility is not a unitary concept; it is multifaceted and depends to some extent on the conceptions that teachers and students hold about their space in the teaching and learning process. Finally, therefore, I shall review a small number of studies that relate to the role of learners' beliefs in language learning, in order to explore how learners conceptualize their responsibility in language learning in accordance with their belief system.

2.1 Linguistics: The Centrality of a Disciplinary Focus

Linguistics is the source discipline that provides L2 acquisition research with a theory of language. Modern linguistics, with a focus on language in its synchronic or static form, eclipsed the nineteenth-century focus on historical philology. It was the Swiss linguist, Saussure (1965), the father of modern linguistics, who first suggested that a synchronic study of language could complement the comparative, historical approach that prevailed up to that time. Modern linguistics, like most fields of scientific enquiry, continues to be characterized by periods of steady growth of the dominant theory, followed by an infusion of new theoretical perspectives, resulting in the introduction of alternative approaches and alternative perspectives to the dominant approach.

In the 1940s and 1950s, structuralism, the dominant linguistic school of the era, drew heavily on the then dominant paradigm in scientific enquiry. Brown (1987, 8) remarks that a focus on the "rigorous application of the scientific principle of observation of human languages" came to characterize research conducted by proponents of this school. The Saussurian dichotomy of *parole* vs. *langue* was strongly rejected by the psychologist Skinner (1957) for Skinner argued that only overtly observable behavior, Saussure's *parole*, could be investigated. Structuralism or descriptive linguistics also implied the careful description of human languages and the identification of the structural characteristics of these languages. Thus, another legacy of this period was a significant body of research on the morphology and phonology of natural languages.

The generative-transformational school of linguistics with Chomsky (1982) as its leading proponent rejected the scientific stance of the behaviorists. Stern (1983) refers to the heyday of the mentalist approach as a period of upheaval, for Chomsky's hypotheses could not be reconciled with the mechanistic behaviorist approach that underpinned Bloomfieldian (1933) structuralism. Whereas structuralists considered the surface structure of language to be important, Chomskyan theory underscored the deep structure of language and posited the existence of a genetically endowed language acquisition device that was creative and generative. By drawing on their innate language acquisition device, speakers could process language at a far more sophisticated level than would be possible if they were constrained to responding to language in a behaviorist way.

The generative-transformational school influenced linguistic theory in yet another way, for an investigation of the deep structure of language meant that two hitherto under-explored fields of linguistic enquiry, syntax and semantics, were brought into sharper focus. Although, Chomsky's theories were later challenged by theories that drew on a more social view of language, modern linguistics owes to Chomsky a focus on the mental processes of language acquisition. Chomsky's theory of government and binding and his elaboration of the concept of universal grammar became critical to the investigation of the psycholinguistic processes of SLA and ultimately led researchers to rethink how language learning could be enhanced.

This very brief overview of two of the major schools of thought in modern linguistics has condensed a long and complex evolution. The primary focus here is to establish the linguistic context in which this study must be situated. What these two vignettes of modern linguistic theory aim to show is that the scientific study of language has been enriched by quite different theoretical concepts and techniques. These theories and techniques have at times complemented one another. At other times, the distinction between the theoretical concepts and techniques has been as stark as the contrast alluded to above between behaviorism and cognitive psychology. However, the pertinent factor continues to be the contribution made by these sometimes quite differing approaches to our overall understanding of a theory of language, and by extension, to a theory of language learning and teaching. Indeed, in the absence of some kind of dedicated research into how language works and the ways in which language learning and teaching can be facilitated, the discipline would lack a theoretical base and consequently the appropriate tools to analyze what Lodge (2000, 112-13) calls "the complexity and mysteriousness of natural languages."

Current linguistic research continues to improve our understanding of the systemic nature of language. Investigation into language as a system has meant a clearer understanding of the phonetics and phonology, morphology and syntax and semantics of natural languages. But the contribution of linguistics has not been confined to these traditional areas of enquiry. Lodge (2000, 121) refers to the "enormous progress" that has been made since the 1960s in both psycholinguistics and sociolinguistics. Psycholinguistics, or research into acquisition, production and processing, has provided the bridge between a general theory of learning—psychology—and linguistics. Sociolinguistics, for its part, has been instrumental in elaborating a theory of language use in society.

To sum up, whether the object of enquiry has been aspects of our biological nature, such as the age, or sex of the speaker; or whether scrutiny has turned to the influence of our social nature on the process and product of acquisition, linguistic enquiry has contributed to a better understanding of the phenomenon of language and the intersecting domains of language learning and teaching. To reiterate, linguistics is the broad discipline that provides the framework for arriving at a theoretical understanding of learning and teaching of first or subsequent languages.

2.2 Learner-Centered Approaches

Foreign language education has additionally been influenced by instructional approaches that filter in from the wider curriculum. Thus, foreign language education has not been immune to the shift in the instructional focus in the classroom. Where before the focus was on a transmission model of teaching and the chief concern was with the provision of content information, curricular approaches are now giving equal, if not primary focus, to the place of learning and the role of learners in the instructional process. The label "learner-centered approaches" reflects the change of perspective inherent in this paradigmatic shift. According to Lambert and Mc Combs (1998, 9), since a learner-centered approach marries a focus on individual learners and a focus on learning, learners must be viewed in a holistic way, i.e. "their history, the environment, their interests and goals, their beliefs", if we hope to have them engage more fully in their learning.

This concern with making instruction more appropriate to learners is not a new one among language educators. Stern documents how reactions against the "method concept" (Stern 1983, 109) in the 1970s spurred a number of new developments in language education. In Europe, van Ek's (1975) Functional-Notional Syllabus took learner needs, rather than structural analysis, as the starting point for syllabuses. In North America, the impetus for more focus on the learner was thought to derive from two sources. On one hand, educators sought to woo learners back to foreign language learning, because the removal of the foreign language requirement had led to declining enrolments. On the other hand, the focus on the individual language learner was in response to a much larger societal phenomenon. A feeling of dissatisfaction and disenchantment among young people gave rise to a period of general student unrest between 1968 and 1972. Educators were forced to adopt curricula that took as their starting point learner needs, rather than teaching objectives. The result was the introduction of new approaches that focused on the individualization of language teaching (see for example, Altman 1970-1971, 1972-1973; Disick 1973; Hanzeli and Love 1971-1972; Phillips 1976). The curriculum emphasis in Europe and the human relations emphasis in North America were just two of the strands that contributed to the increasing focus on the learner's perspective in language learning. Language learning research was also a contributor, particularly Naiman et al.'s (1978) research documented in *The Good Language Learner*.

The renewed focus on learner needs seems once again the confluence of a number of trends in language education. Skehan's (1989, 1991) work on individual learner differences, Moskowitz's (1978, 1999), and Stevick's (1990) writings on humanism in language teaching; and work on learning strategies (O'Malley and Chamot 1990; Oxford 1990; Wenden 1991; Wenden and Rubin 1987) have led to a fresh round of interest in "more learner-centered and participative models" (Candlin 1991, xi). These models focus generally on adapting instructional practice to meet learners' needs, or on the adoption of different curricula for different learners.

A learner-centered model of teaching, then, is another way of organizing teaching to be more inclusive of the learner. Nunan (1988) posits that a key concept in a learner-centered curriculum is that it focuses on the collaboration between teachers and learners. Ultimately, teacher-learner collaboration implies new roles for the teacher. Teachers should show flexibility in response to learners' needs and teaching should be structured to promote self-direction on the learners' part (Tudor 1996). The redefinition of teachers' roles is to be accompanied by a parallel redefinition of learners' roles, for learners in the learner-centered classroom are to be active agents of their own learning. It is still the teacher, however, who assumes primary responsibility for the instructional process, for it is she who controls the learning process, albeit while encouraging greater learner participation. Thus, while learner-centered approaches represent a considerable shift away from transmission models of teaching, the locus of control for teaching and learning still lies mainly with the teacher.

Kohonen (1999) lists seven dimensions (table 2.1) according to which teaching and learning models can be categorized as belonging to more traditional approaches (teaching as transmission[1]), or at the other end of the continuum, as belonging to experiential (i.e. learning by doing) approaches (transformative learning). While generally, learner-centered approaches are situated on the experiential approach/transformative learning end of the continuum, there is one important "assumption in instruction" among the seven identified by Kohonen (1999, 281) that is not usually stressed in learner-centered approaches. Most learner-centered approaches stop short of giving learners control of the process of their learning. Research has shown, however, that it is important that learners be agents of their own learning for a number of reasons.

Table 1: A teaching/learning model adapted from Kohonen (1999)

ASSUMPTIONS IN INSTRUCTION: SOME DIMENSIONS	EXPERIENTIAL APPROACH: TRANSFORMATIVE LEARNING
1. Dominant conceptions of learning	Socio-constructivistic and humanistic theories of learning
2. Power relation and teacher's role orientation	Partnership, teacher to facilitate learning (mainly in various cooperative groups); teachers working in collaboration
3. Learner's role	Active participation, both alone and in cooperative teams

Continued on next page

Table 1 – *Continued*

ASSUMPTIONS IN INSTRUCTION: SOME DIMENSIONS	EXPERIENTIAL APPROACH: TRANSFORMATIVE LEARNING
4. View of knowledge and curriculum	Construction of personal knowledge in process; dynamic, looser curriculum organization
5. Learning experiences and outcomes	Emphasis on process: self-esteem, learning skills, social and communication skills
6. Control of process and motivation	Learner in charge; self-organized learning; internal locus of control, intrinsic motivation
7. Evaluation	Process-oriented; authentic assessment; reflection of process, self-assessment; criterion-referencing

A second reason why the control of process and motivation should be included in any learner-centered approach comes out of research into autonomy and motivation (Dickinson 1995). While learner-centered theory provides a partial answer to facilitating learners' involvement in their learning, learner autonomy seems more promising to address both the issue of learners' involvement in their learning, and learner role and responsibility in the classroom (table 2.2). Dickinson contends that three key concepts in learner autonomy, namely, learner independence, learner responsibility, and learner choice are also identified as central to motivation in the literature on cognitive motivation.

In his review of the literature on autonomy and motivation, Dickinson cites research conducted by Wang and Palinscar (1989). According to these researchers, learners who accept responsibility for their own learning success feel a sense of competence when they are successful; moreover, this sense of success enhances their competence, and ultimately their motivation.

Dickinson's arguments about the efficacy of learner autonomy are also premised on research by Deci and Ryan (1985) into intrinsic motivation. The findings of this research suggest that intrinsic motivation results in more effective learning and that it is promoted in cases where the locus of control rests with the learner.

Finally, Dickinson reviews studies on attribution theory (e.g. Child 1994). Attribution theory examines learners' perceptions of the causes of their past successes or failures, how their perceptions of these causes affect their expectations, and the influence of these expectations on future performance (Arnold and Brown 1999).

Dickinson draws the following conclusions based on the research reviewed:

> learning success and enhanced motivation is conditional on learners taking responsibility for their own learning, being able to control their own learning and perceiving that their learning successes or failures are to be attributed to their own efforts and strategies rather than to factors outside their control. (174)

In summary, an ideal learning situation for learner growth and development seems to be one that not only encourages the personal involvement of the learner through her collaboration with the teacher, but, moreover, one that supports the learner as decision maker, organizer and controller of her learning. Hence, learning is promoted where the locus of control, i.e. the belief that events that one experiences are under one's own or internal control, rather than under the control of other people or outside forces, rests with the learner (Wittrock 1986).

Table 2: A comparison of learner-centered and autonomous approaches based on the seven dimensions identified by Kohonen (1999)

EXPERIENTIAL APPROACH: TRANSFORMATIVE LEARNING	LEARNER-CENTERED APPROACHES	AUTONOMOUS APPROACHES
Socio-constructivist and humanistic theories of learning	✓	✓
Partnership, teacher to facilitate learning (mainly in various cooperative groups); teachers working in collaboration	✓	✓
Active participation, both alone and in cooperative teams	✓	✓
Construction of personal knowledge in process; dynamic, looser curriculum organization	✓	✓
Emphasis on process: self-esteem, learning skills, social and communication skills	✓	✓

Continued on next page

Table 2 – *Continued*

EXPERIENTIAL APPROACH: TRANSFORMATIVE LEARNING	LEARNER-CENTERED APPROACHES	AUTONOMOUS APPROACHES
Learner in charge; self-organized learning; internal locus of control; intrinsic motivation	x	✓
Process oriented; authentic assessment; reflection of process; self-assessment; criterion-referencing	✓	✓

2.3 Learner Autonomy

Proponents of autonomy stress that autonomy is not a new concept. Furthermore, they warn that autonomy should not be seen as the latest "method" in language teaching. This point needs to be made, given what Maley (1984) sees as the discipline's tendency to jump on bandwagons, to accept uncritically, and to see salvation in the most current approach to language teaching. It is clear, nonetheless, that autonomy has been gaining more adherents recently. Little (1991, 1) addressing this issue says that autonomy has attained the "buzz-word" status enjoyed by communicative and authentic in the 1980s.

The new urgency in exploring how learner autonomy can promote better learning is not only a phenomenon of language teaching, but seems to be a part of the general dissatisfaction with a transmission model of teaching and its inappropriateness to contemporary society. Both Cranton (1994) and McLaren (1999) call for an approach to learning premised on transformative action, the very antithesis of the "banking concept of education in which the scope of action allowed to students extends so far as receiving, filing, and storing deposits" (Freire 1972, 46). Knowles (1988) argues that the assumptions about the traditional purpose of education are no longer valid in the dynamic era in which we live. He makes a compelling case for lifelong learning, since it is no longer possible for people to function for the rest of their lives on the store of knowledge acquired by the end of the period of formal schooling. In short, he advocates a different kind of curriculum, one that focuses on learning "how to" in the early stages of higher education, with a gradual shift to self-directed learning in subsequent phases.

Autonomy as discussed in this literature review is premised on the learner assuming responsibility for her learning. Most definitions of learner autonomy include the assumption of responsibility as a key concept, as for example, the three cited as follows:

The main characteristic of autonomy as an approach to learning is that students take some significant responsibility for their own learning over and above responding to instruction. (Boud 1988b, 23)

[autonomy is an] ability to take charge of one's own learning... an ability ... not a type of conduct ... (Holec 1981, 3)

Essentially, autonomy is a capacity - for detachment, critical reflection, decision-making, and independent action. It presupposes, but also entails, that the learner will develop a particular kind of psychological relation to the process and content of his learning. (Little 1991, 4)

Thus, while most learner-centered approaches seem to focus on the teacher making her teaching more effective, autonomous approaches tend to speak directly to the learner and her learning.[2] This has led to some criticism that approaches to autonomy do not see a role for the teacher in the instructional process. It is a fact that some approaches to autonomy envisage the possibility of learners learning independently of a teacher; but the absence of a teacher is not a defining feature of autonomy.

Much of the research into autonomy (Boud 1988a; Broady and Kenning 1996a; Holec 1981; Holec and Huttunen 1997; Wenden 1991) has underscored the need for teachers to embrace new roles. Consequently, far from having a reduced role, teachers are expected to have an expanded role, for the necessity of providing scaffolding as students become autonomous—given that students are seldom ready or willing to assume responsibility for their learning—cannot be underestimated. Cotterall (1995); Knapper (1988); and Knapper and Cropley (1991) all emphasize this point.

This discussion of teacher and student roles and responsibilities is therefore grounded in an approach to learner autonomy. Not only does the L2 acquisition literature on learner autonomy emphasize the primacy of learner responsibility, learner independence, and learner choice, as students become agents of their own learning, but, somewhat paradoxically, the bond between teachers and students in the transition to autonomy is often stressed. When we consider that the integration of technology is both premised on, and expected to lead to, less teacher involvement, we can conceive of the difficulty in achieving the right balance between teacher and student roles/responsibilities in an autonomous approach that integrates technology.

2.4 Defining Autonomy

As I stated earlier, autonomy has long been an important goal in education (see Benson and Voller 1997a; Boud 1988b; Candy 1988). Its origin, as Broady and Kenning (1996b) point out, however, is as a legal-political term. The multiple definitions of autonomy reveal that like Canale and Swain's (1980) definition of communicative competence, autonomy is a very broad term, and that a working definition of autonomy is perhaps the first issue we need to address when trying to promote autonomy. Oxford (2003, 75) underscores this point, arguing that autonomy "is still beset by conflicting ideologies, roiling inconsistencies, and fragmentary theories," adding further, "even the most basic terminology is full of semantic conflicts." The multiplicity of terms and ideologies is undoubtedly at least partly due to the fact that unlike communicative competence, autonomy cannot be defined in purely linguistic terms, because of its political, psychological, and social overtones.

2.4.1 The Versions of Autonomy
Critical pedagogy theorists argue that the adoption of certain radical political ideals into education is often to their detriment, resulting in their being "domesticated" (McLaren 1999, 51), stripped of their essentially social and political overtones. Pennycook (1997, 40) insists that this is what has happened to autonomy. He argues that the mainstreaming of autonomy has led to its transformation from a "more radical social and political concept ... to ... an issue principally of individual development, learner strategies and self-access."

   Benson and Voller (1997b) express a similar concern. They claim that it is sometimes difficult to recognize autonomy as a "product of socially liberating education" from the way it is practiced in some classrooms (5). They contend that, frequently, classroom-based autonomy has lost its concern with freeing learners from external control and giving voice to their communicative agendas. But these educators, like other critical pedagogues, argue that freedom from external control is the right of the individual and, hence, the practice of autonomy in the classroom must support that right. One objective of education should be to empower learners and help them adopt a critical stance to issues of power and authority. Language learning, as one aspect of education, can help to accomplish these ideals. Furthermore, the exercise of the learners' autonomy must not be confined to the classroom, so that learners must be encouraged to "pose their own problems through the second language" and make the link between classroom autonomy and autonomy in the world at large (Pennycook 1990, 311).

A second version of autonomy sees autonomy as primarily a psychological concept. Psychological versions of autonomy are premised on a view of knowledge, which contends that "social reality is constructed by the individuals who participate in it" as "individuals gradually build their own understanding of the world through experience and maturation" (Gall, Borg, and Gall 1996, 18). Consequently, a psychological/constructivist approach stresses learner autonomy in the classroom, shared responsibility between teacher and learner, and the joint construction of knowledge. Autonomy is viewed as both process and product, according to this perspective.

A psychological/constructivist approach to autonomy is seen by some as a step beyond the technical/positivist approach, which is traditionally concerned with teaching learners strategies to provide them with the tools to become autonomous in the period after their formal instruction. Autonomy in the latter perspective is therefore a goal, the product of classroom learning, but it is never actualized in the classroom. As a result, learners assume full responsibility for their learning only in the period following the end of their formal study.

Benson's (1997, 18) contention that there are three "versions" of autonomy implies that learner autonomy will be manifested differently in different contexts. Those who subscribe to a view of knowledge as an objective reality will favor technical versions of autonomy, i.e. passing on to learners the technical ability to learn on their own. Where knowledge is viewed as a socially constructed reality, psychological versions of autonomy will prevail e.g. the concept of each learner's idiolect. Finally, if knowledge is seen as "competing ideological versions of … reality expressing the interests of different groups" (Benson 1997, 22) political versions of autonomy will be preferred e.g. autonomy as a means to help students create "insurgent voices" (Pennycook 1997, 49) and enable "empowerment" (Kenny 1993, 431).

Although the classification suggested by Benson can help us to have a firmer basis for evaluating the different approaches to autonomy (see Oxford 2003, for a typology that introduces four perspectives on autonomy), Benson is careful to add that it is unlikely that proponents of autonomy set out to implement a technical, or psychological, or political version.[3] In a very general sense, though, the way in which learner autonomy is conceptualized in European contexts relates most closely to a psychological/constructivist approach to autonomy. Whereas, the North American tradition in strategy research (O'Malley and Chamot 1990; Oxford 1990; Wenden 1991; Wenden and Rubin 1987) has resulted in a more positivist/technical orientation to work conducted there.

In practice there is seldom, if ever, pure versions of autonomy, since most proponents of learner autonomy draw on key concepts from the three versions. Thus, Holec, for example, though a proponent of learner autonomy as a psychological construct, assigns an important role to learner training in learning how to learn. Holec's vision of autonomy also has clear social and political consequences. Holec (1981, 34) dismisses the possibility of autonomy and self-direction as only classroom-based phenomena: "Can an individual 'live' in a state of partial autonomy such as would relate solely to his learning of languages in a general environment of dependence and passivity?" While Wenden (1987) though best known for her research into learner strategies, argues strongly for the inclusion of a psychological component in strategy training for autonomy. She thinks that students must "become critically reflective of the conceptual context of their learning" and that

> Facility in the use of self-instructional techniques must be accompanied by an internal change of consciousness. Otherwise, attempts at strategy training will meet resistance and be doomed to failure. (12)

In this study, the discussion on learner autonomy draws mainly on the conceptualization of autonomy by Holec (1981); and his associates Moulden (1980, 1990, 1993); Gremmo and Riley (1995); and Riley (1989, 1997a, 1997b). Holec's definition of autonomy stresses the distinction between autonomy as a capacity (the ability to take charge of one's learning) and self-directed learning, i.e. learning conducted on an autonomous basis. He draws an analogy between an autonomous learner and a person who knows how to drive. But, just as someone who knows how to drive may opt to drive or not drive on occasion, so too the autonomous learner can opt for self-directed learning or other-directed learning as she sees fit. This explains why, according to Holec, the defining characteristic of the fully autonomous learner is that she is not only capable but also confident and willing to engage in self-directed learning.

There is one important limitation, however, in trying to adopt Holec's conceptualization of autonomy and that is that the context that has inspired Holec's conceptualization of autonomy is quite different from the context where I plan to integrate autonomy. It is unlikely that the CRAPEL model of autonomy can be transplanted wholesale into my classroom situation (A number of recent works explore the interface between culture and autonomy. See Benson, Chik, and Lim 2003; Holliday 2003; Palfreyman 2003; and Smith 2003 on the issue of culture and autonomy). The learners at the CRAPEL are usually self-selected, mature learners (cf. Moulden 1993) who are likely to be responsive to a practice inspired by andragogy. Although these learners may not have acquired the capacity to be autonomous in the course of their previous schooling, they are usually highly motivated and understand the value of acquiring language proficiency for integrative or instrumental reasons in a multilingual Europe. They are therefore willing to engage in a practice, which supports their personal and societal goals. In many ways, these learners are quite unlike many of the students in my classroom, whose motivation for further study is uncertain, who live in a society that places little value on foreign language learning, and who doubt that their foreign language proficiency will be an asset in finding employment (see item no. 19 BALLI survey). I have had to bear these limitations in mind, as I tried to introduce this innovation to promote autonomy.

Pennycook (1997) is harshly critical of what he judges to be a too-ready presumption that innovations can transfer from one context to another. He sees this as a particular weakness in discussions that imply that learner autonomy is good for all learners in all contexts. While I think there is a lot of merit in Pennycook's argument, like Riley (1997a) and Little (1999) I remain convinced that a context-sensitive version of autonomy is possible. I consider a context-sensitive version of autonomy not only possible, but necessary for students who will need to be active agents of their learning in and out of classrooms in the 21st century. I agree with Benson (1997) that one way to safeguard against the implementation of an approach to autonomy that is inappropriate to the context is to choose a level of engagement suitable to the teacher and students.

A psychological/constructivist version of autonomy seems well suited to what I was hoping to achieve in promoting learner autonomy among my students. Proponents of psychological versions of autonomy see autonomy as a psychological relation between the learner and what is to be learned. They contend that it can develop anywhere and it can be transferred to situations outside the classroom. This perspective of autonomy also underscores the fact that autonomous learners have the skills for, and an appreciation of, the importance of lifelong learning (Knapper 1988; Trim 1996, 1997).

2.4.2 Implications of a Psychological Approach to Autonomy
The main thrust of a psychological approach is to develop the learners' capacity for autonomy and to become aware of the role played by attitudinal factors in the process. This approach stresses that autonomous learners have both a capacity for active learning and an attitude towards learning which leads them to take responsibility for their learning. Little (1996) contends that adopting a psychological approach to autonomy is recognizing that

learner autonomy has both affective/motivational and metacognitive dimensions. It presupposes a positive attitude to the purpose, content and process of learning on the one hand and well-developed metacognitive skills on the other. (204)

Research that has contributed to an understanding of the relationship between attitudinal factors and autonomy has tended to examine the part played by factors internal to the learner or by environmental factors. Wenden (1991) posits that seven factors influence learner attitudes towards autonomy: socialization process, conflicting demands, complexity of roles, lack of metacognitive knowledge, learner helplessness, self-esteem, and self-image. Cotterall (1995), for her part, has identified six factors—role of the teacher, role of feedback, learner independence, learner confidence in study ability, experience of language learning, and approach to studying—that she suggests may indicate learners' readiness to assume responsibility for their learning. Press (1996), however, found that ethnicity was not a predictor of the attitudes that learners bring to autonomy, while a number of authors (Holec 1981; Pierson 1996; Thomson 1992) posit that the learners' previous schooling determines the attitude that they are likely to hold to autonomy.

2.5 Models of Teacher/Learner Interaction in Autonomy

Further support for the importance of education/socialization in the shift to autonomy comes from Higgs (1988). Higgs contends that the learning experiences of both teacher and learner are likely to influence the attitudes that they bring to learner autonomy. Broady and Kenning (1996b) claim that the conception of teachers' roles gives rise to certain expectations of behavior and that learners are unlikely to be willing to adopt what they see as the teacher's responsibilities. Thus, as learners move to autonomy, there will be a high degree of anxiety when they are asked to change and accept roles that are not traditionally part of their repertoire. In addition, much has been written on the difficulty experienced by students as they make the "cross-cultural" adjustment (Kelly 1996, 98) from secondary school to university and their need for appropriate support. This added constraint will need to be addressed in an intervention to promote autonomy in first-year undergraduate students.

Another dimension of the teacher-learner interface in autonomy is revealed when we look at research conducted by Pierson (1996) among Hong Kong Chinese learners. Pierson's research reveals the complexity of promoting autonomy in a very examination-oriented educational culture. It seems that students' natural tendency to see their teachers as "omniscient authority" (Jehng, Johnson, and Anderson 1993, 28) is exacerbated in a culture where students depend on their teacher's management of their learning to achieve success (see Greaney and Kellaghan 1995). This finding is likely to be very relevant to the students in this study who, as I have argued, are products of such an environment.

Pierson's findings suggest that learners who have been socialized in a very competitive environment will measure their teachers' efficacy by the extent to which these teachers can guarantee examination success. The danger here is that many students will fail to distinguish between examination success and individual learning, because they see them as one and the same thing. Teachers' instructional effectiveness and students' learning are inextricably meshed in such a scenario, and many students find it difficult to separate the teaching from the learning process in an educational system that promotes high-stakes testing. This is in direct contrast to Wittrock's (1986) argument that posits distinct roles for good teaching and good learning in achievement.

A final aspect of the teacher-learner relationship that needs to be considered in autonomy is the motivational factor. The students' diaries, one of the sources of data in this study, revealed that in many cases, the students' initial interest in foreign language study was sparked by a teacher whom they admired. The foreign language teacher was often credited with playing a critical role in motivating learners, in encouraging them to persist with language learning, and in influencing their love of, and positive attitude to, the target language and its speakers. For many students in this study, the goodness of the fit between them and their secondary school teacher depended on two factors: the teacher's instructional effectiveness, because of the highly competitive nature of the educational system and the quality of the relationship that existed between the teacher and the student.

Not surprisingly, the literature on learner autonomy identifies the teacher-learner relationship as an important theme. Wright (1987) has written extensively on the role of teachers, the nature of the teacher-learner relationship and its significance for classroom learning. Boud (1988b) for his part singles out teachers' attitude to their students as the most important factor in enhancing the relationship that is shared by teachers and students.

To sum up, although there can be little argument that the metacognitive dimension of learner autonomy is essential, an equally persuasive argument exists for focusing on the affective and motivational components of learning to learn, in the shift to learner autonomy (see for example, Henner Stachina 1986-1987). This focus has been gaining even more prominence in the growth of a new body of research on counseling for autonomy (Bailly 1993; Crabbe, Hoffmann, and Cotterall 2001; Gremmo 1993; Hoffmann 1999; Kelly 1996; Mozzon-McPherson 2001; Mozzon-McPherson and Vismans

2001; Pemberton et al. 2001; Riley 1997b; Schaefer Fu 1999; Toogood and Pemberton 2002; Voller, Martyn, and Pickard 1999).

The renewed focus on counseling has been given a boost by the spread of self-access centers in many European and Asian contexts. But it is perhaps a reflection, as well, of the growing understanding of the need to adopt a gradual approach and give learners the scaffolding, a "safety net" (Cornwall 1988, 247) to ease their transition to their new role. As more and more educational institutions integrate autonomy into their practice, some of the difficulties that may have been less apparent in the earlier experimental type settings, where learners were in the main highly motivated, are starting to appear. Although Holec (1981) clearly identified both psycho-social support and technical support as necessary to usher the traditional learner from dependence and passivity to autonomy and self-directed learning, the theorizing about the proper level of support for the affective well-being of learners seems a development of the last fifteen or so years.

The role of counselor, for example, has been receiving attention in more recent literature on autonomy, because of the need to define the roles and responsibilities of the person who does not have a teaching role (see Dickinson 1999). Counseling the autonomous language learner is still a relatively new field[4] and as a result there is vibrant debate as those involved in counseling try to select the most appropriate label for the person who counsels. In different contexts, that person is referred to as a counselor, an adviser, a helper, a facilitator, a mentor, a consultant, or a knower. All these terms reflect the dual role of the counselor as guide-facilitator and expert in learning.

The skills required of the counselor, the objectives of the counselor, and the behavior of the counselor are other issues of debate, according to Voller (1997). There is some similarity between the counselor role in a self-access center and the counselor/knower in Curran's Community Language Learning as a supportive, non-judgmental helper (see Stevick 1990; Omaggio Hadley 1993). At the root of the debate on the name and tasks carried out by the counselor are questions on the role and the responsibility of the counselor and her interaction with learners.

A number of writers have described in some detail what an appropriate teacher-learner relationship might look like. Underhill (1999) distinguishes the "Facilitator" from the "Lecturer" or the "Teacher". The Lecturer, according to Underhill's framework, is the teacher in any educational setting, with knowledge of the topic, but no special skill or interest in acquiring skills to enhance her delivery. The Teacher has both knowledge and skills, but does not attempt in any systematic way to explore either her teaching or her students' learning at a deeper level. Underhill sees the Facilitator as the ideal. She is someone whose pedagogical approach subsumes lecturer and teacher competencies, but according to Underhill (1999, 126), she does this while remaining attentive to "the psychological learning atmosphere and the inner processes of learning on a moment to moment basis." It is this caring stance coupled with her teacher competence that enables student autonomy.

It is the Facilitator who most closely resembles the teacher role described by Boud (1988b). In addition to her tasks as Lecturer and Teacher, the Facilitator is also concerned about "the relationships in and between people in the group, the degree of security felt by individuals... the quality of listening and acceptance, the possibility for nonjudgemental interaction, the way the needs for self-esteem are met, and so on" (Underhill 1999, 130). Underhill believes that a serious flaw in many efforts to promote autonomy is that educators adopt a Teacher technique in order to achieve Facilitator ends.

Voller's (1997) analysis of the roles of teachers in approaches that seek to promote greater learner involvement looks at teacher types in terms of the psychosocial and technical support they provide. The facilitator, according to Voller, is perceived as having two complementary roles. The first role enables the facilitator to provide psychosocial support, while the second role allows the provision of technical support. Among the psychosocial features of the first role are the personal qualities of the facilitator, a capacity for motivating learners, and an ability to raise learners' awareness. The technical role encompasses activities that are usually associated with learner training, such as helping learners to plan and carry out their independent language learning needs, helping learners evaluate themselves, and helping learners acquire the skills and knowledge needed to implement their language learning and evaluation.

The counselor is the term used by Voller to describe the role held by educators who interact on a one-to-one basis with learners, usually in the context of a resource or self-access center. The role of the counselor is patterned on a psychotherapeutic model. According to Kelly (1996):

> Counselling acknowledges the difficulty individuals experience in achieving their autonomy and self-direction and has developed helping techniques to facilitate personal growth. (97)

There is little difference between the roles and responsibilities of the counselor as described by Kelly and the role of facilitator as described by Voller and Underhill. The most salient difference is that the facilitator interacts with groups of students, in or out of the classroom, while the counselor interacts with the individual learner in a self-access facility.

The teacher as resource is the third way in which the teacher's role and responsibility in learner autonomy has been characterized by Voller. According to Voller, it is the situation in which the teacher works, whether it is classroom/group-learning situations or self-access situations that determines whether the teacher's role as resource or guide or expert or knower is considered her main function.

Holec (1996) makes a distinction between the dual responsibilities of the trainer/adviser who as trainer trains in self-directed learning and whose role as adviser is to give advice. In Holec's framework, the materials supplier acts as a human resource, as well as a source of technical knowledge and skills. Her role is to supply resources to enable self-directed language learning. One person can in some cases hold the trainer/adviser and materials supplier role. In other cases, different individuals may look after different tasks (see Morrison 2002; Serra 2000; Toogood and Pemberton 2002;and Victori 2000, for discussions on roles and responsibilities within self-access systems).

A third set of perspectives on teacher-learner relationships is to be found in a seminal article by Oxford et al. (1998). These authors use educational metaphor to examine how "concepts of control and power" in classroom interaction are carried by a range of different metaphors (16). The supportive, caring relationship between teacher and learner, reminiscent of the teacher in Boud (1988b), the facilitator (Underhill 1999) and the facilitator and counselor in Voller (1997), is conveyed by metaphors of *the Teacher as Nurturer, Lover or Spouse, Scaffolder, Entertainer* and *Delegator*" (Oxford et al. 1998). These metaphors belong to the Learner-Centered Growth perspective (other perspectives are education as Social Order, Cultural Transmission and Social Reform), which is described in the following terms:

> the underlying theme [of the Learner-Centered Growth perspective] is that the teacher facilitates the full and harmonious development of the learner's inner powers … By fostering the right conditions to promote these inner potentialities, in accordance with the developmental needs of the student, the teacher follows the logic of nature, rather than … the structure of knowledge in the curriculum. (27)

As many writers have suggested, the traditional teacher role is no longer appropriate in a learning situation that tries to support autonomy. The teacher who is committed to learner autonomy has changed her "representation" (Holec 1987, 152) of what it means to be a teacher. She cannot dismiss her responsibility to instruct, but in her role as instructor, she is keen to develop a relationship where teachers and learners are co-constructors of knowledge and share responsibility for any learning that takes place.

I think that models of teacher-learner interactions, such as those suggested by Underhill (1999) and Oxford et al. (1998), as well as those found in descriptions of counseling by Kelly (1996) and Gremmo (1993) can be appropriate models for teaching-learner interaction in classroom-based autonomy. Ehrman's (1998, 104) warning against the "abandonment of a learner not ready to set goals, self-evaluate, design activities, or manage feelings" serves as a reminder that psychological preparation for autonomy must integrate the metacognitive and the affective and motivational. Higgs (1988) and Cornwall (1988) are two writers who also stress the need for teacher guidance and support in fostering students' autonomy.

To summarize, the teacher who wishes to promote autonomy will try to meet the learners' affective and motivational needs in the course of the innovation. This, as I have shown, is an important dimension of the enhanced role of the teacher in autonomy. In addition to this psychological training for autonomy, the other area in which the teacher intervenes is in providing methodological training for learner autonomy. It is to this aspect that I now wish to turn in the literature review.

2.6 The Teacher's Responsibility in Autonomy

2.6.1 The Provision of Psycho-social Support

Holec (1981) theorizes that the acquisition of autonomy can best be conceptualized in terms of two processes, both of which need to take place simultaneously. He calls the process by which teachers help students examine their preconceptions about languages and language learning and their role in it, a gradual "deconditioning" (Holec 1981, 22) process. This psychological preparation for autonomy concentrates on raising students' metalinguistic awareness, i.e. helping them to have increasing insight into how language is organized, how language is used and how second languages are learned and metacognitive awareness—how to use different learning resources, strategies and techniques for language learning and insight into their own learning style (see Broady and Kenning 1996b; Scharle and Szabó 2000). As part of the psychological preparation for autonomy, teachers are expected to help students come to a better understanding of their role in learning and their ability to learn and take responsibility for learning (Wenden 1991) and the levels of control that they may exercise (Benson 2001). It is in this area of intervention that teachers will need to draw on a range of counseling and facilitating skills in order to support students as they embark on the road to autonomy.

2.6.2 The Provision of Technical Support

The second component of autonomy is the gradual acquiring of the knowledge, skills, and confidence needed to assume responsibility for one's learning. This suggests a second area of responsibility for teachers, for the task will be theirs to provide the methodological training for students who need knowledge and skills to become autonomous.

The tension referred to earlier, between psychological versions of autonomy and technical versions of autonomy, comes into play when we examine the teacher's responsibility for facilitating the gradual "deconditioning" process and the gradual acquisition process. The latter process, which is commonly labeled strategy training, has come to be equated in some quarters with learner autonomy. This movement does not find favor with those who stress that training the learner for autonomy must include a psychological component, as well as a methodological component. Indeed, Holec (1981) and other proponents of psychological versions of autonomy, for example, Dickinson and Carver (1980) and Huttunen (1996) see learner training more holistically, as being made up of both psychological and methodological preparation, corresponding in other words to both the gradual "deconditioning" process and the gradual acquiring process.

Ellis and Sinclair (1989, 2) offer a definition of learner training which includes the psychological and the methodological dimension:

> Learner training aims to help learners consider the factors which affect their learning and discover learning strategies which suit them best, so that they may become more effective learners and take on more responsibility for their own learning.

Other researchers have also defined what they see as necessary to a program of learner training. Huttunen (1996) sees the development of learning awareness, of language awareness, of self-confidence as a person and as a learner, and metacognitive, cognitive, social and affective learner strategies as reflecting a focus on learning to learn for autonomy. Finally Wenden (1991) summarizes the three categories to be included in a program of learning training: (1) cognitive and self-management strategies; (2) knowledge about learning, which is sub-divided into person, strategic, and task knowledge; and (3) attitudes towards personal responsibility and personal capability.

Yet, issues surrounding learner training remain some of the most contentious in the discussions on learner autonomy. On the one hand, general criticisms are leveled against learner training initiatives, because it is argued that they confirm the view of learner autonomy as the antithesis of pedagogy[5] and therefore inappropriate in instructional practice. More specific criticisms come from those, for example, Rees-Miller (1993) who contend a lack of empirical evidence about the effectiveness of learner training and query the advisability of devoting instructional time to learner training instead of language learning. On the other hand, proponents of learner autonomy who have different conceptions of what it means to be autonomous because of their particular ontological and epistemological stance debate the contents of a learner-training program. Teachers who wish to promote autonomy will not find ready-made answers to the issues and can only hope to apply a context-sensitive version of learner training, based on their understanding of some of the criteria that need to be considered. Scharle and Szabó's (2000) handbook, for example, aims to give practical guidance in this regard.

Sheerin (1997, 60) uses the term "learner development" in preference to the more widely used learner training, because she considers that training connotes too instrumental a view of the process and does not sufficiently accommodate the developmental aspect of the learner's growth. Like Sheerin, other researchers have sought to bring clarification to some of the issues surrounding learner training. Wenden (1987) provides a comprehensive treatment of the components of a learner training program and also a yardstick for assessing such programs. She has identified four criteria according to which learner training may be assessed: (1) explicitness of purpose, (2) content of training, (3) integration, and (4) evaluation. Holec (1996) explores the timing of learner training: independently of language training, either before or in parallel with it, integrated with language training, or a combination of the two modalities. While Fernández-Toro and Jones (1996) posit that learner training is perhaps best suited to learners who have reached intermediate level proficiency and beyond.

Sinclair and Ellis (1992) and Sinclair (1996) looked at the integration of learner training in published materials. Sinclair and Ellis use eight criteria to examine the integration of learner training in published material. Some of the criteria noted by Wenden above are also used here to evaluate learner training in published textbooks, e.g. (1) explicit focus on learning, (2) pairing of cognitive and metacognitive strategies (Wenden's content of training), and (3) integration. There are some areas of overlap in Wenden's fourth criterion, evaluation, and Sinclair and Ellis's self-assessment and monitoring. But some criteria mentioned by Sinclair and Ellis, e.g. accessibility, variety, opportunities for self-direction, and reference are peculiar to the promotion of learner training in textbooks. Another important consideration raised in Sinclair and Ellis, but which is also of concern in learner training in the classroom, is whether training can be conducted more effectively in the L1 or L2.

Sinclair (1996) focuses primarily on the explicitness of learner training in published and self-access materials. She also explores the difficulty of maintaining the balance between the learner training content and the language learning content in textbooks. Although, if one were to consider the foreign language as both medium and content of learning, especially for more advanced language learners, one could say that learning training content pitched at an appropriate level are in fact additional samples of authentic language for language learning. Wenden (1991) is another researcher who addresses this issue of the balance between learner training and language learning, and in particular, the difficulty of spending instructional time on learner training in the face of learners' skepticism about the usefulness of training.

A less controversial way in which the classroom teacher is expected to intervene is in helping learners acquire linguistic autonomy. The teacher who seeks to promote learner autonomy has, in fact, two main objectives in her teaching: helping learners develop linguistic autonomy and learning autonomy. Holec (1981) sees both linguistic and learning autonomy as necessary and complementary to the learner's acquisition of autonomy. The literature on learner autonomy tends however to emphasize the development of learning autonomy, and with good reason, since this is the area that has traditionally been neglected in language learning. Yet, the teacher's responsibility in fostering linguistic autonomy, bearing in mind the relationship between linguistic autonomy and communicative competence remains an important dimension of the teacher's responsibility (Benson 2002).

Holec (1981) lists five areas in which the teacher has traditionally intervened to control learning. The teacher or educational institution defines the objectives, selects the resources, selects methods and techniques, monitors the acquisition procedure, and evaluates acquisition. Thus, from the start of the learning program to its end, the teacher/educational institution is the chief decision-maker and never relinquishes control of the decision-making process to students.

On the other hand, in learning conducted on an autonomous basis, students are the decision-makers and the teacher acts as facilitator and guide, supporting students and giving them help and advice to achieve learning and linguistic autonomy. Accordingly, when the teacher helps students to define their objectives, this entails helping them define objectives based on their communicative needs. In the selection of resources, the teacher can act as resource and materials supplier, supplying information on the possible sources of authentic and didactic learning materials. In her role as knower and adviser, a teacher can promote autonomy by helping students decide on the methods and techniques that will enable them to reach their linguistic and communicative objectives and by helping them learn how to monitor their progress. Finally, the teacher can help students assess the results obtained, based not on an external standard, but on criteria which they have jointly determined as appropriate to the students' communicative agenda.

Although, from a theoretical standpoint, I have looked at learning autonomy and linguistic autonomy as discrete areas, I think it will be difficult, in practice, to isolate those activities that the teacher should adopt to foster learning autonomy from those that foster linguistic autonomy. The fundamental issue, I think, is to recognize the role of learning *and* linguistic autonomy in students' overall autonomy and to understand the teacher's responsibility in autonomous language learning as she tries to shift the locus of control from herself to the students.

2.7 The Learner's Responsibility in Autonomy

The autonomous learner has to accept responsibility for her learning in the five areas defined by Holec (1981). But accepting responsibility for her own learning does not absolve the learner from being a participant in the learning community to which she belongs. Freire's (1972) advocacy of the joint ownership of the process of learning points to another issue which merits attention as we examine how the literature on learner autonomy treats the re-configuration of the learner's role in autonomy.

The tension between the individual and social aspect of autonomy is one of the recurring themes in the literature. Critical pedagogy theorists are in the vanguard of the opposition to a brand of autonomy that is too focused on individualism (see for example, Benson 1997; Pennycook 1990, 1997). The focus on the individual in autonomy also lays it open to charges of cultural inappropriateness, as for example in cultures that are collectivist in character. Riley (2003) explores another dimension of the individual vs. the collective debate, moving beyond the notion of the individual per se to notions of self and personhood and their cultural variations.

On the other hand, Aoki and Smith (1999); Esch (1996); Littlewood (1999); Palfreyman and Smith (2003); and Smith (2003) highlight research that challenges the view of an inherent cultural bias in the theory and practice of autonomy. From a communicative perspective, Little (1991, 1996, 1999) among others, stresses interdependence in autonomy, since language development requires social interaction. Finally, research on cooperation and collaboration in language learning (Crandall 1999; Dörnyei and Malderez 1999; Nunan 1988, 1996) points to the value of collaborating with other language learners to achieve performance goals.

Higgs (1988) reconciles the individual-collaborative dimensions of autonomy by suggesting that the autonomous learner can opt to conduct her learning independently, or choose alternative modes of learning which may be more appropriate to her learning goals. This does not imply, however, that the learner can simply transfer over-reliance on teachers to over-reliance on her peers. If the learner wishes to participate fully as an equal partner in learning, she must first give up her dependence and passivity and replace these by more active involvement in her own learning. The shift from dependence to independence can only occur gradually and this shift still stops short of the way interaction should occur in a classroom supportive of autonomy. Boud (1988b) sees the shift from dependence to interdependence as a four-stage process, with learners moving through stages of counter-dependence and independence before attaining interdependence.

A stress on the social character of autonomy helps the learner to appreciate that, in order to achieve both learning autonomy and linguistic autonomy, the support of the learning community is invaluable. The growth of tandem learning schemes both in face-to-face and virtual modes reflects the need to "anchor their [the students'] learning in social relations" (Esch 1996, 44). Even within the context of independent learning in a self-access center, it is important that learners invest in supportive relationships with other learners who may have similar goals. Esch (1996, 44) refers to this notion as "shareability."

Esch's notion of "shareability" is an important concept for a learner who needs to assume responsibility for her learning. Boud's (1988b) inventory,[6] as well as Holec's (1997) description of the tasks that the autonomous learner may be called on to perform could seem quite daunting to the learner who has little experience in managing her own learning. If, however, the learner sees her peers as a resource in her language learning, the feeling of anxiety may be lessened.

A learner who is used to seeing her peers as competitors instead of collaborators may overlook them as a resource in her acquisition of learning and linguistic autonomy. That learner will need to change long-standing assumptions about the nature of classroom learning and the nature of classroom relationships. Thus, the learner's representation will need to change, not only in relation to the teacher-learner relationship, but also in relation to learner-learner relationships in the classroom. In a very fundamental sense the learner will have to see herself and her role in language learning differently.

2.8 Adopting and Adapting to Autonomy

One implication of adopting autonomy as an approach to language learning is that it is no longer possible to prescribe what the language learner will do.

While it is possible to categorize the domains of intervention of the learner, those areas that the learner can potentially control, the fully autonomous learner will personalize her learning program based on her own objectives. Little (1996) in a slight modification of Holec's framework lists four areas in which the learner may decide to exercise her autonomy. An autonomous learner may (1) determine her objectives, (2) define the content and process of her learning, (3) select her methods and techniques, and (4) monitor and evaluate her progress and achievements. In theory then, no two learners will follow the same learning path, since no two learners will have exactly the same learning objectives, nor choose the same route to accomplish their goals.

Little contends that the promotion of autonomy is conditional on factors such as the institutional framework, the learners' age, competence and previous background. While the initial decision to promote autonomy may be the teacher's, there is much scope for negotiating how autonomy will be implemented in a learning partnership with advanced learners. It is highly unlikely that there has always been a perfect fit between the learners' own objectives and course objectives in any given course, in all the areas identified by Little. Adult learners have always contrived to balance course goals and their own goals—for pragmatic reasons (scheduling and financial constraints); for affective reasons (their attitudes to the teacher or content, motivation, anxiety and so on); for cognitive reasons (their learning style, their perceptual preferences, and so on). The ways in which learners choose to exercise their personal autonomy may not always have been explicit.

Integrating learner autonomy in a language-learning curriculum for undergraduate students gives learners the opportunity to reflect and make conscious and informed decisions about their language learning goals. Instead of practicing a kind of autonomy by default—absence, little motivation, other-directed learning—autonomous learners can decide their level of engagement with a clear understanding of the link between objectives/content and process/methods, and techniques/progress and achievements. An autonomous learner will have the possibility to make informed decisions and to negotiate, as she has always done, though this time explicitly, how she will reconcile course objectives and her own. The locus of control for learning will be in the hands of the learner, who is capable and willing to make decisions based on her needs.

The exercise of autonomy as an individual concept must however be balanced against autonomy as a social concept. The learner who understands her role in a classroom learning community is not only cognizant of her own needs, but is also aware that an attempt must be made to cater for the needs of the other participants in learning. The rules of mutual dependence imply that learners must negotiate and collaborate with each other to co-construct their classroom learning. The horizontal relationship between learners and teacher should allow a learner to appreciate the teacher's responsibility to her instructional role. If, for example, the teacher is able to negotiate some of the assessment criteria and conditions, but not others, because of institutional policy, the learner is aware of the premises on which the teacher is acting. She will not interpret the teacher's action as an attempt to wrest away the locus of control from her. The exercise of autonomy as a social concept must be predicated on negotiation, collaboration, and the shared responsibility for the learning process.

Autonomy conceptualized in this way is therefore conditional rather than absolute and must be negotiated with other learning partners to accommodate learner independence, learner responsibility, and learner choice for all participants in learning. The learner must assume responsibility for her own learning but, as a participant in the learning community, she also has a responsibility to her learning partners. The learner cannot ignore her social responsibility to her learning partners in the exercise of individual freedom and individual choice (Dam 1995).

Another aspect of the individual/social tension in learner autonomy is likely to derive from what Benson and Voller (1997b, 11) call the "situational autonomy" caused by computers and new technologies. Moreover, Benson and Voller (1997b) and Esch (1996), among others, raise the specter that situational autonomy may not result in greater individual autonomy for learners, but merely result in transferring the locus of control from teacher to technology. Thus, while the impetus for change from transmission teaching may come from technology and may seem to support new teacher and learner roles in the classroom, both autonomy itself and the social aspect of autonomy can be compromised by the integration of technology which is not premised on a strong educational rationale.

To counter a new kind of dependence and to ensure that the change in the way learners conceptualize their responsibility in the classroom results is lasting change, attitudinal change must be an important consideration in a shift to autonomy. Holec (1981) and Riley (1989) maintain that learners need to change their representation of their role and responsibilities in language learning in order to assume more responsibility for their learning. Cornwall (1988) agrees, but underscores the difficulty of changing one's personal construct. He opines (Cornwall 1988, 247), "This personal construct cannot be lightly abandoned on the say-so of another or because of the sudden appearance of new kinds of demands."

2.9 Learner Beliefs

One way in which attitudinal change may be brought about in learner autonomy is by helping learners explore their underlying beliefs about their role in language learning, a thesis shared by Cameron (1990); Cotterall (1995, 1999); and Horwitz (1987, 1988, 1999). Wright (1987, 1990) makes the point that role is a complex factor and the covert nature of beliefs about roles adds to that complexity. In much the same way that teachers have a fairly coherent set of beliefs about their role, according to Pajares (1992) and Richards and Lockhart (1994), so too do learners.

Sakui and Gaies (1999) suggest that every discipline that deals with human behavior and learning attaches considerable importance to the role of learners' beliefs. This, they say, is because beliefs are both outcomes of previous learning and determinants of subsequent learning. A number of studies have in fact shown the salience of learners' beliefs to their language learning, and ultimately to their development of learner autonomy. White's (1999) study revealed a relationship between learner beliefs and locus of control, tolerance of ambiguity and what she calls the learner-context interface in self-instructed learners. Cameron (1990) contends that learners' beliefs not only influence their approach to learning, but also can enhance the quality of thinking and task engagement.

Cotterall (1995), as previously discussed, sees a clear link between learners' beliefs and their potential for autonomy. She claims that beliefs may either contribute to, or impede the development of, the potential for autonomy. Finally, Wenden (1987) argues that the learners' socialization process may have led to the acquisition of beliefs that encourage dependence rather than independence. These beliefs must be subject to re-examination and re-interpretation, or if necessary they must be completely recast.

One of the instruments used in this study, the Beliefs About Language Learning Inventory (BALLI), was developed by Horwitz (1988) to elicit learners' beliefs about: (1) the role of aptitude, (2) the difficulty of language learning, (3) the nature of language learning, (4) learning and communication strategies, and (5) motivation and expectations. Horwitz stresses the utility of the BALLI as a research instrument that allows researchers to catalogue learner beliefs. But Horwitz also envisages a role for the BALLI in promoting more effective teaching and learning. Teachers who are aware of their students' beliefs can find opportunities to have students critically examine and revise their beliefs, if these beliefs seem inimical to their language learning.

Since Horwitz's landmark study in which she examined the beliefs of beginning university students of French, Spanish, and German in the US, a number of other researchers have used the BALLI to catalogue the beliefs of students and their teachers. Kern (1995) examined the beliefs of French learners and instructors also in the US. He was particularly interested in comparing the beliefs of the students in his study with those in the original Horwitz study. He examined student and instructor beliefs over the course of one semester of instruction. Yang (1992, 1999) examined the beliefs of Taiwanese EFL students in relation to their use of learning strategies. Finally, Park (1995) examined the beliefs of Korean EFL university students in relation to their strategy use.

Although Horwitz warns that the BALLI may be culturally inappropriate outside the context in which it was developed, the growing number of studies (Horwitz 1999 lists thirteen studies) that have used the BALLI indicate that the question of the generalizability of the BALLI is less of an issue now than it was in 1988 when the instrument was first developed.

Other researchers who address the issue of learner beliefs in their research share Horwitz's basic premise that learners have a set of beliefs, distinct metacognitive knowledge that can be accessed. Most theories of learner beliefs draw on cognitive psychology theories that focus on the learner's acquired knowledge about learning. Wenden (1998) stresses that metacognitive knowledge is fact based, not necessarily complete, focused on a particular task, and can be revised through instruction. Consequently, she draws an important distinction between learner beliefs and metacognitive knowledge.

While Horwitz and others, for example Victori (1999b) and Victori and Lockhart (1995) accept learners' beliefs as evidence of their metacognitive knowledge, Wenden, and other researchers (for example, Sinclair 1999) in the tradition of Flavell (1979), argue that metacognitive knowledge is divided into knowledge on one hand and beliefs on the other. The distinction is an important one, for Wenden (1998) argues that beliefs are more diffuse, more idiosyncratic/subjective, may be broader in scope, are valued by learners and, as a result, are likely to be held more tenaciously than knowledge.

This is not the only area of debate as regards learner beliefs. Grotjahn (1991) advocates that the study of learner beliefs could be better served by being grounded in the Research Programme Subjective Theories. According to this research paradigm, subjective theories, i.e., "implicit", "naïve", "private" or "everyday" theories

> can roughly be characterized as complex cognitive structures that are highly individual, relatively stable, and relatively enduring, and that fulfil the task of explaining and predicting such human phenomena as action, reaction, thinking, emotion, and perception. (188)

Grotjahn contends that ignorance of a teacher's or learner's subjective theories may mean that classroom innovation may be doomed to failure because of the lack of knowledge about an individual's perspective as well as her expectations and beliefs.

Benson and Lor (1999) on the other hand, propose that the study of learner beliefs can be greatly aided by drawing on research conducted in educational psychology within a tradition known as Student Approaches to Learning (Watkins 1996). They propose that what learners think the objects and processes of learning are, in other words, their conceptions, are a higher and more abstract order of representations than what learners hold true about these objects and processes (their beliefs). The third element of their framework contrasts a surface or quantitative, as opposed to a deep or qualitative approach to learning. From this research perspective, beliefs represent a first level of data analysis. But it is the learner's conceptions about the nature of foreign language, what it is and what the process of learning consists of, that need to be modified if teachers wish to bring about attitudinal change.

Learner representations is another term used in the literature to refer to metacognitive knowledge. Riley (1989) is but one example. The term learner representations comes from constructivist psychology and underscores the part played by learners' perceptions in their vision of reality. Rézeau (1999, screen 1) describes *"les répresentations des apprenants"* as a body of concepts, or pseudo concepts, which learners use in order to grasp new information and construct their knowledge. He suggests that these beliefs may constitute an epistemological obstacle, implying that learners must change their beliefs in order to understand and learn.

Other terms in use in the literature to refer to learners' perceptions of their language learning include learners' philosophy of language learning (Abraham and Vann 1987) and folklinguistic theories of language learning (Miller and Ginsberg 1995). This profusion of terms and theories shows that the study of learner beliefs is a very dynamic area in language learning. At our present state of understanding of learners' metacognitive knowledge, it is impossible to state definitively whether learners' beliefs are metacognitive knowledge or a subset of metacognitive knowledge. What emerges clearly from research being conducted into learner beliefs, however, is that despite these areas of debate and despite the complexity of the beliefs/attitudes/behavior relationship, the salience of learner beliefs to their language learning cannot be disputed.

In conclusion, it is for the aforementioned reason, the salience of learner beliefs to their language learning that proponents of learner autonomy contend that the study of learner beliefs is central to the discussion on learner autonomy. While it is very difficult to describe the relationship between beliefs and autonomy in terms of a simple causal relationship, if we proceed with an abundance of caution, we can try to interpret how certain learner beliefs may influence the attitudes that learners hold. It may then be possible to make some hypotheses about the implications of these beliefs and attitudes on an autonomous approach to learning. Riley (1997, 128) argues that it is important to understand the subjective reality of learners, because "it is their [the learners'] beliefs that hold sway over their motivations, attitudes and learning procedures." This is the most convincing argument about the importance of learner beliefs and this is why proponents of autonomy see the need for further research in this area in order to deepen our understanding of the salience of learners' beliefs to their learning and to their autonomy.

NOTES

1. Voller (1997, 99-100), citing Barnes, distinguishes between transmission teachers and interpretation teachers and posits: "In terms of teacher beliefs and the locus of control it would appear that writers on autonomy are firmly positioned at the responsive, interpretation end of the continuum."

2. Nunan (1996, 14) offers the term "learning-centredness" to describe an approach where learning is focused on content learning and the learning process. He sees autonomy as an end-goal, something that is acquired gradually with considerable teacher support. Learning-centeredness is therefore the route via which autonomy (an end-goal) is acquired.

3. Wenden (1999 a) and Aoki (1999) offer plausible explanations of how separate research strands have now converged under the umbrella of learner autonomy.

4. Gremmo and Riley (1995) date the first appearance of counseling as sometime in the 1970s. They call it the first form of learner training.

5. Although autonomy was first conceptualized by Holec in the context of adult education and consequently is inspired by principles of andragogy, research reported in Dam (1995); Dam and Legenhausen (1996); Holec and Huttunen (1997); and Little, Ridley and Ushioda (2003) reveals that learner autonomy can be successfully integrated at the primary and secondary level.

6. Some of the tasks include identifying learning needs, setting goals, planning learning activities, finding resources needed for learning, selecting learning projects, creating "problems" to tackle, choosing where and when they will learn, determining criteria to apply to their work, engaging in self-assessment, deciding when learning is complete and reflecting on their learning processes.

Chapter Three

ADOPTING A RESEARCH PERSPECTIVE

The study reported here was the major component of an intervention to promote autonomy (appendix A) in first-year students of French at the University of the West Indies, St. Augustine, Trinidad and Tobago, in the 1997/98 academic year.

3.1 Participants

The participants in this study were an intact class of first-year students of French. Thirty-nine students were enrolled in the first semester course, though only thirty continued to the second semester. The majority (N=38) were secondary school graduates, who had studied French for at least seven years, or approximately 500 hours. All the students, except two,[1] were L3 speakers of French. However, all students were expected to have an adequate command of French, because classes were conducted in the target language.

Thirty-seven of the thirty-nine students were female. The majority (N=35) were also traditional age students. The non-traditional students were between thirty-five and fifty-eight years old. Students came from diverse socioeconomic backgrounds. But all the L3 speakers were high achievers (among the top 25% of secondary school entrants), who at 11+ had been placed in grammar schools or modern secondary schools, the traditional sector schools where French is taught.

3.2 Setting

This study was conducted at the University of the West Indies, St. Augustine. The Faculty of Humanities and Education, the home of the foreign language program, offers three-year degree programs (majors) in French and Spanish, as well as free-standing electives or minors in French, Spanish, and Portuguese. Of the Faculty's 306 undergraduate entrants in 1997/98, thirty-nine entered the French program, as majors or minors in French.

Five lecturers taught French: three taught language and two taught literature. All were full-time academics, except one, a French national who was jointly attached to the French Embassy and the University during the period of his civilian service. All the lecturers were native-speakers or had near-native speaker fluency. All had done some or part of their training in France.

3.3 The Teacher/Researcher

My membership in this academic community as one of the lecturers in French language meant, however, that I balanced two roles during the study. On one hand, I was grammar and writing instructor for two out of the six contact hours that the course met each week. The in-course activities to promote learner autonomy were integrated into these classes. I also exercised overall responsibility for the first-year French language courses. On the other hand, I was a researcher working in a qualitative, naturalistic paradigm.

When I began the research, I was aware that I might experience some conflict in reconciling the demands of being teacher and researcher, what Hornberger (1994, 689) calls "the insider/outsider dilemma." But since the purpose of the study was to explore an issue related to my students' learning, that dual responsibility was inevitable. The tension between the researcher and the teacher roles was, nevertheless, one of the limitations of this research. I had an ethical and professional obligation to students as participants in a qualitative study. But, primarily, my responsibility was to facilitate students' second language acquisition and manage environmental conditions to promote acquisition. I needed to balance both sets of responsibilities.

Sometimes, this balancing act affected the research process. I had, for example, planned to administer the BALLI in the third week of teaching. I was forced to delay its administration until the seventh week, a more appropriate time because of the number of late admissions that year. Another source of concern at the inception of the research was how students who were extrinsically motivated might react to a study that promised no immediate benefits to their proficiency. The students' reactions proved that my anxiety was misplaced, as the following extract from my informal notes revealed:

October, 10, 1997
The other incident, more positive this one, was when I spoke to L. about my plans to have the Spanish students do the BALLI. He consented and added that he was aware that I had started my research because the students had said to him that they were helping Mrs. Carter in her research. Goes to show that we imagine the worst and the reality is far more pleasant. It was good to hear that they feel that they are helping ... I suppose it makes them feel empowered that they too can contribute and [are] not confined to being on the receiving end of my wisdom, but that I too can learn/be helped by them. The [diary] entries of course continue to be fascinating with each writer indulging totally in sharing her unique perspective on things.

In conclusion, I hope that my teacher role gave me an emic, or insider's perspective during the research process. Peshkin (1993, 28) writing in defense of the "goodness" of the qualitative paradigm, suggests that it is "a type of research that gets to the bottom of things, that dwells on complexity, and that brings us very close to the phenomena we seek to illuminate." I felt that my dual status as teacher and researcher afforded me that opportunity and sharpened rather than dulled my researcher's perspective.

3.4 The Researcher-as-Instrument

The researcher in a qualitative study is the primary research instrument and therefore has as much responsibility to provide information about herself as she does about any of the instruments used in the study, according to Johnson and Saville-Troike (1992); see however, Bogdan and Biklen (1998) for a more nuanced discussion of this issue. LeCompte, Preissle, and Tesch (1993) posit that the metatheoretical predispositions as well as the personal and professional interests of the researcher inform key decisions made during the entire research process.

My background is similar to the participants in a number of respects. Like most of the participants in the study, I too am female and a non-native speaker of French, a national of Trinidad and Tobago. Like them, I acquired French at secondary school, before continuing my study of French, one year later, at the baccalaureate and then master's level, at the Université de Franche-Comté à Besançon. Upon my return from France, I taught at the secondary level for twelve years before being offered a full-time post at the University in 1991. For several years I also taught French on a part-time basis to adult students in a state-funded language school.

Of the three modern languages to which I have been exposed—Spanish at secondary school and first-year university, Portuguese briefly at university —French is the only one that I use regularly and the only one in which I am very proficient. But French is much more than an intellectual or professional engagement because, for over thirty years, it has played a significant role in many areas of my life. My attitude to learning and teaching French is therefore based on the sum total of my experiences as a learner and teacher of French in L1 and L2 contexts.

I think that I am an autonomous language learner; though I am unsure to what extent my autonomy was fostered by my having to survive academically in an L2 context. I do believe, however, that the long-term engagement that language learning requires makes special demands on foreign language learners. I advocate learner autonomy for my students because I think it is a competency that foreign language learners need to acquire if they wish to maintain a high level of motivation.

3.5 Data Collection

3.5.1 Research Instruments

During the study I used two types of written instruments (see table 1) to collect data on students' attitudes and beliefs. The students' diaries allowed me to collect longitudinal data, while the second group of instruments, that is pre-course and post-course questionnaires, and the Beliefs About Language Learning Inventory (BALLI), allowed me to collect cross-sectional data at different points of the study. Each instrument had certain methodological strengths and weaknesses. But I felt that, in combining these two types of instruments, I would be able to balance the limitations of one against the other and enhance the data collection process.

Table 3: The Instruments

INSTRUMENT	DESCRIPTION	DATE ADMINISTERED/ DURATION	DATA ELICITED
Personal Information Questionnaire	Fifteen-item questionnaire using a mixture of ten closed questions (items 1-8; 10 & 11) and five open-ended questions (items 9 and 12-15)	From September 08, 1997	a) biographical information (items 1-7) b) information on current proficiency (items 8 & 9) c) information on current studies (items 10-12)

Continued on next page

Table 3 – *Continued*

INSTRUMENT	DESCRIPTION	DATE ADMINISTERED/ DURATION	DATA ELICITED
			d) reasons for continuing study (item 13) e) expectations about university life (item 14) f) future aspirations (item 15)
Learner Diaries	Structured and unstructured entries in L1 or L2; five sentences long	A minimum of two entries a week from September 22/23, 1997	Self-report on personal variables in in-class and out-of-class language learning
BALLI	Thirty- item inventory twenty-six Likert scale items, ranging from (1) strong agreement to (5) strong disagreement (items 1-3; 7-28; 30); two items requiring student ratings (items 6 & 29); two items were open-ended (items 4 & 5)	October 21-22, 1997	Learners' beliefs about (a) the difficulty of language learning; (b) foreign language aptitude; (c) the nature of language learning; d) learning and communication strategies; (e) motivation and expectations
Course Evaluation Questionnaires	Twelve- item questionnaire using seven open-ended questions (items 1, 3, 4, 8, 9, 10 & 12); four closed questions (items 2,5, 6 & 7);	December, 1997	(a) reflection on course objectives and personal objectives (items 1-4) (b) evaluation of course components (items 5- 9) c) suggestions for improvements to the course (items 9 & 10)

Continued on next page

Table 3 – *Continued*

INSTRUMENT	DESCRIPTION	DATE ADMINISTERED/ DURATION	DATA ELICITED
	and one item that elicited both a closed and open-ended answer (item 11)		(d) student definition of success in course (item 11) (e) impact of course on short term and long term language goals (item 12)

3.5.2 Personal Information Questionnaires

The Personal Information Questionnaire (PIQ), the first instrument (appendix B) that I used to collect data was modeled on two questionnaires described in Whalen et al. (1994). The PIQ consisted of fifteen items and used a mixture of closed and open-ended questions to elicit biographical information and information on students' foreign language proficiency, their rationale for advanced language study, and their aspirations as language learners.

All thirty-nine students completed a PIQ. Most of them completed the PIQ during the first class meeting for the course. Some students preferred to take time to reflect on their answers, especially in response to items 9 and 12 to 15 (open-ended questions) and so chose to complete the questionnaires at home and return them later. However, all the questionnaires were completed in September 1997.

I used the PIQ to gather biographical information on students. The PIQ also allowed me to have academic information and make interventions to support students' learning. An example will serve to illustrate this point. Although students qualify for university matriculation and therefore entrance into F14A (the first semester course) if they have two passing grades (grades A to E) in the GCE Advanced Level Examinations, students with the lowest grades, not surprisingly, often experienced the most difficulty. Many of these students failed F14A and were unable to continue into Semester II, or failed the second semester course and could not continue into Year 2. Not infrequently, students chose to abandon French when this happened. Knowing this allowed me to track students and offer them help and advice in their language learning.

While entering grades were frequently a predictor of success, the information that students gave in response to the attitudinal questions of the PIQ sometimes proved more revealing than their assessed aptitude. Thus, while a student's poor GCE results may have been due to student/ teacher/ course-related factors, the student who wrote, "I could [sic] honestly say that

I have not picked up a French book since I finished exams on 24th June, 1997", in response to item 9 of the questionnaire, was probably revealing beliefs or representations about the nature of language learning that could influence her performance in higher education.

3.5.3 Learner Diaries

The second instrument used for data collection was a learner diary (appendix A). Students kept a diary of their language learning from September to December 1997. In my notes, I reflected on the irony of compelling students to keep a diary in an intervention intended to promote learner autonomy, and therefore learner freedom and learner choice. The dilemma posed was, of course, how to ensure that students would supply me with the data that I needed for the study, without some element of external motivation. It was easy to have students complete a questionnaire during class-time. It was less easy to have them keep a diary on their own time, even with a minimum requirement of two entries per week. Fry (1988) notes that diary keeping is time consuming and that initial enthusiasm may give way to fatigue. I knew this from the experience of a pilot project the previous year. Of the thirty-two students registered for F14A in 1996/97, only three submitted diaries. I did not wish to risk the same lack of success, since the diary was to be the primary data collection instrument. Reluctantly, I had to make the diary a course assignment in 1997/1998.

Some Methodological Issues. Diaries have become important tools in SLA research since they allow researchers to have access to individual variables that can seldom be accessed in other ways. Cohen and Hosenfeld (1981) call diaries a form of retrospective self-observational data. Diaries are the preferred method of collecting mentalistic data "where a holistic exploratory investigation of the learning/acquisition process is pursued" (Matsumoto 1994, 369). One characteristic of learner diaries that makes them particularly appropriate for a study on learner autonomy is that the act of keeping a diary engages students as participant observers in ethnographic research on their own learning. A diary study, "an account of a second language experience as recorded in a first-person journal" (Bailey and Oschner 1983, 189) is the methodological tool used to document and analyze the contents of a diary.

A diary study is an ethnography, the "detailed study of a particular society or social unit" (Erickson 1986, 130) although, like all ethnographies, diary studies are by definition case studies, since they are reconstructions of a single culture (LeCompte, Preissle, and Tesch 1993). Many of the early diary studies were participant studies where researchers studied their own language learning (e.g. Bailey 1983; Schumann 1980; Schumann and

Schumann 1977). In non-participant studies, the student's role as researcher is an important one, for it is the student-researcher who becomes the primary instrument for data collection.

However, this strength of diary studies, as an aid to learner introspection, is also a potential weakness and issues of the quality of the diary studies may arise. Bailey and Oschner (1983) contend that few authors have the necessary methodological training to adequately collect data. One way to overcome this limitation is to have diarists use a very structured approach to delimit the scope of their introspection (see for example, Matsumoto 1987, 1994, 1996; Palmer 1992).

Cohen and Hosenfeld (1981) also advise researchers that a more focused data instrument might make the data easier to analyze and ultimately more meaningful. Nonetheless, I opted to have students use a mixed approach (structured and unstructured entries) for two reasons. Firstly, because I was more interested in what individual attitudes and beliefs would emerge in students' entries when they volunteered information on their language learning. Secondly, I felt that too structured a task could deter students from keeping a diary. Students were therefore given rather loose guidelines about possible topics for their entries. I asked them to write fairly structured entries on three occasions. All students were asked to begin by writing autobiographies to document their language learning history. Their second and third structured entries were based on an in-class and an at-home task, respectively. These three entries used external elicitation as opposed to the majority of diary entries that used internal elicitation.

Another methodological issue was whether the diaries would be done in the students' L1 or L2. The literature on diary studies advocates the use of the L1 when researchers and learners share the L1. The concern here for Hilleson (1996) and Matsumoto (1996) is that the quality of the learners' reflection would depend on their L2 proficiency. In this study, students invariably used both languages. In cases where students wrote in French, I made it clear that there was neither penalty nor reward for L2 writing. Furthermore, I did not intend to "correct" their expression (a promise which I was able to keep for the most part), because that was not the object of this writing exercise. The excerpts that appear in chapter 4 have not been edited for grammatical accuracy. The degree of accuracy reveals students' linguistic mastery at that stage of their linguistic development.

A few students kept electronic diaries that they e-mailed to me. There were several research advantages to this. Data collection was easier and the data less bulky when diaries were submitted via e-mail. I did not have to decipher handwriting in the electronic diaries, nor was there any need to photocopy the extracts at the study's end. All the entries were automatically dated, unlike the handwritten entries that sometimes contained no date, just journal number 2 etc. E-mail diaries also promoted a more spontaneous exchange. I often tried to respond to any queries or concerns students raised in their diaries. I was able to do this more quickly with electronic diaries. With the paper diaries, my replies had to wait until the next writing class or office appointment. I felt that electronic diaries enhanced the "ongoing dialogue" (Fry 1988, 166) between students and myself even more than did paper-based diaries. Additionally, the use of e-mail for diary keeping was one small area where technology was integrated into students' learning. The advantages that students derived from using technology—more teacher-student interaction, more learning opportunities and more affective support—confirm what has been said in the literature by authors like Gaspar 1998; Beauvois 1992; Marsh 1997; and Warschauer 1997 about Computer-Mediated Conferencing (CMC).

My decision to make the diary a course requirement also gave rise to an ethical issue since student participation was not voluntary and therefore the students' motive for keeping the diary could be questioned. I tried to balance this limitation by awarding only five marks for the completion of the diary. Completed diaries had to include the students' autobiographies and entries covering four periods. Students were asked to write a minimum of five sentences at least twice a week in each period. Twenty-six students submitted completed diaries.

To give back to students some of the autonomy that I felt I was taking away by not making the diaries voluntary, I gave them some flexibility in submitting their entries. All autobiographies had to be submitted by October 01 and the final entry had to be submitted by December 05, 1997. But students could choose to submit the remaining entries at any date. Although the flexibility I gave to students made my task of collecting their diaries more difficult, I felt that students needed to have some measure of freedom in deciding if and when to participate in the research.

There is one final caveat concerning the methodology of diary studies and that pertains to the research cycle, which Bailey (1983) outlines. A diary study is a five-stage process. Diarists first write their autobiographies; then they record their feelings about their current language learning in a "confidential and candid diary" (Bailey 1983, 72); next, the private diary is revised for public perusal; the researcher studies the primary data; and finally, she presents an analysis with or without illustrative data.

Traditionally, the researcher's stance is non-interventionist during the first three stages; she intervenes only at the fourth and fifth stages. My intervention at the second stage of these diary studies, particularly with the electronic diaries, was an approach more akin to Spack and Sadow's (1983) description of dialogue journal writing. Towards the end of the semester, I was not able to read and return the diaries as quickly as I had at the beginning, so the dialogue between the students and myself lessened. There was another small variation in the Bailey model, since there was no revision of the private diary into a public document. Although Bailey suggests that there is little editing in the public version. However, I concealed the students' identities by assigning them fictitious names in the study.

3.5.4 The Beliefs About Language Learning Inventory (BALLI)
Instrument number three in this study was the BALLI (appendix C), a research and teaching tool developed by Horwitz. The BALLI was developed in response to a concern similar to mine—an enquiry into students' beliefs about language learning and the influence of these beliefs on students' learning. The inventory was initially developed out of free-recall protocols of English as a Second Language (ESL) and Foreign Language (FL) teacher educators and student and teacher focus groups in the United States. Horwitz subsequently refined the inventory to produce one with thirty-four items.

The BALLI used with these students was a thirty-item questionnaire. Twenty-six of the thirty items used a five-point Likert scale. Two items, (item 6) and (item 29) elicited student ratings and two items (item 4) and (item 5) were open. Thirty-five[2] students completed the BALLI, down from thirty-nine with the PIQ. The BALLI was completed in week seven of the semester. Completion time averaged about twenty-five minutes, at the end of which normal teaching and learning activities resumed.

Some Methodological Issues. I selected the BALLI because it was a valid and reliable instrument. It had been field tested with a variety of populations, as the studies reviewed in chapter 2 show and it had been used successfully in non-US contexts. The BALLI seemed appropriate to elicit the kind of data that I wanted to collect. Therefore, once I obtained permission from Horwitz, I proceeded to use the BALLI as one of the instruments to gather data on students' beliefs.

I made some changes to the BALLI. I omitted items 12, 18, and 21, which looked at students' communication in second, as distinct from foreign language contexts. I also decided to exclude item 15, leaving it for an open-ended questionnaire to be distributed later in the study. I replaced American by British spelling. I do not think that these minor changes[3] affected the validity and reliability of the instrument, but have no empirical evidence to support my contention, since this amended version was not field-tested.

There are several methodological advantages to using a structured questionnaire and the BALLI conformed to all of these. Briefly, they include ease of administration, cost-effectiveness and the elicitation of data that are uniform and standard. Conversely, structured questionnaires with a high degree of explicitness and few open questions have a number of limitations (Seliger and Shohamy 1989). Victori (1999b) contends that such questionnaires lend themselves to difficulties with interpretation; contain leading questions, i.e. the focus and wording of the prompt may lead respondents to suggest answers that they may not otherwise have suggested; and restrict respondents to chose a compromise answer because they are unable to elaborate on their answers. In chapter 4, I shall return to some of these difficulties, because there was some evidence that they affected a few respondents.

In spite of these limitations, the BALLI's utility in the study weighed against its disadvantages. The ease of data collection and data analysis with the BALLI greatly facilitated the research process. The BALLI allowed me to have a snapshot of the students' beliefs about language learning and this was its chief advantage. A final advantage of the BALLI was that it allowed me to triangulate the data obtained from the diaries and the unstructured questionnaires.

3.5.5 Course Evaluation Questionnaires

A twelve-item course evaluation questionnaire (appendix D) containing a mixture of closed and open-ended questions was the last instrument used to collect data during F14A. Distribution of the questionnaire took place in the week beginning December 01 and completed questionnaires were returned by December 05, 1997. Unlike the personal information questionnaires, the course evaluation questionnaires were anonymous, so that it was not possible to measure how individual students' attitudes had evolved from the beginning to the end of the semester. What emerged then was a group view of how students felt the course contributed to their language learning, and a group self-evaluation of their growth over the thirteen-week semester. Twenty-two students (N=35) submitted course evaluation questionnaires.

By the end of the first semester, four sets of data, derived from the personal information questionnaires, the diaries, the BALLI and the course evaluation questionnaires had been collected and the first phase of the data collection process came to a close.

3.6 Data Collection in Semester II

Data collection in the second semester was conducted in a manner similar to what has been described for Semester I. Given that the first year course was a two-semester course, F14A and F14B, and with no repeaters re-joining the program, there was no further need to distribute personal information questionnaires. The PIQ was the only instrument that was not re-administered in Semester II. Students continued to keep their diaries. The BALLI was re-administered and course evaluation questionnaires were distributed at the end of the second semester course, according to the schedule outlined in table 4.

Table 4: Instruments used in Semester II

INSTRUMENT	DESCRIPTION	DATE ADMINISTERED/ DURATION	DATA ELICITED
Learner diaries	Structured and unstructured entries in L2; five lines long	January-April, 1998	Reflections on the grammar project; personal variables in language learning
BALLI	Thirty-item questionnaire (as for semester I)	April, 1998	Learners' beliefs about: a) the difficulty of language learning; b) foreign language aptitude; c) the nature of language learning; d) learning and communication strategies; e) motivation and expectations
Course Evaluation Questionnaires	Ten-item questionnaire using five closed questions (items 2-3,4-6 & 7); and five open-ended questions (items 1, 5, 8-10)	April, 1998	a) reflection on course and personal objectives (items 1-4); b) definition of an autonomous learner (item 5); c) student performance in the course (items 6-7); d) good/bad aspects of the course (items 8-9); e) further comments (item 10)

3.6.1 Learner Diaries

I made two changes to the diary studies in the second semester based on feedback that I received. Students were asked to write their entries in French. They were also required to include reflections on a grammar project on which they worked (appendix F).

The decision to have students write in French stemmed from their positive reaction to keeping diaries in the target language. Moreover, the writing focus in the second semester, business as opposed to general writing, created the need for more general writing wherever possible. The diaries also provided a forum for students to document their efforts on assembling a grammar-workbook (the second semester out-of-class project). Many students opted to work on their own for this project, so they used the diaries to interrogate themselves (and the teacher, although I very rarely intervened in writing in Semester II) on their progress on the project. These changes to the study are summarized in table 5.

Table 5: Methodological differences in diary studies in Semesters I and II

SEMESTER I	SEMESTER II
Mainly internal elicitation (unstructured entries) Some external elicitation (structured entries)	External elicitation (structured entries) and internal elicitation (unstructured entries)
Use of target language optional	Use of target language compulsory
Participation compulsory, but rewarded by a five mark bonus	Participation compulsory, no bonus
Researcher's role mixed: interventionist and non-interventionist stance	Researcher's role mainly non-interventionist

Methodological constraints. Unfortunately, constraints external to the French program (a long period of industrial unrest among administrative and support staff) affected the frequency with which learners were able to submit their diaries. Classes sometimes had to be rescheduled or cancelled at short notice. This, combined with the compulsion to use the L2 and the lack of bonus points, meant that far fewer students submitted their diaries regularly, than had done so in Semester I. These constraints affected mainly the paper-based diaries. The electronic diaries were not affected by the physical constraints.

3.6.2 The Beliefs About Language Learning Inventory (BALLI)

The BALLI was re-administered in Semester II. At the same time I asked students to reply to the question, "Do you feel that you have a foreign language aptitude?" Many students were absent on the day of the follow-up investigation, as this was during the period of industrial unrest and thus the response rate was very low. The six students who completed the BALLI the second time did not change any of their previous answers and only one student wrote a few sentences in response to the open question. Those data were therefore not included in the data analysis.

3.6.3 Course Evaluation Questionnaires

Course evaluation questionnaires (appendix D) were distributed at the end of Semester II. The ten items sought to explore students' reactions to the course. Items 4 and 5 addressed the learner autonomy intervention. The response rate for this questionnaire was high, with twenty-five of the continuing students (N=30), submitting questionnaires.

3.7 Data Analysis

The second stage of the research was the data analysis. A qualitative methodology commonly produces large quantities of written data. The challenge for the qualitative researcher is reducing what risks being an unwieldy and amorphous mass to a manageable framework for data analysis. In this study, I used content analysis to analyze data from pre-course and course evaluation questionnaires. The content analysis of the BALLI was modeled on the approach used in Horwitz (1988). Data from the students' diaries were analyzed in two ways. I analyzed the autobiographies as a separate data set using metaphor analysis, as described in Cortazzi and Jin (1999) and Lakoff and Johnson (1980); while the diaries were analyzed according to the model of diary studies set out in Bailey and Oschner (1983).

3.7.1 Analysis of the BALLI

The data from the BALLI were the first data set to be analyzed. Unlike some attitudinal instruments, the BALLI does not produce a composite score of attitudes towards language learning. What emerge from an analysis of the items are clusters of beliefs according to the five major areas. Accordingly, in responding to items 3, 4, 5, 6, 17, 22, 29, and 30, students revealed their beliefs about the difficulty of language learning. Items 1, 2, 10, 16, 23, 25,

26, and 27 indicated students' beliefs about foreign language aptitude. The nature of language learning was revealed by an analysis of items 8, 11, 13, 18, 20, and 21. Learning and communication strategies were catalogued in items 7, 9, 12, 14, and 15. Finally, items 19, 24, and 28 referred to students' motivations and expectations. The data were reported numerically as a raw score.

3.7.2 Analysis of the diaries

Analyzing the students' diaries proved to be slightly more problematic. While each diary revealed something of the individual's approach to learning French, another picture emerged from the autobiographies when they were viewed as a separate set of data. I first analyzed the autobiographies according to the categories suggested in my directions to the students. I sorted the data into these pre-determined categories based on:

- Their first exposure to foreign language learning (classroom-based or naturalistic)
- The role of the teacher or family members in language learning
- The role of classmates
- The role of affective variables in language learning
- Skill preferences
- Learning strategies
- Other factors that promoted or hindered language learning

Although this was a convenient way of sorting the qualitative data, it did not seem to account for the emerging patterns. I coded the autobiographies a second time using highlighters—blue to code negative emotions, red for positive emotions, purple for references to teachers and so on. This way of processing the information was more effective in revealing significant themes in the autobiographies. I had been struck by the students' references to falling in love with French, but I was unable to find a way to interpret those data satisfactorily. A second and more effective way to make sense of the data came from using metaphor analysis.

Rod Ellis's (1999) paper at the Beliefs Symposium at AILA Japan 99 revealed that he was using learners' diaries to research learners' beliefs. Although Ellis worked with a sophisticated concordancing program and I worked the old-fashioned, pre-technology way, manually sorting and coding the data, there were several areas of overlap in our findings. But more importantly, Ellis's talk convinced me to look again at the autobiographical data through the lens of metaphor analysis. Although I was familiar with work on teachers' metaphors, for example, research conducted by Katz

(1996) and Oxford et al. (1998), it was the work of Lakoff and Johnson (1980) and research in Cameron and Low (1999) that deepened my understanding of metaphor analysis. Over the course of the data analysis, a period of approximately two years, I had grown very familiar with the data, as I returned to them time and time again, trying to tease out the patterns in the diaries. I had become quite familiar with what I was seeing, however, it was metaphor analysis that provided the tools to help me interpret and theorize the data.

The final phase of the data analysis was the selection and in-depth analysis of the diaries of a few learners. Which diaries? Which learners? All the diaries seemed to offer very rich qualitative data. All revealed fascinating insights into the thinking of these first-year students. Choosing the "best" data was difficult. Nonetheless, I proceeded in a linear, step-by-step fashion, selecting first, completed Semester I diaries, then from these, I eliminated those diarists who did not keep a diary in Semester II. At the next step, I selected students with GCE Grades A to C, those who are usually most likely to do well in the first-year courses. Finally, I selected a small subset of three diaries based on the qualitative data they contained. Two of the diaries were selected because the diarists were typical cases of first-year undergraduates, but the third was a unique-case selection.

The three diaries selected were analyzed following the procedure recommended by Bailey (1983). The final treatment carried out on this small sample of diaries was an analysis to see whether there was any fit between the beliefs referred to in the diaries and the beliefs catalogued by the BALLI.

3.8 A Qualitative Methodology

In this study, both data collection and data analysis procedures relied on a qualitative research methodology. Erickson (1986) and Davis (1995) remind us that qualitative research techniques do not constitute a research method. It is the focus and intent of the study, rather than the techniques employed that constitute a qualitative methodology. Allwright and Bailey (1991, 51) concur, stating that "the goal in naturalistic enquiry is to understand what happens in the individual classroom." In this study, a qualitative naturalistic methodology was thus appropriate to explore how students' conceptions of responsibility for learning influenced the roles they were prepared to adopt and ultimately, influenced their willingness to be autonomous learners. Studies such as these that purport "to describe educational settings and contexts, to generate theory, and to evaluate programs" are labeled educational ethnographies (LeCompte, Preissle, and Tesch 1993, 8).

There are, however, a number of techniques upon which a qualitative research methodology relies and these were integrated into the study. An important issue in conducting field research in qualitative paradigms is prolonged observation of the "context", i.e. the environment in which the behavior occurs. My knowledge of the informants in this study came from approximately fifty contact hours of classroom or field experience, during the period of data collection. Generally, I was able to fulfill one condition of internal validity in the qualitative paradigm, that is, long-term observation. In addition to long-term observation, internal validity in the data analysis was derived from data triangulation.

Another way in which qualitative data can be verified is by the inclusion of other researchers in data collection and data analysis. Internal validity may be derived from peer examination of the data or participatory or collaborative modes of research. Although I worked as an independent researcher, my supervisor was often involved in key decisions that I made during the research process. The following extract from my informal notes indicates something of his role as non-participant observer at different stages of the study:

23/09/97
Spoke with I. today. He was having misgivings about the either or in French, although I thought he agreed to my Fr./Eng. option. He shared his experience with the scanner, its lack of fidelity and felt a hand-held one, at the present time was not perfected enough. I threw out the idea of a qualitative data package, stressing that I knew that the technology while it had certain advantages, had certain limitations.

This kind of collaboration with my supervisor helped me to gain another perspective on the research process and helped to validate the decisions that I made during data collection and analysis. Other colleagues also provided critical assistance at various stages of the study. My participation in various symposia and conferences at which I presented some of the data and the feedback from colleagues on those occasions served as debriefings by peers.

Another procedure that is often recommended in qualitative paradigms is doing member checks, that is, ensuring the accuracy of the information by receiving feedback from the informants. I was not able to do this during the data collection period. But during the data analysis, one of the three non-traditional learners, referred to earlier, e-mailed the following response to the draft of an article[4] that I sent her:

Chere Madame,
I have just skimmed thru' the article & my initial response to it is "How I wish I had something like this to read BEFORE I started this programme, or even at the end of yr 1!!!!!".
I know I need to read it thoroughly, but even from skimming thru' I know that if I had this kind of understanding of my own situation at the beginning, the anxiety would have been considerably less, and I would have been able to channel that energy into actual learning instead. I know there's only a few weeks left, but I still think the knowledge is helpful, even at this stage.
Also, it has strongly re-enforced to me the absolutely necessity of Linguistics for the foreign-language learner.
It would be nice if all mature students could have a copy of something like this before embarking on the degree programme.
Thanks

This student's reactions support what has been said about the goals of qualitative research. For LeCompte, Preissle and Tesch (1993), the goals of qualitative and other interpretive approaches are:

1. Comparison of results to similar and dissimilar processes and phenomena;
2. Development of workable and shared understandings regarding regularities in human behavior in specific settings.

Summarizing what I have said thus far, I wish to conclude by reiterating that qualitative and quantitative paradigms operate on very different premises. Qualitative research advocates a different role for the researcher and the researched; a different approach to data collection and data analysis; no conventionalized mode for presenting findings, diversity reigns (Bogdan and Biklen 1998) and ultimately different criteria for judging the results of the research.

While the quantitative paradigm stresses validity, reliability and generalizability, the qualitative researcher does not seek the objective reality of the quantitative paradigm. My intention is to convey the subjective, multiple realities of the participants. My responsibility is to do so with a high degree of accuracy and in a manner that is reliable and able to withstand verification. Finally, my task as a researcher in the qualitative paradigm is to arrive at a valid interpretation of the findings. These are the goals that I hope to achieve in the following chapter, which presents the findings of the study.

NOTES

1. There were two speakers with native speaker proficiency at the start of the course. The 20 year-old male, a native of Rwanda had completed his secondary education in Trinidad. He was a part-time student, who only completed the first semester. The 58 year-old female, was a German L1 speaker, who had lived and worked in French-speaking Switzerland for 20 years. She, however, withdrew from the University after one week. The majority of students were L1 speakers of Trinidadian English.

2. One student had withdrawn from the course and three were absent and subsequently withdrew.

3. Creswell (1994) warns that when a modified instrument is used the original validity and reliability may be distorted and it is necessary to reestablish validity and reliability.

4. The case study is reported in Carter (1998).

Chapter Four
DEVELOPING LEARNER AUTONOMY
IN LANGUAGE LEARNING

In this chapter, I present and discuss the findings of the study. In keeping with the order in which the data were analyzed, I begin by looking at the results of the BALLI questionnaire. For reasons of clarity, the implications of the results will be discussed after the data for each section have been presented. Secondly, I will examine the student autobiographies to explore what they reveal about the students' learning histories. Finally, I will do an in-depth analysis of a small sample of three diaries.

4.1 Results and Discussion of the BALLI

4.1.1 The Difficulty of Language Learning
The students surveyed overwhelmingly (N=31) supported the belief that there is a hierarchy of difficulty when it comes to language learning. No one strongly disagreed with this statement, although a small number of students (N=3) neither agreed nor disagreed and one student disagreed. This item (item 3) was one of a very few items for which there was almost universal support.

The belief in a hierarchy of difficulty when it comes to language learning is not peculiar to the students in this study. Bauer and Trudgill (1998, xvi) in fact contend that the notion that some languages are harder than others is one of the "myths," one of the "well-established ideas about language" that ordinary people have. Phillips and Stencel (1983) shed some light on the source of such beliefs. These authors posit, for example, that the relative simplicity of Spanish grammar in the early stages makes Spanish more accessible than French to English speakers. This in turn leads to the perception that Spanish is easier than French as an L2 for native speakers of English.

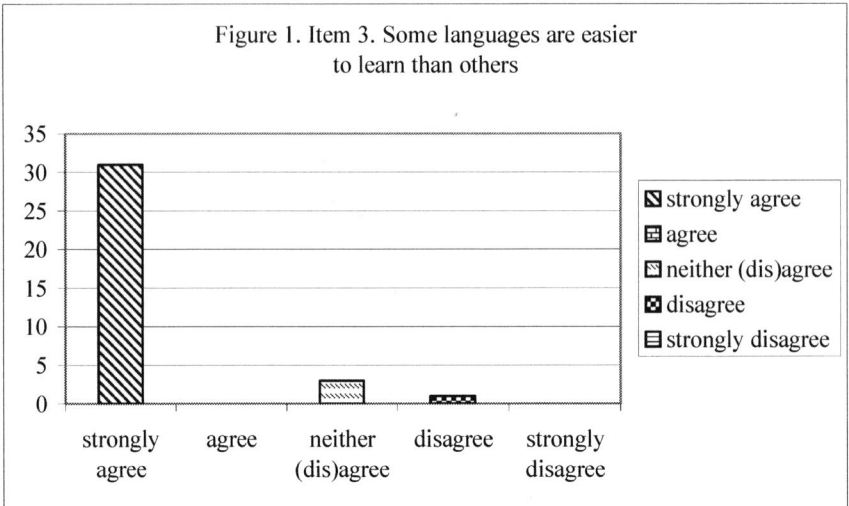

Figure 1. Item 3. Some languages are easier to learn than others

Items 4 to 6 of the questionnaire attempted to get further insights into students' beliefs about a hierarchy of difficulty. Item 4 asked students to identify a language that was difficult to learn and item 5 asked for a language that was easy to learn. Item 6 required students to judge how easy or difficult it was to learn the target language. No student listed Spanish as a language that was difficult to learn. On the other hand, a variety of languages, ranging from Arabic to Russian were said to be difficult to learn. Five students felt that Chinese was difficult to learn and five felt that Japanese was difficult to learn. The languages that students rated next as being most difficult to learn after these two less commonly taught languages were English (N=4) and French (N=3).

Although, in many instances, the languages identified as being difficult were those that used different writing systems from English, for example, Hindi, Arabic, and Russian, the fact that students identified French (N=3) and English (N=4) as difficult languages suggests that students used several criteria to judge difficulty. Hence, the difficulty of the grammar of the language, as Phillips and Stencel (1983) suggest, could well have inspired students' answers. With a questionnaire of this type, it is impossible to know exactly what criteria students applied to arrive at their judgment of difficulty. Interestingly, one student tried to ensure that she was not misunderstood on this point. Instead of choosing an easy and a difficult language, she wrote:

> I don't really think that it's a matter of being easy/difficult, but more so a question of which language the person is more exposed to: this would make for an easier/quicker understanding of the language.[1]

This student's felt need to clarify her answer reveals one of the limitations of questionnaires, a point alluded to in chapter 3. Unless students are asked to think aloud and explain their choice or the researcher does follow-up interviews (and both these techniques have the potential to contaminate the data), it is difficult to do more than speculate as to what led students to choose one option over another.

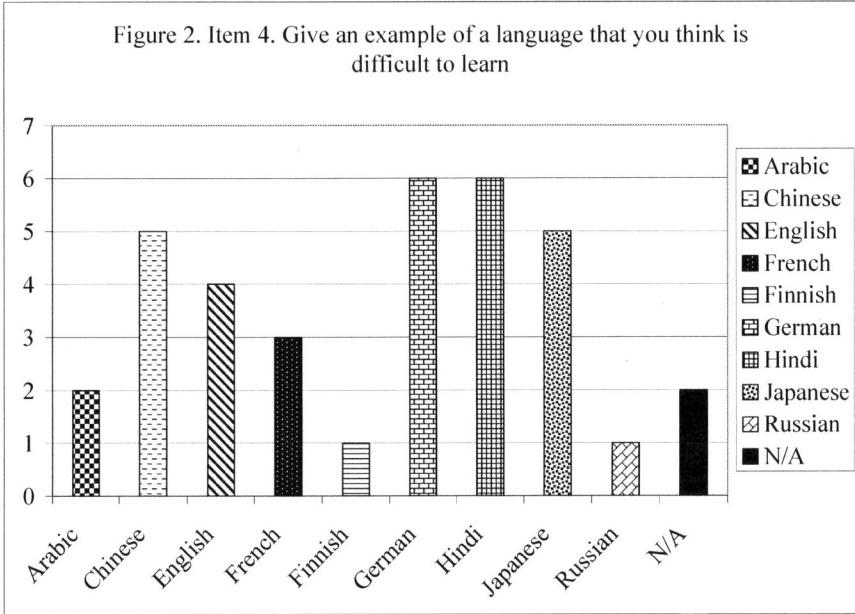

Figure 2. Item 4. Give an example of a language that you think is difficult to learn

Item 5 asked students to name a language that was easy to learn. A majority of the students (N=18) felt that Spanish was easy to learn. Only one student gave the example of French as an easy language to learn. This was in sharp contrast to the answers given in item 6. In item 6, one student labeled French a very difficult language and fifteen felt that it was a language of medium difficulty. In other words, thirty-one of the thirty-five students surveyed ranked French as difficult rather than easy.

The students' perception of the difficulty of French as opposed to the ease of Spanish is significant when one considers how these perceptions might influence students' attitudes. How is their perseverance for French language learning likely to be affected by these perceptions? Will difficulty of learning have the same impact on students who are intrinsically and extrinsically motivated? What will be the relationship between such perceptions and instrumental or integrative motivation? In short, how does the fact that students find the second foreign language more difficult than the first foreign language govern both their overall motivation and their day-to-day experience of French as a foreign language?

Earlier in this study, I examined some of the contextual factors that govern the teaching of French in Trinidad and Tobago. An area worth exploring in future research might be the relationship between contextual factors and the strongly held belief that Spanish is easier than French.

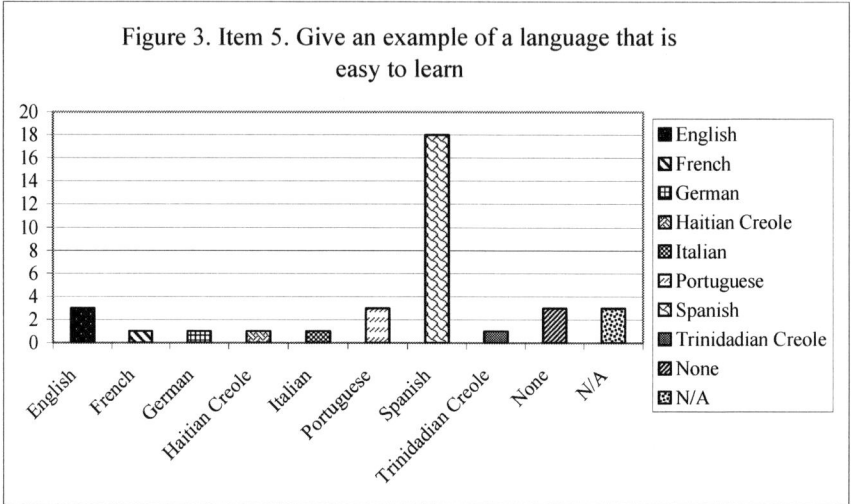

Figure 3. Item 5. Give an example of a language that is easy to learn

Is difficulty/ease primarily a function of the grammatical systems of the two languages, that is, a linguistic phenomenon? Is difficulty/ease related to the status of the languages in the education system—Spanish, primary foreign language, compulsory in all public secondary schools, as opposed to French, second foreign language, taught in selected schools—a social phenomenon? Is the perception that Spanish is easier than French related to the sociolinguistic environment and the proximity of Spanish-speaking nations?

Sealey (1983, TS-4) draws attention to the role of the Venezuelan-inspired parang as a "national cultural form" and the effect of this continuing contact with Spanish language and culture on the sensitivity to Spanish in Trinidad and Tobago, lending support to the student's perception, cited earlier, according to which ease or difficulty could be linked to the degree of exposure to the target language. It seems that a number of factors, some internal to the language, others related to the role and status of (the) language(s) in the society may explain why students perceive French to be more difficult than Spanish.

Under the category of beliefs pertaining to the "Difficulty of Language Learning", the BALLI also sought students' views on the relative ease or difficulty of certain skills. Item 17 investigated whether students thought that it was easier to speak or understand a foreign language, while item 22 probed the difficulty of developing reading as opposed to writing skills. A majority of students (N=19) disagreed that speaking was easier than understanding, with eleven of them disagreeing and eight strongly disagreeing. These students far outnumbered those who agreed (N=5). A significant number (N=11) of the students surveyed were, however, undecided about the comparative ease or difficulty of these skills.

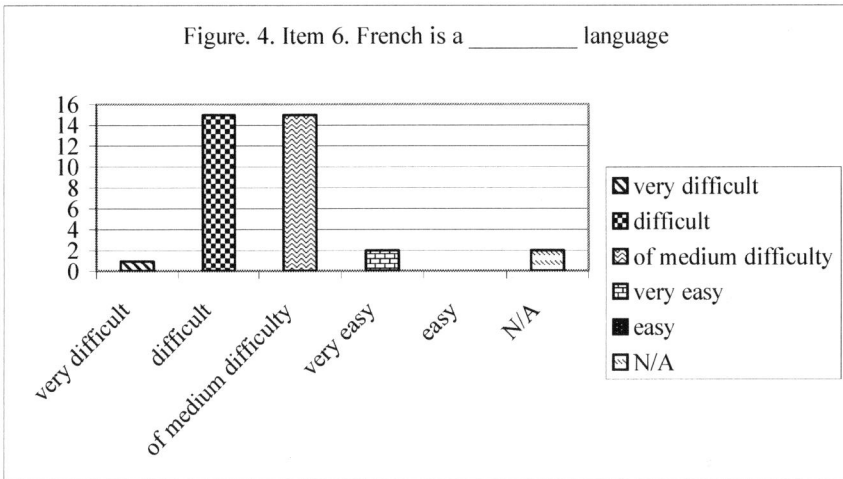

Figure. 4. Item 6. French is a _____ language

In answer to item 22, the greatest number of students, twenty-nine out of thirty-five, thought that it was easier to develop reading skills than writing skills in a foreign language. Seven students strongly agreed; the majority (N= 22) agreed. Two students were neutral on the issue but five disagreed that it was easier to develop reading skills than writing skills in a foreign language. However, no one strongly disagreed. The trend noted in item 17 was therefore confirmed in item 22, with students assessing the receptive skills of understanding, i.e. listening and reading, as being comparatively easier than the productive skills of speaking and writing.

It is difficult to decide whether these beliefs spring from a perception that it is easier to develop the skills associated with receptive tasks, or whether an affective characteristic, such as anxiety influences how learners interpret different classroom tasks. A brief review of the literature relating to these two notions could bring us to a better understanding of the possible source of the students' beliefs.

First of all, research on how learners process aural and written input has changed much of our thinking about how comprehension takes place. In her very comprehensive review of the research on listening comprehension, Rubin (1994) lists several factors that are presumed to affect listening comprehension. These are:

1. Text characteristics (variations in a listening passage/text or associated visual support);
2. Interlocutor characteristics (variation in the speaker's personal characteristics);
3. Task characteristics (variation in the purpose for listening and associated responses);
4. Listener characteristics (variation in the listener's personal characteristics); and
5. Process characteristics (variation in the listener's cognitive activities and in the nature of the interaction between speaker and listener).

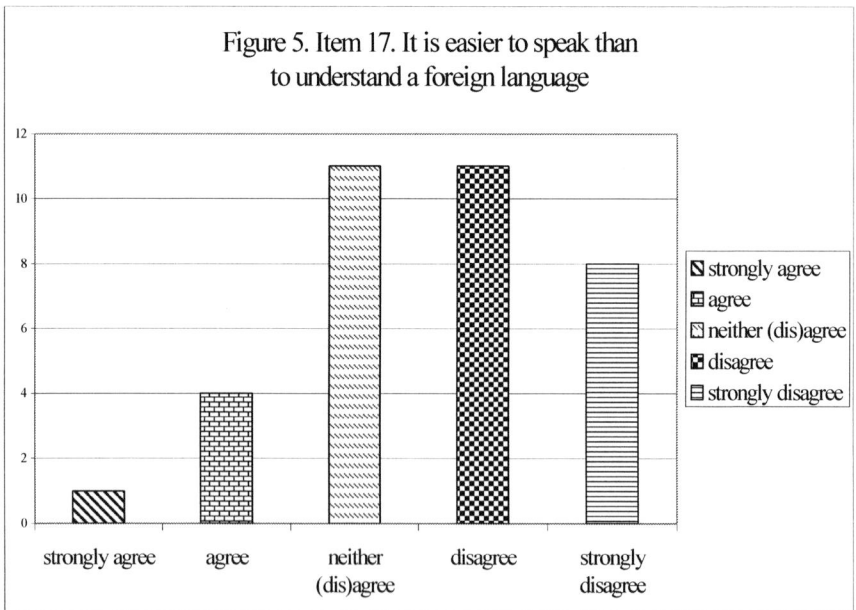

Figure 5. Item 17. It is easier to speak than to understand a foreign language

Rubin's (1994) review of over one hundred studies which report on the variety of factors affecting listening comprehension underscores the complexity of comprehending aural input. Swaffar and Bacon (1993, 126) in reviewing the research on reading and listening comprehension, also list some of the factors that are thought to influence these two skills. They identify the text's sociolinguistic context, its rhetorical organization, its lexicon, style and morphosyntax, and the effect of instruction in strategy use, as some of the "learner-extrinsic factors that may affect the comprehension process." In Swaffar and Bacon's view, life was easier for both the teacher and researcher in the period prior to the foundational L1 work in psycholinguistics which now informs second and foreign language research design. It was easier because listening and reading were regarded as automatic recognition skills and not as activities that were open to influence by cognition and affect.

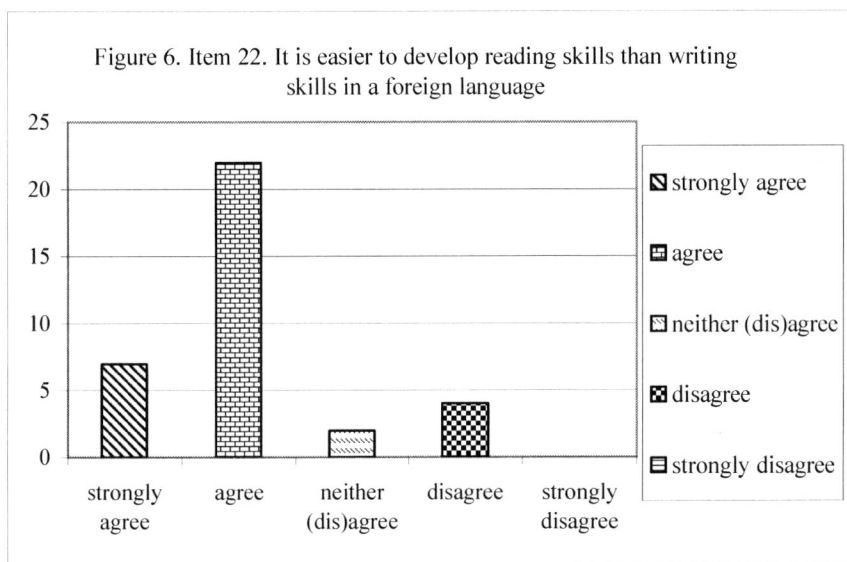

Figure 6. Item 22. It is easier to develop reading skills than writing skills in a foreign language

Life was easier for students also, though for another reason. The use of didactic texts that were standardized in terms of morphosyntactic as well as lexical features seemed appropriate when the task of listening was conceived of as registering and replicating aural input. By contrast, the use of authentic texts in the classroom often requires students to respond as active participants, whose task it is to construct meaning on the basis of what is read or heard. According to this view, comprehension is an interactive process requiring learners to be creative and to make meaning out of texts.

Gass and Magnan (1993) contend further that since comprehension requires students to produce meaning from texts, there is room to see reading and listening as productive skills. But students who think that the object of comprehension is to register and replicate are likely to underestimate the task demands and engage in a level of processing well below what is required. Consequently, such students may interpret the task and, by extension, the process of comprehension, as easier than they really are, because their perception of the difficulty of the task is premised on their perception of the nature of the task.

In the absence of empirical evidence, it is impossible to say whether the majority of beginning university students see comprehension as registering and replicating (passive/receptive skills) or as interpreting and creating meaning (active/productive skills), although anecdotal evidence suggests that the first view prevails. What I can say, though, is that in spite of the students' claims that it is easier to acquire listening and reading skills than speaking and writing skills, their classroom test results do not reveal better performance in the area of listening and reading.

The foregoing discussion is not meant to imply that students are wrong when they perceive speaking and writing as more difficult to acquire than listening and reading. The students' perceptions or beliefs about what is easy or difficult for them cannot be disputed. What seems to be the issue here is whether students have the "metacognitive knowledge about task demands or goals" (Flavell 1979, 907) in the comprehension skills. It is important to recall arguments about the need to distinguish between metacognitive knowledge and beliefs. When the source of students' perceptions is a lack of metacognitive knowledge, there is room for giving students metacognitive knowledge about task demands or goals. Thus, one way to have students reexamine their invalid beliefs is by sharing the appropriate metacognitive knowledge with them.

As was true for listening and reading, a variety of factors, some extrinsic, some intrinsic to the learner, influence the production of oral and written discourse. Here again if students could be made aware of the exact nature of the learning task and taught how to manage the task while engaged in it, the perceived difficulty of these skills may be lessened.

Cognitive strategy training rests on the assumption that learners can be taught how to use what Wenden (1991, 19) refers to as "mental steps or operations ... to process both linguistic and sociolinguistic content." Strategy training also acknowledges the role of metacognitive or self-management strategies used by learners to oversee and manage their learning. Successful strategy use, it is often emphasized, is consistent with the application of the appropriate strategy to the task. What this means is that learners must be aware of the repertoire of available strategies and be able to select the most appropriate strategy, in keeping with their assessment of the task to be performed.

The social and affective strategy of self-talk is perhaps one strategy that could be usefully adopted by all learners who find production tasks demanding. Tasks that are regarded as more challenging are likely to produce greater anxiety in students than tasks that are regarded as easy. Anxiety, here, is judged as being linked to the nature of the task, state anxiety, rather than being a personal characteristic, "a more permanent predisposition to be anxious", trait anxiety (Scovel 1978, 137). State anxiety is thought to be a complex factor that could prove to be either a positive or negative force in language learning. Positive anxiety—facilitative anxiety—enhances L2 performance because students are encouraged to make a greater effort to respond to the learning task. In contrast, students who think that a task is too difficult are more anxious when called upon to perform that task. It is hypothesized that the negative or debilitating anxiety produced on such occasions causes learners to flee a learning task that they perceive as too difficult. Learners who know how to engage in self-talk could use this strategy to great effect when confronted with difficult production tasks.

There is sufficient anecdotal evidence in the qualitative data of the students' diaries to support the contention that too high levels of anxiety lead to poor performance. It seems that students perform less well in those skill areas that they find difficult, in part because the high level of anxiety that they experience inhibits their performance. Indeed, Krashen's affective filter hypothesis (Krashen 1981, 1982) is premised on this observation. A vicious cycle is set up, whereby poor performance leads to greater anxiety which, in turn, spells poor performance, so that students' fears about a lack of competence could be eventually realized. In summing up, it is evident that the students' beliefs about the difficulty of oral and written production are important because of their potential impact on their self-concept as language learners.

The remaining items examined under the category of the "Difficulty of Language Learning" addressed the issues of the rate of learning (item 29) and the students' potential for becoming proficient (item 30). Students were unequivocal in their belief that the rate of language learning depended on the target language and the individual language learner. A clear majority (N=30) felt that it was difficult to predict how long it would take someone to learn to speak a language very well at the rate of one hour per day. At least one respondent selected each of the options suggested—less than a year (N=1); 1-2 years (N=1); 3-5 years (N=2); 5-10 years (N=1). Nonetheless, this item was significant in that the majority of answers were bunched in one category. Students preferred not to speculate on the rate at which a foreign language could be learned. Instead, they overwhelmingly rejected finite periods, opting rather for an answer that implied that language learning was an open-ended task, dependent on the individual learner and the target language.

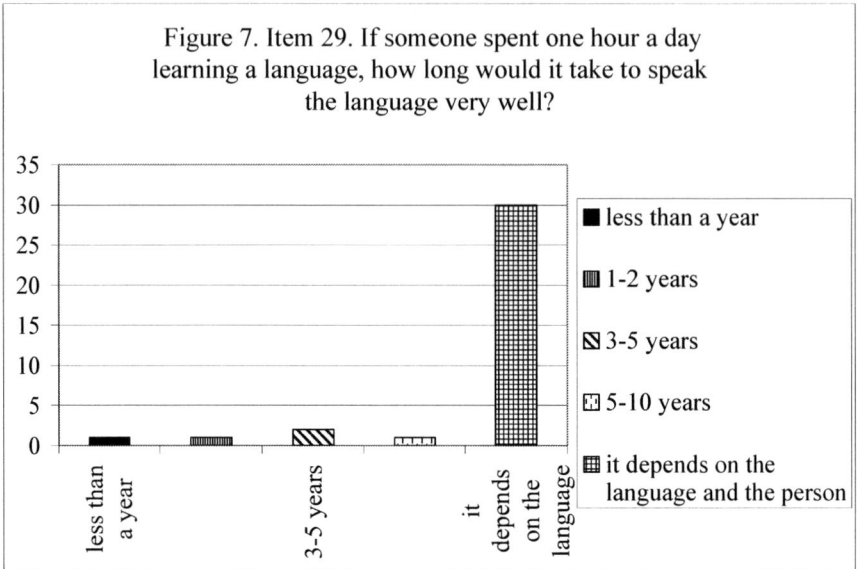

Figure 7. Item 29. If someone spent one hour a day learning a language, how long would it take to speak the language very well?

- ■ less than a year
- ▥ 1-2 years
- ◪ 3-5 years
- ▣ 5-10 years
- ▦ it depends on the language and the person

Item 30 asked students to assess their chances for learning to speak the target language very well. It is a very positive sign that, notwithstanding the students' assessment of French as a difficult language and their rejection of the idea that it was easier to speak than to understand, the students' self-concept about their potential for success is intact. Whereas many of the other items in this category—items 3, 6,17, 22, and 29—asked students to speak for the idealized foreign language learner, item 30 asked students to speak on their own behalf. They answered an emphatic yes, with twenty-five students strongly agreeing that they would ultimately learn to speak French very well.

Major trends in the data and their implications. An investigation of learner beliefs is an important dimension of an intervention to promote autonomy. Through the BALLI, both the students and I were able to gain an insight into some of their perceptions. Becoming aware of some of the perceptions, for example the perception of the relative difficulty of French as compared to Spanish, is useful in helping me to appreciate some of the underlying attitudes and beliefs that influence students' behavior. In other cases, for example the students' beliefs about the difficulty of productive as opposed to receptive skills, there is room for me to intervene and provide metacognitive knowledge in order to confront beliefs that could prove inimical to foreign language learning and learner autonomy.

The students' belief in the comparative facility of receptive skills as against productive skills is, as we have seen, not a belief that is fully supported in current research. If, however, students persist in thinking in this way, it is quite likely that they will not activate the necessary cognitive strategies to be efficient listeners and readers. While such behavior may not prevent the successful completion of tasks at lower levels of proficiency, where comprehension is chiefly registering and replicating, at higher levels where learners are expected to make inferences and engage in a more analytical reading of texts, their deficiencies could become apparent. The consequences of these beliefs for the students' assumption of autonomy must be underscored. It is doubtful whether students could develop the kinds of attitudes and behavior consistent with autonomous, self-directed learning in their execution of comprehension tasks, if their self-concept of their role is premised on a misunderstanding of what constitutes effective comprehension.

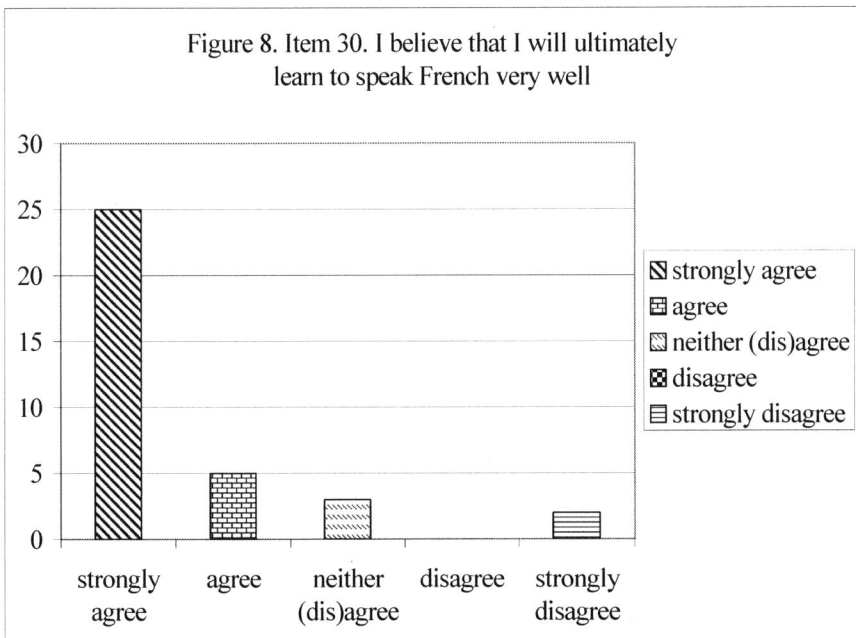

Figure 8. Item 30. I believe that I will ultimately learn to speak French very well

It is evidently for reasons such as these, that the link between evaluation and autonomy has often been emphasized. Autonomous learners are those who are capable of assuming responsibility for their learning, even though they may not always choose to exercise that autonomy. Students who are teacher-directed need their teacher to perform the roles of diagnostician and planner. Students who are autonomous are able to fulfill these roles themselves. In assessing the demands of a task and the effort they need to make for the successful completion of the task, autonomous learners are therefore more capable of assessing whether their efforts fall short and begin to adopt the necessary remedial measures to achieve the successful completion of the task. On the other hand, students who are not self-directed are not inclined to perform the evaluative function themselves and are even less apt to know how to progress from their present to a higher level of mastery. Promoting learner autonomy in the receptive skills might entail raising students' awareness about the requirements of these skills, thereby helping them to be better prepared to accept the diagnostician and planning roles in furtherance of their objectives.

Another area that warrants attention in the analysis of the students' replies to the "Difficulty of Language Learning" is the students' belief in their potential for achieving oral proficiency. Given the students' categorization of oral proficiency as a more difficult skill than aural comprehension, it may be worth exploring whether they are able to perform the diagnostician and planning roles to realize their goal in this aspect of their communicative competence.

Beyond their belief about the difficulty of this skill, do students know how to proceed to rise above the obstacles that they envisage? How does one acquire oral proficiency? Is it a function of the strategies employed—the exploitation of social, communicative and affective strategies as O'Malley and Chamot (1990) contend; exposure to comprehensible input as Krashen (1981, 1982) contends; or negotiated interaction resulting in what Swain (1999) labels "collaborative dialogue"? How much interaction with native speakers is necessary?

There is still considerable debate among researchers about which of a variety of factors enhances oral proficiency. Yet, students who ignore the full range of possibilities for improving their oral proficiency may employ a limited range of strategies and fail in their efforts to acquire the desired level of proficiency. Students who are not flexible and cannot discard unproductive strategies are equally likely to be hampered in their efforts to improve proficiency. If the failure to employ appropriate strategies results in poor performance, with students failing to attain the level of proficiency that they deem desirable, their belief in the difficulty of the skill is likely to be reinforced. The end result may be that the students' initial positive outlook on their potential for achieving oral proficiency could be severely dampened by their repeated failure to improve their oral competence. When this happens students are likely to lose motivation to continue to improve their language learning.

Students who are unaware of how their attitudes and beliefs can stymie their genuine desire to improve their proficiency need the opportunity for introspection to reflect on the attitudes and beliefs that they hold. Language learning methodologies, even learner-centered methodologies, have not traditionally made a case for the development of metacognitive and metalinguistic awareness as part of language learning. The results of this study suggest, however, that there is a role for the integration of metacognitive and metalinguistic awareness in language learning.

Proponents of autonomous approaches, especially those who subscribe to psychological versions of autonomy advocate the integration of a specific focus on awareness, both metalinguistic and metacognitive awareness, into autonomous approaches to language learning. Broady and Kenning (1996b) suggest that learners could be helped to develop an awareness of how to use different learning environments and resources. They also see room for developing learning strategies and the insight into one's own learning style as part of an approach that seeks to promote learner autonomy.

4.1.2 Foreign Language Aptitude

The next cluster of items told us whether students thought that there was equal potential for achieving proficiency in L2 learning scattered among the population. The category "Foreign Language Aptitude" examined whether students believed that some learners are likely to be more successful than others, due to factors such as special language ability (item 2), intelligence (items 23 and 25), sex (item 16), and so on.

A majority of the students (N=27) believed that children have an advantage over adults in language learning (item 1). Almost equal numbers of students strongly agreed that this was so (N=13) and agreed that this was so (N=14). Just one student indicated that she disagreed. One student indicated that she strongly disagreed and six students neither agreed nor disagreed.

Snow and Hoefnagel-Höhle (1978) conducted a large-scale investigation into second language learning in a natural situation. They indicated that while there seemed to be some clear-cut results about child, adolescent, and adult second language acquisition in different domains, the difficulty lies in interpreting the meaning of the results. They advise caution in interpreting their preliminary results and suggest that more empirical work needs to be conducted to ensure that claims for the superiority of child language acquisition will be premised on empirical data rather than speculation and anecdotal evidence.

Figure 9. Item 1. It is easier for children than adults to learn
a foreign language

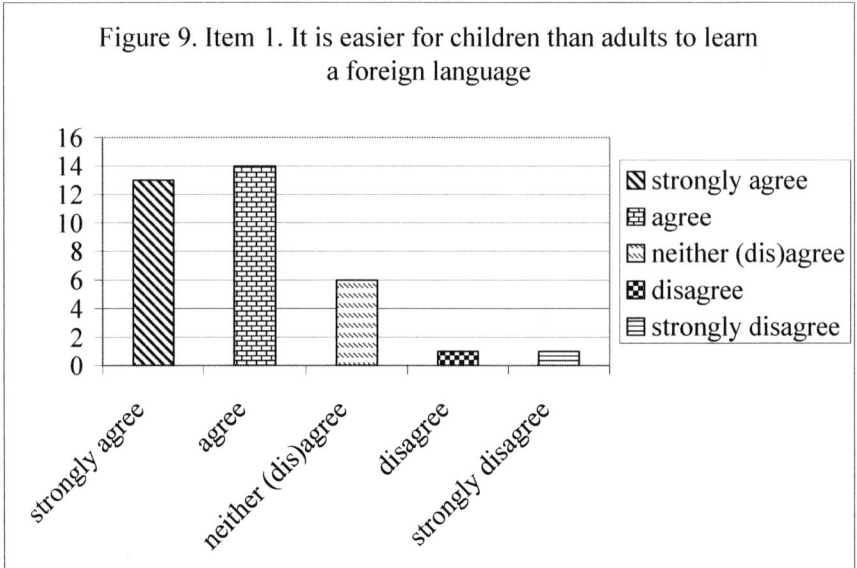

It is precisely the tendency to over-generalize and make false analogies that Brown (1987) condemns in his comparison of child and adult second language acquisition. He maintains that too often claims for the superiority of child language acquisition have been based on the comparison of child first language acquisition (FLA) and adult second language acquisition (SLA). Consequently, while children do seem to be able to master the phonology of the language more successfully than adults, there are several factors that make it difficult to endorse wholeheartedly the superiority of children as foreign language learners.

Brown does, however, concede that a comparison of SLA in children and adults points to a number of differences. By looking at neurological, psychomotor, cognitive, affective and linguistic considerations that affect SLA in adults and children, Brown is able to give a more fine-grained analysis of some of the ways in which acquisition takes place in older and younger individuals. While there seems to be a definite role in second language acquisition theory for the importance of age as a learner characteristic, there is not as yet sufficient evidence to state unconditionally that children learn foreign languages more easily (or more successfully) than adult learners.

Item 2 examined whether students felt that some people had a special ability that helped them learn a foreign language. Although the majority of students (N=23) agreed with this statement, roughly one third of the students expressed dissent. Six students neither agreed nor disagreed with the statement in item 2, while five disagreed and one strongly disagreed. The answers given to item 27 indicated, however, a majority belief in the existence of a general language ability. The notion that there exists a general language ability, a biological endowment shared by all human beings was reflected in the almost universal support (twelve students strongly agreed and twenty agreed) given to the statement "Everyone can learn a foreign language." No one disagreed with this proposition and only a few students were neutral (N=2) or disagreed (N=1). If the respondents' view on items 2 and 27 are examined together, it appears that almost all the respondents (N=32) accepted that everybody can learn a foreign language, whereas about three-quarters of them (N=23) agreed that some people have a special ability or gift above the rest.

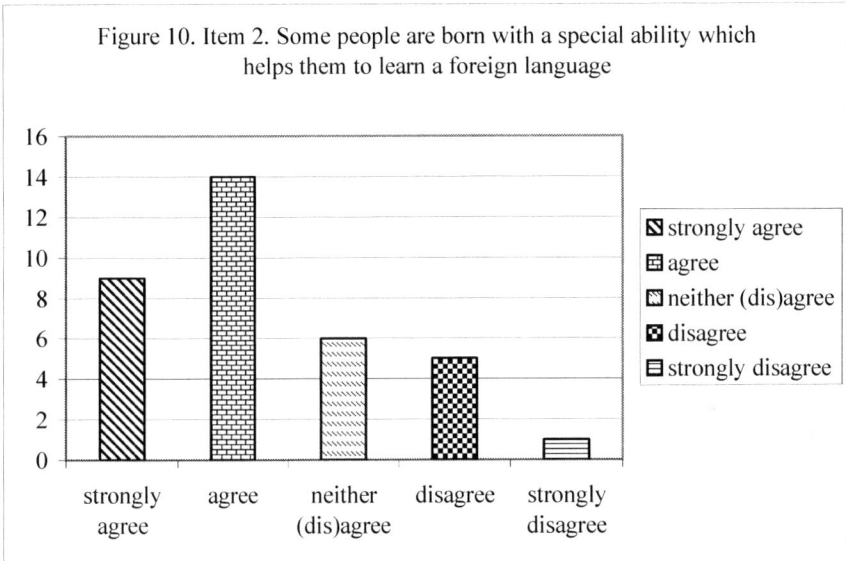

Figure 10. Item 2. Some people are born with a special ability which helps them to learn a foreign language

The debate about whether foreign language aptitude is found universally in the human population, or whether it is the gift of the linguistically endowed is not of recent vintage. As far back as 1967, Carroll (1967-1968) sought to disambiguate the issue, focusing instead on the consequences for foreign language learning. He concluded that, while foreign language aptitude relates to an individual's capacity or general ability to learn a foreign language and to be successful in the undertaking, the degree of proficiency attained by a foreign language learner does not depend solely on high foreign language aptitude. Exposure, for example, through study abroad could redress the imbalance for the low-aptitude student.

Item 10 sought to find out whether students thought that foreign language learning could be facilitated if the learner already spoke one foreign language. The majority of students agreed (N=12) or strongly agreed (N=7) that an L2 speaker could acquire L3 competence more readily than a monolingual speaker could acquire L2 competence. But, there was considerable disagreement on the issue. Just under a quarter of the students were unsure and chose the option neither agreed nor disagreed. While an equal number of students (N=8) disagreed or strongly disagreed that this was so.

Figure 11. Item 27. Everyone can learn a foreign language

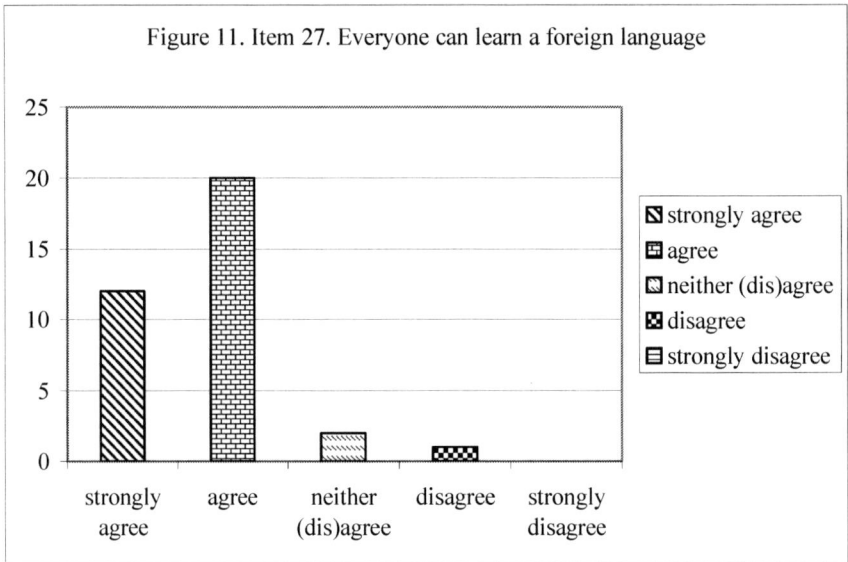

The students in this study have very little first-hand experience of multilingualism in their daily lives. Thus, though they seem prepared to accept foreign language aptitude as a universal phenomenon, their hesitation to agree with this proposition betrays a gap between their received knowledge and their experiential knowledge concerning multilingualism. In contrast, learners who live in multilingual societies would probably not doubt the linguistic potential of the multilingual speaker over the monolingual one.

The students' responses to item 10 revealed the importance of societal beliefs in forming students' attitudes to, and beliefs about, foreign language learning. Horwitz (1987) stresses the importance of taking into account the pervasive societal beliefs about language learning. Learners who develop a receptivity to foreign languages because of the educational context and the larger social context of their language learning are more likely to be confident about their ability to acquire multiple languages.

Figure 12. Item 10. It is easier for someone who already speaks a foreign language to learn another one

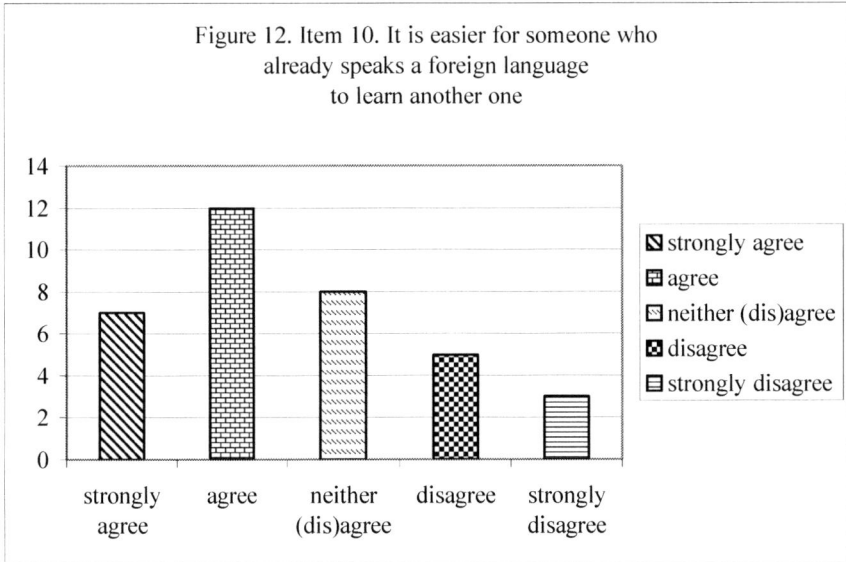

Cook (1993) draws on a study by Koenig, Chia, and Povey (1983) to defend a similar view. As Cook reports, a native of the Cameroon uses, on a daily basis, four or five languages chosen from the two official languages, the four lingua francas, and the 285 native languages. By contrast, monolingual speakers or foreign language learners who have little experience of multilingual contexts tend to regard their state as the norm and see multilingualism as a phenomenon. Sridhar (1994) chides linguists for sometimes acting as though they too share this belief.

The importance of the context of language learning and its impact on students' beliefs was again highlighted in item 26. In responding to the statement "People in Trinidad and Tobago are good at learning foreign languages", the majority of the students (N=24) neither agreed nor disagreed. No one strongly agreed. Eight students agreed, but three of them disagreed. No student strongly disagreed.

While the expression of neutrality might simply be a case of prudence on the part of the students who were hesitant to interpret "good at learning foreign languages", it nonetheless pointed to a lack of confidence in their fellow citizens' ability as language learners. Thus, although the students thought that everyone had an aptitude for foreign languages and they themselves felt capable of achieving high levels of proficiency, they were unsure whether the same was true for others in their country.

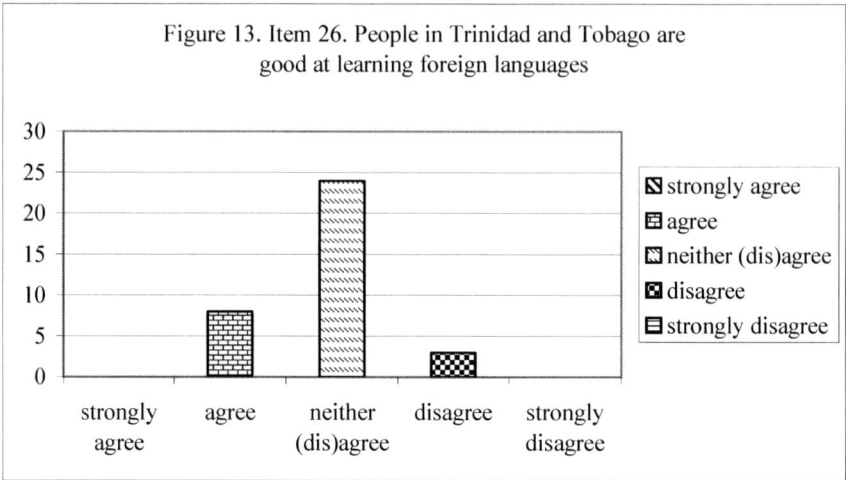

Figure 13. Item 26. People in Trinidad and Tobago are good at learning foreign languages

The belief that people in this country are poor language learners is especially unfortunate, when accounts of 19th century Trinidad refer to it as Babel-like country. According to Gamble (quoted in Carrington, Borely, and Knight 1974, 12):

> There are men from all quarters of the globe, and with little exaggeration, it may be said that in Trinidad, all the languages of the earth are spoken.

One hundred and fifty years ago, the society was characterized by vibrant multilingualism. As recently as early in the 20th century, Trinidad English/Trinidad French Creole bilingualism was a feature of the sociolinguistic landscape. This "multi-competence" (Cook 1993, 244) gradually disappeared in favor of monolingual competence in Trinidad English and English-lexicon Creole varieties. In the absence of such models of "multi-competence", a quarter of the undergraduate language learners in this study (N=8) concluded that people in their country are inept at foreign language learning.

Item 16 tried to ascertain whether the students felt that women learn a language more easily than men. The largest number of students opted for the middle ground and so eighteen of them said that they neither agreed nor disagreed. Only one student strongly agreed and four students agreed. Of the twelve students who disagreed, eight disagreed and four strongly disagreed.

Figure 14. Item 16. Women learn a language easier than men

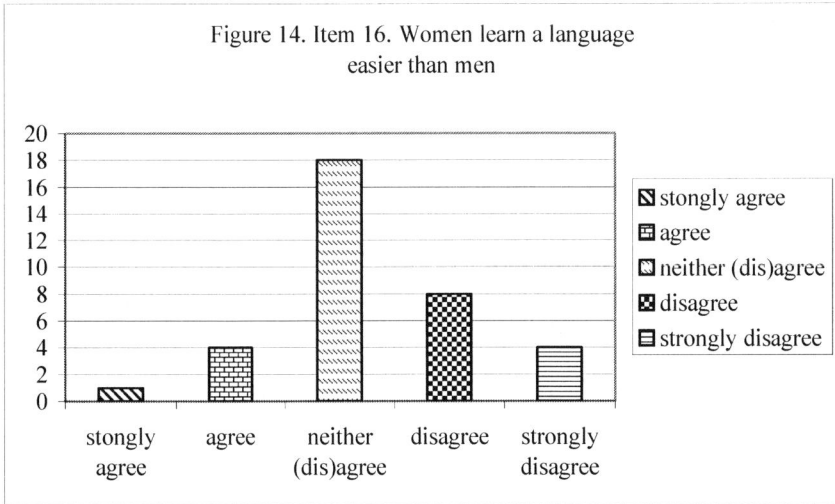

It is not surprising that the majority of students are unaware that there are empirical data showing that women employ (a) more strategies and (b) a greater variety of strategies in their language learning than men. These are thought to be positive traits because research has shown that a correlation exists between wide and effective strategy use and successful language learning. It is hypothesized that the good language learner is one who knows how to appropriately deploy a range of strategies. There are several reasons why this largely female cohort of students may be unaware of their special advantage in language learning.

Firstly, the results of research on learning strategies have probably not filtered down into the average foreign language classroom in this educational context. Foreign language teachers, generally, have few opportunities to remain current with the latest research and instructional practice in their field. There is no mandatory pre-service teacher training for secondary school teachers, although teachers may opt to pursue an in-service diploma in education after two years of service.

However, once teachers complete the diploma and return on a full-time basis to the classroom, there is little time and impetus for them to develop and maintain a research interest. Not many foreign language teachers have the kind of school setting that encourages them to be reflective practitioners. The result is that, cut off from the active researchers at the School of Education of the University of the West Indies, the majority of teachers have little opportunity to update their language teaching/learning theory on an ongoing basis. Thus, although strategy research has been integrated into classroom practice in many language-teaching contexts, notably in Europe, North America and Asia, locally it is probably the exception rather than the norm.

Secondly, it is not improbable that a foreign language teacher who is aware of such research might prefer to downplay this advantage of the female language student. In this educational context, like in many others, foreign language teaching is largely a female profession. Moreover, the majority of advanced foreign language learners are also female. In a climate where educators and the general public are rightly concerned about male underachievement, as noted by Miller (1998), teachers may refrain from doing anything that may lead the rare male advanced learner to feel that he has less potential to be successful at foreign language learning than his female counterpart. But be it for this reason or the reason given above, the options selected by the students reveal that they are unaware of research by applied linguists such as Bacon and Finnemann (1992), and Ehrman and Oxford (1989), that shows that female learners are potentially more successful at classroom-based language acquisition.

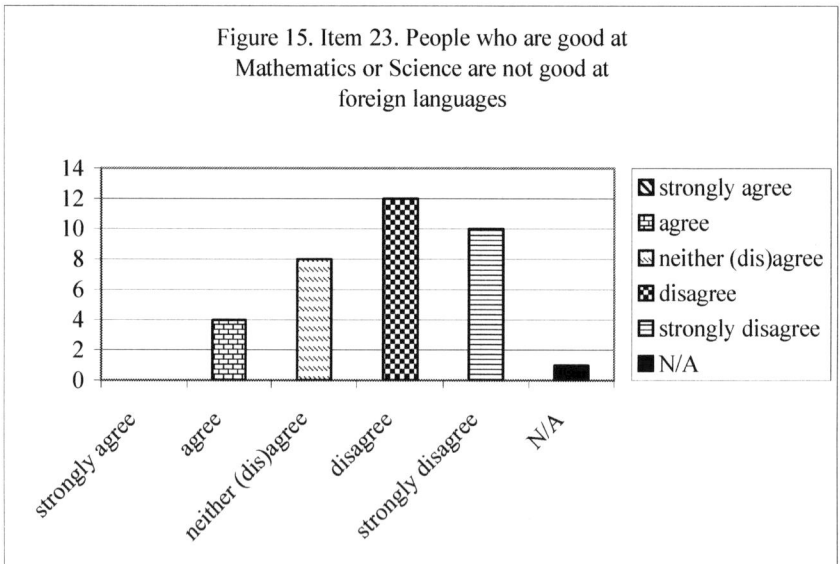

Figure 15. Item 23. People who are good at Mathematics or Science are not good at foreign languages

It is not unusual to hear people claim that good mathematicians and scientists are poor linguists and vice-versa. Item 23 sought to investigate whether students thought that there was any merit in this statement. Of the thirty-five respondents who completed the questionnaire, no one strongly agreed with this statement. One student gave no answer. The largest number of students (N=12) disagreed with this statement and ten students strongly disagreed. Only four students agreed that mathematicians and scientists are poor linguists. The wide spread of answers for this item revealed that there were no group beliefs about scientific as opposed to linguistic competence.

About a third of the students (N=11) neither agreed nor disagreed that people who speak more than one language are intelligent (item 25). The same number of respondents, however, did not agree with this statement; six disagreed and five disagreed strongly. The next highest number of answers came from the nine students who agreed with the statement. A small number of students (N=3) strongly agreed. One student did not select any option. As was noted for item 23, the students selected a wide range of answers. Here, there was an almost clear division into three categories of respondents: those who were neutral (did not agree nor disagree), those who agreed or strongly agreed and those who disagreed or strongly disagreed.

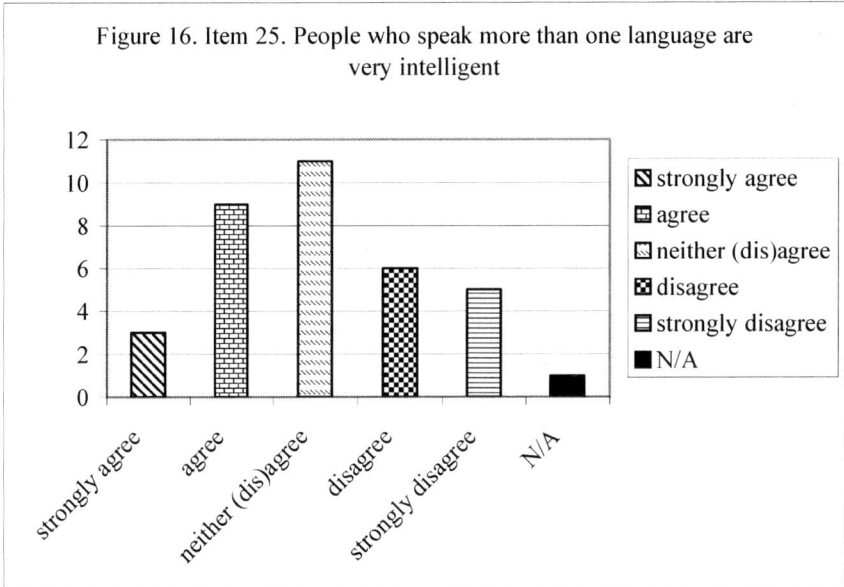

Figure 16. Item 25. People who speak more than one language are very intelligent

Major trends in the data and their implications. The items in this category of beliefs required students to move beyond their assessment of their own competence and their opinions about the difficulty or facility of different skills and make judgments about some of the factors that influence foreign language aptitude.

The students' beliefs about a foreign language aptitude can be discussed according to the categories to which they assigned the various items. Thus, there was strong support for the notion of a universal foreign language aptitude. Additionally, students thought that an optimal learning age, a special language aptitude and bilingualism, as opposed to monolingualism, were factors positively associated with foreign language aptitude. The majority of students neither agreed nor disagreed that women and people in their country are good at learning foreign languages. The majority of students disagreed that language-learning aptitude was incompatible with mathematical and scientific aptitude. Finally, almost equal numbers of students agreed as disagreed on the relationship between bi/multilingualism and intelligence.

It is difficult to know what conclusions to draw from some of the answers given by the students. Can we speculate, for example that, because students subscribe to the idea of an optimal age for learning that they think they are somewhat handicapped in achieving foreign language proficiency because they began their language learning as adolescents rather than as children? How do we reconcile the students' belief about their individual potential for success and the absence of this potential among their compatriots? What I can say about the students in this study is that their long apprenticeship as foreign language learners, seven plus years, has allowed them to form a set of stateable beliefs about what facilitates or hinders foreign language learning.

One area that is important for the analysis is what the students' answers revealed about the "group language learning self-image", the label used by Horwitz (1987, 122). The contrast between the students' strong belief in the universality of foreign language aptitude and their neutrality about Trinidadians and Tobagonians' potential for success at foreign language learning was, to my mind, an interesting one. If I extrapolate from the statements made in items 26 and 27, it seems that students are saying:

1.   Everyone can learn a foreign language.
2.   People in Trinidad and Tobago can learn a foreign language.
3.   But/however, people in Trinidad and Tobago are not particularly good at learning foreign languages.

In her study of beginning foreign language learners, Horwitz posits that when students have a negative group self-image, they may hold negative expectations about their capability as members of that particular group. Given the students' responses to item 30, we can speculate that this is less likely to be so for advanced learners. Advanced learners, like these undergraduate students who have known considerable success, may be more confident about their potential for individual success, despite not having a very positive group self-image[2]. Nonetheless, the importance of the learning-group self-image remains an important consideration for the long-term language confidence of the students.

An important issue for autonomy is whether the practice of autonomy can help learners to continue learning beyond the end of their formal schooling. Autonomous learners need to be self-sustaining. They must be able to continue to use the learning resources around them to maintain and improve their proficiency. It is possible, though, that while students may be confident about their ability to be proficient at foreign language learning during the period of formal instruction, this could change once they reintegrate into the wider community. Detached from the institutional language learning community and the group solidarity that it provides, foreign language learners may not find the wider society sufficiently supportive of their language learning needs. If this were to happen, the poor group language learning self-image might influence the learners' self-perception of their foreign language competence and impact on their long-term motivation and perseverance for language learning.

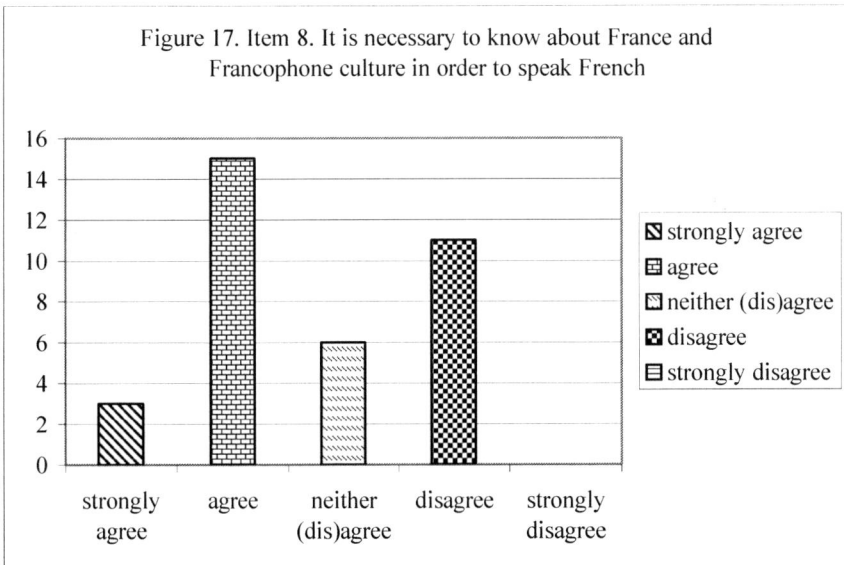

Figure 17. Item 8. It is necessary to know about France and Francophone culture in order to speak French

4.1.3 The Nature of Language Learning

The third category of beliefs addressed (1) the relationship between the culture of the target language country and language learning (items 8 and 11); and (2) the importance of vocabulary (item 13), grammar (item 20) and translation (item 21) in language learning. Under the category of the "Nature of Language Learning", the BALLI also encouraged students to reflect on whether foreign language learning was the same as learning other school subjects (item 18).

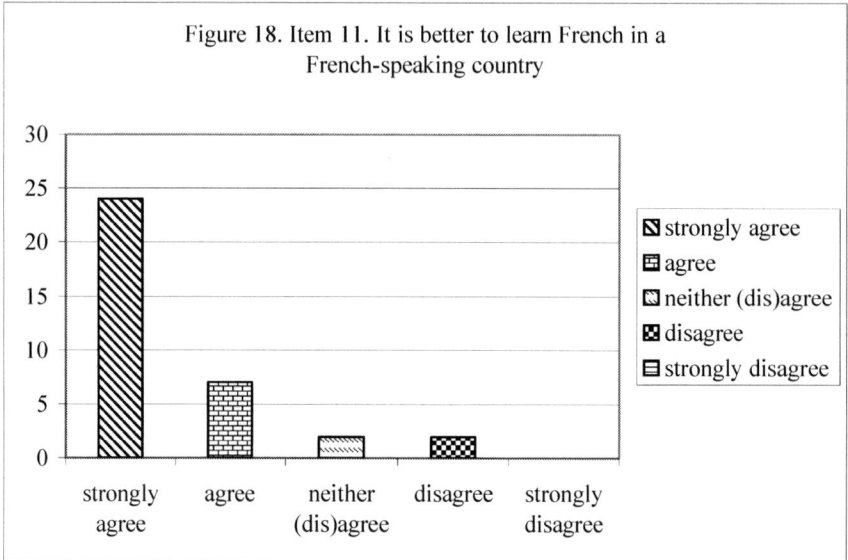

Figure 18. Item 11. It is better to learn French in a French-speaking country

A small majority of students (N= 18) felt that it was necessary to know about France and Francophone culture to speak French (item 8). Only three students strongly agreed, though fifteen agreed. Of the remaining students, six neither agreed nor disagreed and eleven disagreed. No one strongly disagreed. It is somewhat surprising that, in an era when foreign language learning is premised on language learning for communication, the students' answers revealed that almost half of those surveyed attach little importance to the role that the target language culture plays in language learning.

If we were to accept the students' statements at face value, their belief about the importance of culture appears to be at odds with much current research on the importance of culture and inter-cultural communication in language learning. Authors like Seelye (1984) and Morgan (1993) have emphasized the importance of assigning a role to the L2 culture, what Morgan (1993, 63) defines as "the way of life, the conventions of behaviour, value systems, way of viewing the world, the institutions, etc."

It is possible that students do not ascribe a major role to culture in their language learning. But I think a more compelling reason why students professed so little interest in culture is that students and researcher attach different interpretations to the word culture (the question of differing interpretations in questionnaires was one of the limitations discussed in chapter 3). Hence, while the focus in this item was on culture, the students were most probably thinking of Culture—the fine arts, geography and history, aspects of culture that have too often been the object of classes on culture to the detriment of "those aspects of life that concern most of the people most of the time" (Seeyle 1984, 8). But, given the students' preference for learning the L2 in the target language country (see item 11), I think students would be more willing to admit a role for culture in their language learning.

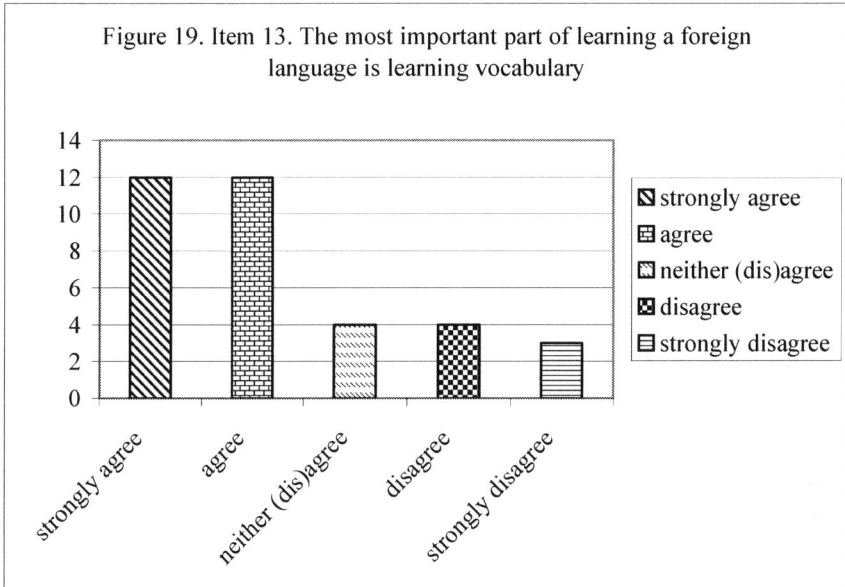

Figure 19. Item 13. The most important part of learning a foreign language is learning vocabulary

Item 11 asked students to state whether it was better to learn French in a French-speaking country. The fact that most of the students strongly agreed (N=24) and seven of them agreed, showed that students were aware of the benefits of being exposed to the target language country. No one strongly disagreed with this statement, though two students neither disagreed nor disagreed and two students disagreed.

The role of vocabulary in language learning was explored in item 13. One fifth of the students disagreed (four disagreed and three strongly disagreed) that the most important part of learning a foreign language was learning vocabulary. A majority of them (N=24), however, equally divided between those who strongly agreed and those who agreed, thought that vocabulary was the most important part of foreign language learning.

Figure 20. Item 20. Learning another language is mostly a matter of learning grammar

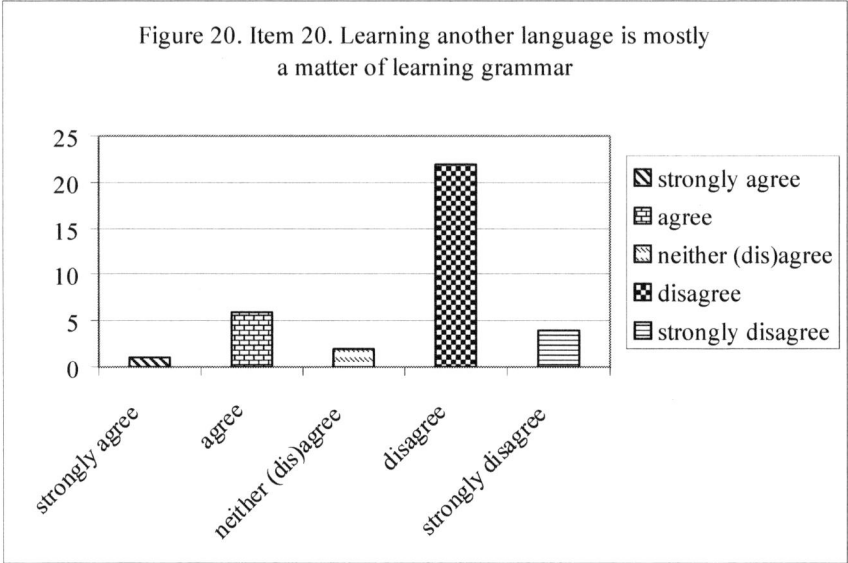

In contrast to the beliefs about the importance of vocabulary, very few students felt that learning a foreign language was mostly a matter of learning grammar rules (item 20). The largest number of students (N=26) disagreed or strongly disagreed with this statement. Only one student strongly agreed that language learning was chiefly about learning grammar rules. Six students agreed and two students neither agreed nor disagreed.

The students' beliefs about vocabulary and grammar relate to one of the most controversial areas in the Communicative Language Teaching Approach. Earlier approaches to Communicative Language Teaching came into prominence at a time when there was widespread criticism of structural approaches to language learning. The traditional focus on grammar shifted to a focus on meaning, in keeping with the new trend that valued the meaning potential in L2 learning. Since then, the debate about the place of grammar in a model of communicative competence has been an ongoing one. Both at the level of the researcher and at the level of the classroom practitioner, there is considerable debate about what weighting should be given vocabulary or grammar to achieve communicative competence in classroom-based acquisition.

On the research side, acceptance of the importance of universals in language learning implies a smaller role for grammar as an object of L2 learning and a larger role for vocabulary (Cook 1993). Krashen's contested Acquisition/Learning Hypothesis also attributes a lesser role to grammar, since Krashen contends that the formal study of grammar, "learning", is unlikely to result in communicative fluency or "acquisition"—a highly debatable contention.

Grabe (1991) underscores the central role played by vocabulary, stressing the importance of a large vocabulary for all language skills, academic performance and related background knowledge. When we investigate the importance of vocabulary from the student perspective, a study conducted by Dickson (1996) among first-year undergraduate students in a British context showed that these students agreed with their UWI counterparts in assigning an important role to vocabulary in developing language proficiency.

However, there is less unanimity about the role of grammar in communicative competence. Earlier approaches, partly because of their focus on promoting fluency, tended to minimize the role of grammar/accuracy. Consequently, the methodology of the day continued in the path of the audio-lingual and audiovisual methods, with the result that deductive approaches to the teaching of grammar and overt error correction were proscribed.

More recently, there has been some evolution in the thinking about how grammar should be integrated into Communicative Language Teaching. Recent research, as for example in Doughty and Williams (1998) acknowledges a clear role for a focus on form in classroom-based acquisition. Advocates of a greater focus on grammar adopt a position that was endorsed by Wilkins (1974) three decades ago when he recognized the importance of grammar in promoting communicative competence. What remain controversial in approaches that promote a focus on form are the kind of grammar instruction and the role of error correction. There is ongoing debate, for example, as to whether grammar should be taught deductively, or whether an inductive approach, with a focus on language awareness and consciousness-raising could prove more useful.

Helping students to explore their beliefs about language learning could include helping them to become aware that a focus on grammar, though not in the narrow sense of memorization of grammar rules, and a focus on vocabulary are equally necessary to communicative approaches to language learning. Classroom activities that encourage students to introspect on how form and lexicon both contribute to creating meaning in texts could help students to discard invalid beliefs.

The belief that the most important part of learning French is learning how to translate from English (item 21) was an idiosyncratic one. Very few students supported this proposition. No one strongly agreed, although two students agreed. One respondent neither agreed nor disagreed and one respondent gave no answer. The majority of students did not share this belief; twenty students indicated that they disagreed and more than a third (N=11) strongly disagreed.

Figure 21. Item 21. The most important part
of learning French is learning how
to translate from English

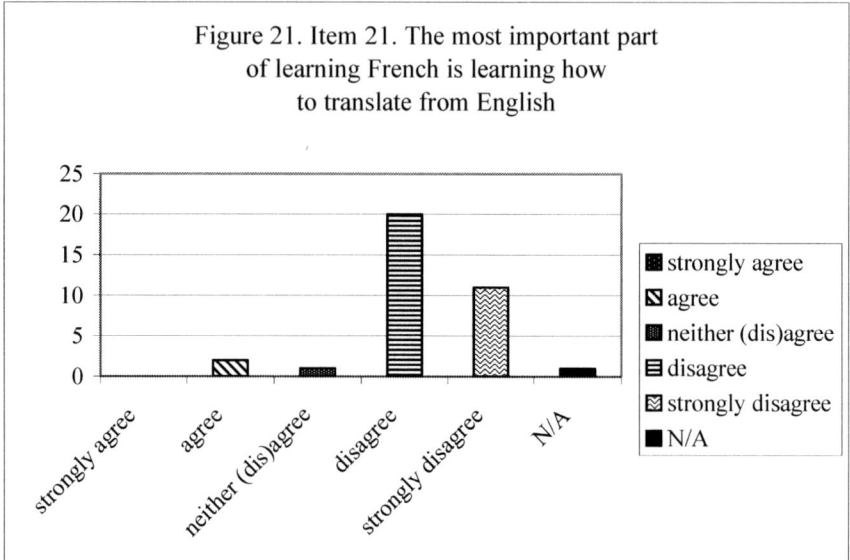

One other item sought to investigate the students' beliefs on the nature of language learning. Item 18 queried whether students thought that learning a foreign language was different from learning other academic subjects. One student strongly disagreed and one student disagreed. Three students neither agreed nor disagreed. A total of thirty students, twenty who said they strongly agreed and ten who said they agreed, defended this statement.

It is posited that L2 learning draws on both a general intelligence and a language-specific aptitude. According to Carroll's (1967-1968) four-factor theory—phonemic coding ability, associative memory, grammatical sensitivity, and inductive language learning ability are the constituent elements of aptitude. It seems, therefore, that students are partly right, for some aspects of L2 learning are indeed unlike other kinds of learning. Phonemic coding, for example, which is defined as the capacity to make sound discriminations and to code foreign sounds in such a way that they can be recalled later is one of the components of aptitude which is undoubtedly peculiar to language learning.

Notwithstanding this evidence of the dissimilarities between learning a foreign language and learning other academic subjects, there is reason to encourage learners to adopt a more holistic approach to learning. Holec

(1981) emphasizes the need to "decondition" learners from restrictive views about learning. Students who keep their knowledge too compartmentalized will not seek to transfer strategies across subject areas. Hence, whereas the active learner might draw on her knowledge of music or mathematics or geography to support her language learning, the learner who approaches each discipline as though it were a discreet domain will not seek to transfer strategies across domains.

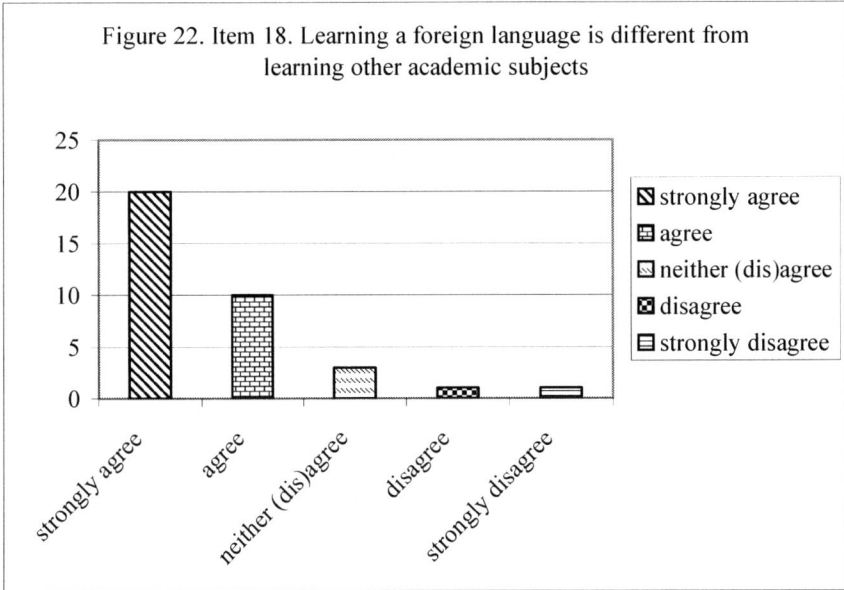

Figure 22. Item 18. Learning a foreign language is different from learning other academic subjects

Major trends in the data and their implications. One characteristic of the students' responses in this section was that, with the exception of item 8, "It is necessary to know about France and Francophone culture in order to speak French", there was a high degree of consensus on most items. Over 60% of the respondents agreed/strongly agreed that (a) it is better to learn French in a French-speaking country (item 11); (b) the most important part of learning a foreign language is vocabulary (item 13); and (c) learning a foreign language is different from learning other academic subjects (item 18). While over 60% disagreed/strongly disagreed that (a) learning another language was mostly a matter of learning grammar rules (item 20); and (b) the most important part of learning French is learning how to translate from English (item 21). Although a few students held opposing views to the majority, the strength and homogeneity of the group beliefs was a significant feature of this set of responses.

The extent to which the students' beliefs about the nature of language learning are the result of their previous learning experience is a point of interest in a study of this kind. The post-A level entrant into the undergraduate program is usually part of a small group of approximately 150 students who sit the terminal GCE Advanced Level Examination (French) in Trinidad and Tobago each year. About a quarter of these students opt to study French language and literature at the University of the West Indies, St. Augustine.

These foreign language learners, because of their shared language learning background, have more in common than a cohort of second language learners: number of years of foreign language study; place of French as L3 in the school syllabus; initial public examination after five years and later after seven years of secondary schooling. These factors, especially given the importance of the public examinations and the wash-back effect of these exams, are likely to result in a high degree of congruence in language teaching/learning methodologies. The similar backgrounds give rise to shared perspectives and may be advanced as one reason why there was such a high degree of consensus about the nature of language learning.

In the light of the above, classroom discussions could prove very effective in helping students explore their beliefs about the nature of language learning and in providing metacognitive knowledge to replace invalid beliefs. Students who have some misconceptions about the role of certain activities—for example that grammar should not be an object of study in communicative approaches—need to be made aware of current second language acquisition and language learning theory to confirm or disprove their beliefs. This "deconditioning" must be a precursor to the process to acquire the knowledge and skills to assume responsibility for their learning.

4.1.4 Learning and Communication Strategies

The next group of answers sought to investigate students' beliefs about several learning and communication strategies. This category of BALLI answers revealed whether students showed a preference, not only for certain skills, but also for certain activities that are found in the communicative classroom.

When asked whether they thought that it was important to speak French with an excellent accent (item 7), twelve of the students strongly agreed and sixteen agreed. No student strongly disagreed, though four students disagreed and three neither agreed nor disagreed.

Communicative approaches, while not undervaluing good pronunciation, attach more importance to the intelligibility of speakers' oral production. Accordingly, in the assessment of oral production, accents are generally evaluated based on whether or not they impede communication and whether the message is comprehensible to all native speakers (NSs) or only to those used to dealing with non-native speakers. Thus the "goodness" of the accent is secondary, since intelligibility is primary.

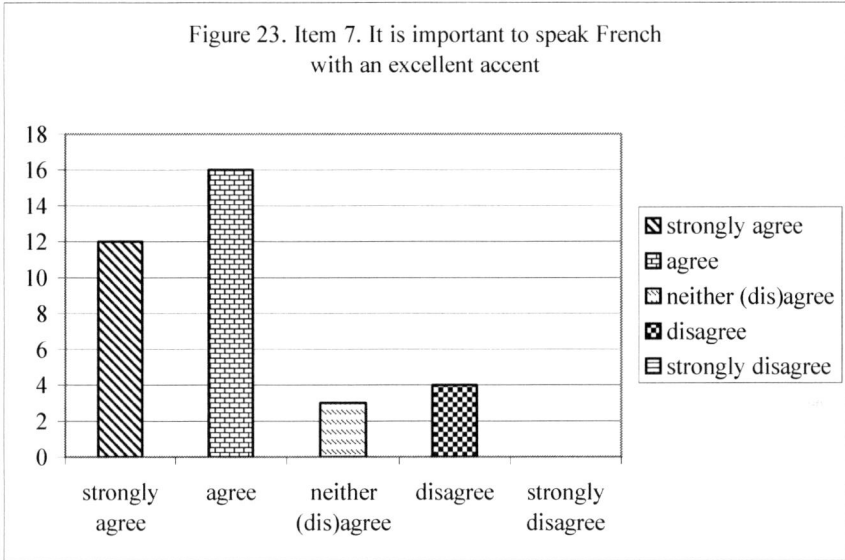

Figure 23. Item 7. It is important to speak French with an excellent accent

It is possible though, that some students are less concerned with the concept of intelligibility to NSs, but more concerned with their teachers' judgment of the importance of "excellent accents". This conclusion is a tentative one and further investigation will need to be carried out to determine whether or not this is so. However, an extract from a student's journal, reproduced here, demonstrates why this student is likely to attend to the quality of the sound she produces in order that her pronunciation and accent be as close to the idealized native speaker as possible.

> I first encountered French, as most other students here at UWI, in my first year at Secondary school ... and to be perfectly honest my first experience was dreadful! I had heard numerous stories about much-hated, strict, disciplinarian French teachers, who insisted on having every syllable pronounced exactly as they wished, or else they drew back in disgust, declared you a hopeless case and more or less branded you an absolute idiot in French...

Students such as this one will no doubt be inclined to agree with the statement made in item 7, because they believe that "an excellent accent" is a necessary component of their oral production.

In contrast to their support for item 7, the majority of students dissented when asked whether learners should refrain from saying anything unless they could say it correctly (item 9). Of the twenty-seven students who disagreed, nineteen disagreed and eight strongly disagreed. Of the remainder, six strongly agreed and two agreed that learners who were unable to speak "correct French" should not speak at all.

Figure 24. Item 9. You shouldn't say anything in French unless you can say it correctly

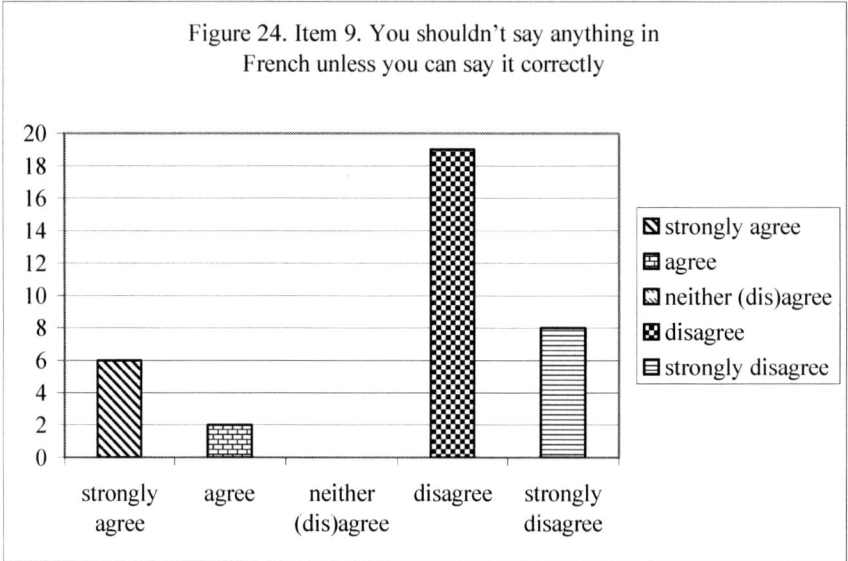

Although accuracy is considered important in making sure that the message conveyed is intelligible, Omaggio Hadley (1993) reminds us that when learners are engaged in creating with the language, the correctness of both oral and written production is sometimes compromised. It is important, for this reason, to balance the demand for accuracy with the demand for giving learners the opportunity for extensive practice using the L2. Learners need to speak, to negotiate meaning, to increase their mastery of the spoken language and, in so doing, they will make errors. It is a very positive sign for these students' oral proficiency if they are prepared to acknowledge the need to speak, even at the risk of making errors.

Item 12 sought to capture students' beliefs on guessing as a communication strategy. A majority of the students thought that guessing was a useful strategy, although about a third did not agree that it was. Of those who approved of guessing, seventeen students agreed and one strongly agreed, while six students disagreed and four strongly disagreed. Seven students neither agreed nor disagreed.

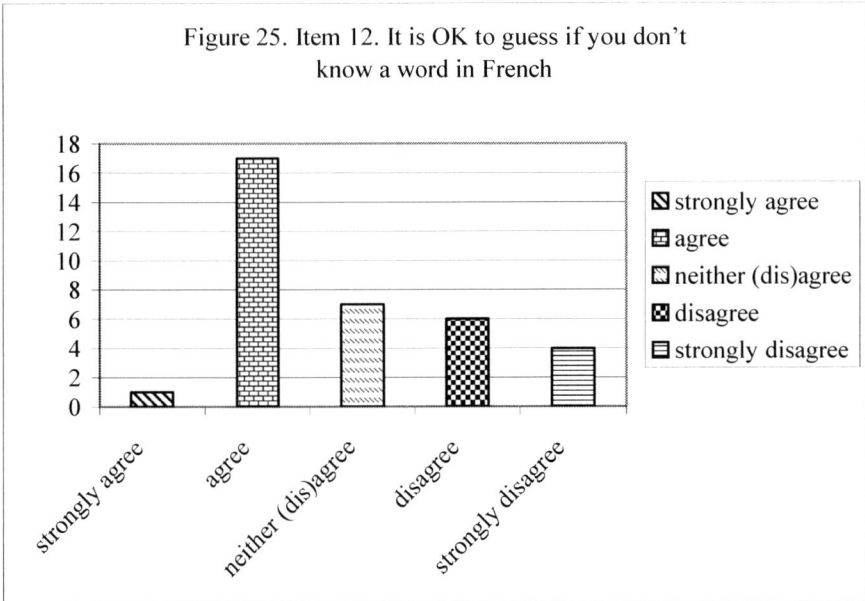

Figure 25. Item 12. It is OK to guess if you don't know a word in French

Naiman et al.'s (1978) research on the good language learner suggests that guessing is a strategy employed by good learners. But, like so many other areas of second language acquisition research, there are several caveats about the adoption of guessing as a strategy. Good language learners make educated guesses in trying to work out the meaning of contextual clues in comprehension. Where production is concerned, guessing may be thought of as an achievement strategy, part of the learner's strategic competence used to ensure that communication does not break down. The utility of guessing as a strategy seems, however, to be linked to the context of use and its frequency. Hence, learners who employ this strategy on a particular task to meet certain communicative needs may find guessing more beneficial than learners who regularly resort to guessing to compensate for linguistic difficulties. The latter practice may indicate a tendency to impulsivity. Guessing, like anxiety, may therefore be analyzed in terms of whether it is linked to a particular task, the learner's state, or whether it is seen as a fairly stable trait of the learner, that is, a dimension of the learner's cognitive style.

All the respondents thought that it was important to practice to become a fluent speaker of French (item 14). This was the only item about which students expressed unanimity, with answers bunched into two categories: thirty-three strongly agreed and two students agreed.

Students were asked whether it was important to practice a lot in order to become fluent speakers of French, a slight deviation from the original item in Horwitz's BALLI. The decision to replace the Horwitz item stemmed from the fact that language laboratories are not generalized in secondary level French language learning in this country. Additionally, while it may be common to have beginning students repeat and practice, this instructional activity is less common with advanced learners. Consequently, these students would have interpreted practice as engage in communication with other speakers of the L2. Thus, by agreeing with item 14, students are in fact confirming their belief in the importance of extensive practice as the way to achieve fluency in oral production.

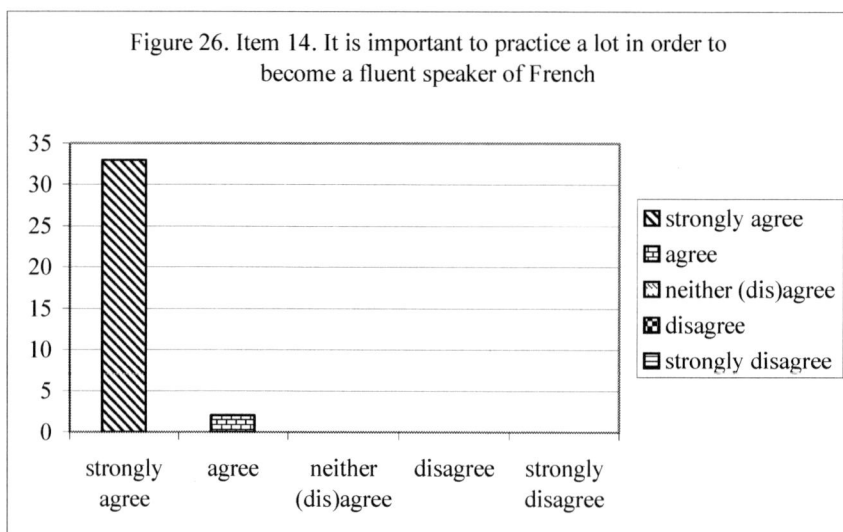

Figure 26. Item 14. It is important to practice a lot in order to become a fluent speaker of French

Finally, item 15, "If you are allowed to get away with mistakes in the early stages it will be hard to get rid of them later", probed students' opinion on fossilization/the value of explicit error correction. There was majority support for the idea that fossilization could occur when no error correction takes place in the early stages of speech production. Of the thirty-two students who thought that teachers should systematically correct errors, twenty-four strongly agreed and eight students agreed. The remaining students neither agreed nor disagreed (N=2) nor strongly disagreed (N=1). No one disagreed

The role of error correction in communicative approaches is, as I noted earlier, a very divisive issue in language learning debates. Corder's (1973) typology of performance mistakes as opposed to competence errors is still valid and with it, an appreciation of the need to treat each category differently. Yet classroom learners have tended to react in one of two ways to what they judge to be insufficient error correction. Whereas some learners respond positively to less error correction—a practice which Krashen (1981, 1982) argues produces less anxiety and helps to lower students' affective filter in teacher-controlled classroom interaction—others, like these respondents, fear that no/too little error correction is detrimental to their long-term accuracy.

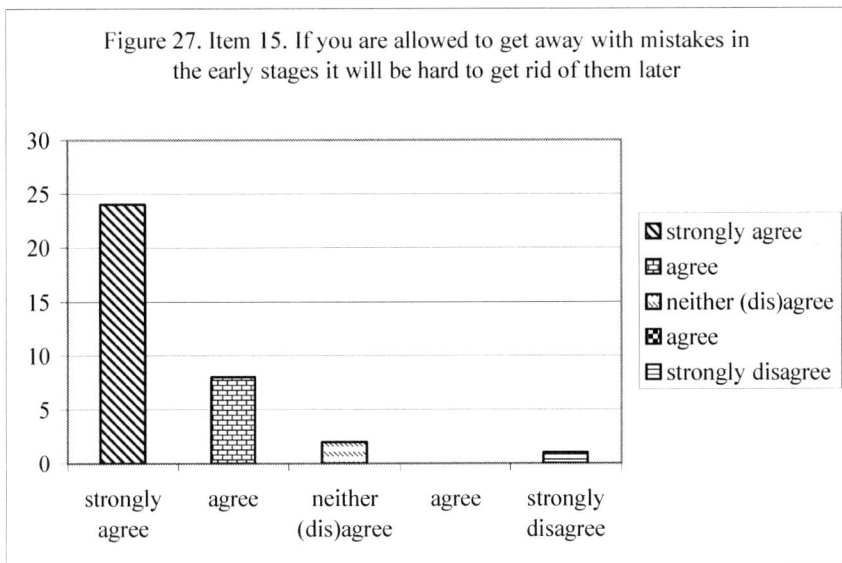

Figure 27. Item 15. If you are allowed to get away with mistakes in the early stages it will be hard to get rid of them later

The latter contention has been borne out by research conducted by Swain (1999) among immersion students in Canada. Immersion students developed a commendable degree of fluency. But, the presence of a number of fossilized forms in their oral production led Swain to reassess the importance of a focus on form in classroom teaching/learning. Empirical evidence such as this has led to a more mitigated view in the accuracy vs. fluency debate, with many theorists now advocating the importance of language awareness or a focus on form to achieve a reasonable degree of accuracy. Kohonen (1992, 29) puts forward a slightly stronger position, one that I share, given my knowledge of the degree of grammatical mastery of the first-year student. He calls for "learner reflection on language structure and an explicit teaching of the systemic structure of the target language, aiming at a conscious control of language."

Major trends in the data and their implications. Students' beliefs about learning and communication strategies are for the most part in keeping with current second language acquisition research about effective production strategies. Their support for a focus on fluency (item 9), guessing (item 12) and an awareness of the importance of feedback suggest that they will adopt the right practices to improve their foreign language proficiency. The only area of dissonance seems to be their belief about the importance of having an excellent accent when speaking French. If, as was hypothesized, students have come to this conclusion based on their previous learning experience, an approach to autonomy could free students of some of their constraining beliefs.

Advanced level learners must have a sufficient understanding of the factors that promote communicative competence to be able to make informed decisions about their desired objectives. Holec (1981) argues that learners should develop their idiolect. What this implies is that self-directed learners will make their own choices about the level of mastery that they wish to acquire. Students who wish to acquire excellent pronunciation will therefore be free to work toward this goal, because this is what they want and not because this is what the classroom teacher has outlined as an appropriate goal. Students who do not wish to strive for excellent pronunciation will be equally free to determine their objectives, but will do so with an awareness of how poor pronunciation may affect their communicative goals. Integrating an autonomous approach into classroom learning can help students to understand more about their learning and communication strategies and help them to choose appropriate strategies in terms of the objectives that they have defined.

4.1.5 Motivation

Items 19, 24, and 28 referred to the final area of enquiry researched by the BALLI questionnaire. Item 19 assessed whether students' French language learning was governed by instrumental needs. Item 24 sought to investigate the importance of foreign language learning in the country where the study was conducted. Finally, item 28 queried whether "It is necessary to speak their language in order to communicate successfully with native speakers."

Just one student strongly agreed that French language learning could serve an instrumental purpose in the society. Ten students agreed that by speaking French well they might obtain employment. The largest number of students (N= 16) neither agreed nor disagreed that French language learning served an instrumental purpose. Approximately a quarter of the students disagreed with this contention, five strongly disagreed and three disagreed.

These figures confirm the anecdotal evidence that the majority of students who pursue French language study at UWI St. Augustine, do so more because of integrative motivation, than instrumental motivation. While Spanish, the first foreign language, is thought to be a valuable asset on the job market, there seems to be no such impetus for French language study. This is perhaps the reason why so few students think that a high level of proficiency in French will improve their marketability when they seek employment.

Figure 28. Item 28. It is necessary to speak their language in order to communicate successfully with native speakers

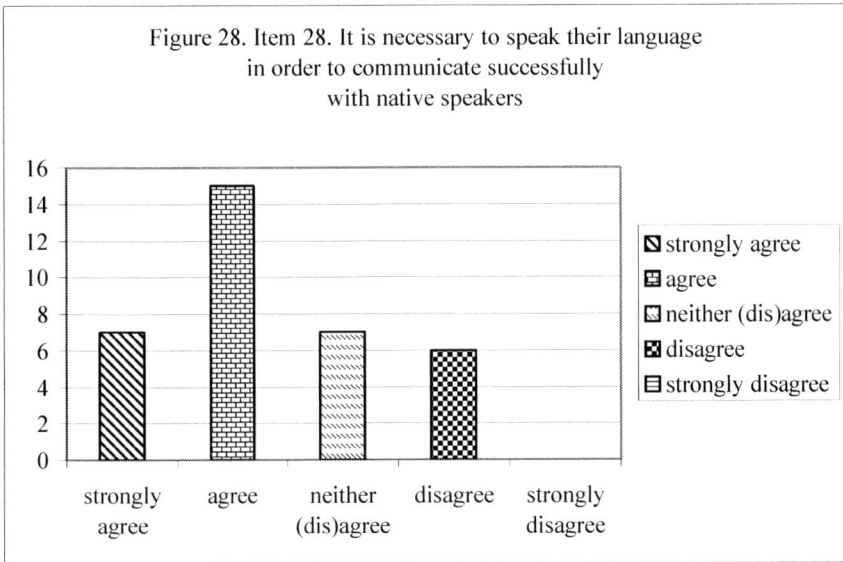

In contrast to the students' rejection of French language learning for instrumental reasons, there was strong support for learning French for integrative reasons. The majority of students agreed that one needed to speak the L2 to communicate successfully with L2 speakers (item 28). Twenty-two students expressed this view, seven students strongly agreed and fifteen students agreed. While no student strongly disagreed with this view, there were a few dissenting voices. Six of the respondents disagreed and seven were neutral on the issue.

Finally, item 24 encouraged more reflection on the thorny issue of the social context of language learning. Fourteen of the thirty-five respondents disagreed that their fellow citizens place a lot of importance on learning foreign languages and ten strongly disagreed. Small numbers of students, however, expressed an opposing view: one strongly agreed and two agreed. Eight students were noncommittal, choosing neither to agree nor disagree.

Figure 29. Item 19. If students learn to speak French very well, it will help them get a job

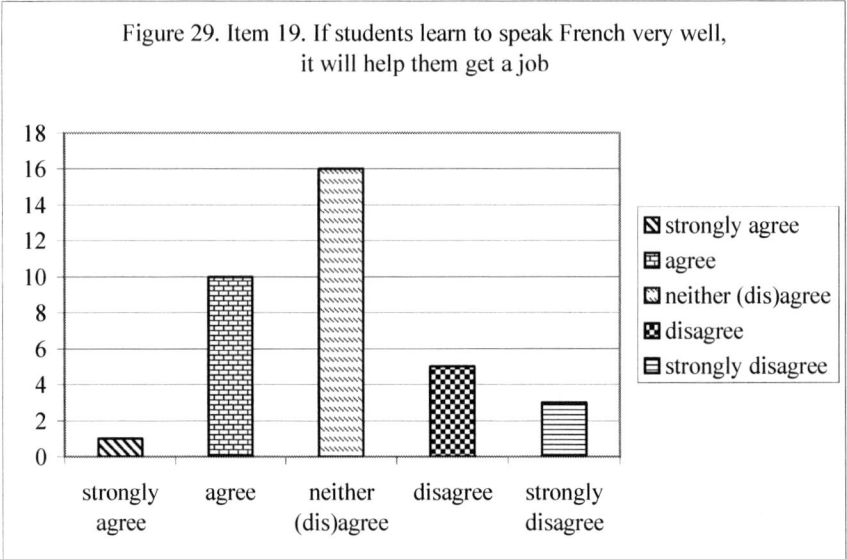

Major trends in the data and their implications. The answers in this section on motivation addressed the fundamental issue of the reason why students in this study are engaged in foreign language learning at the undergraduate level. Although many of those who advocate foreign language learning in the Caribbean do so on utilitarian grounds (Bourne 1993; McIntyre 1995; Yetming 1995) stressing the need for this competency in a world economy driven by globalization, French language learning is seen by many as an affective, not a pragmatic engagement. Thus, while most students of Spanish may feel that there is a direct link between their course of study and their future employment, the majority of students of French in this study would not support such a direct link.

The question remains how does this affect students' willingness to acquire learner autonomy? One school of thought is that a language student who is less focused on utilitarian goals will be less motivated by the extrinsic goal of career rewards than the intrinsic goal of mastery of the subject for its own merit. On the other hand, we might hypothesize that a student who sees competence in the foreign language as leading to well-defined career goals may be more willing to strive for a higher level of proficiency, for the higher her proficiency, the greater the likelihood of accomplishing her career goals. The need for firmer conclusions about the link between student motivation and student performance suggests that the area of student motivation is one that could be fruitfully explored in future research on factors affecting learner autonomy.

Figure 30. Item 24. People in Trinidad and Tobago
place a lot of importance on learning
foreign languages

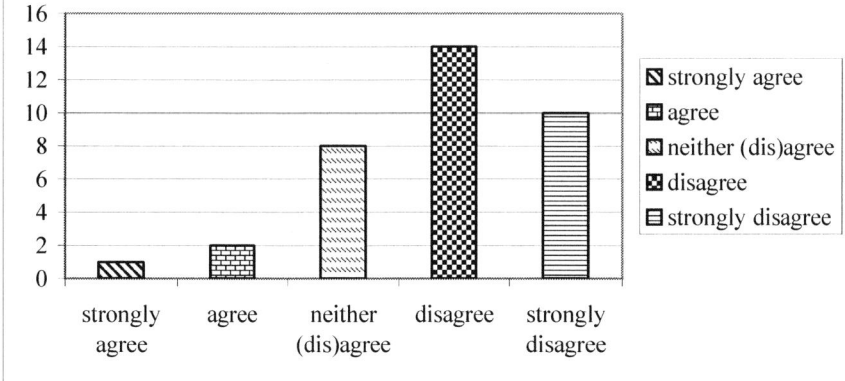

4.2 The Learner Autobiographies: What's Love Got to Do with It?

Twenty-eight students submitted autobiographical accounts of their language learning history. The autobiographies varied in length and the amount of detail included, so that while the shortest autobiography was just 98 words long, the longest was 853 words. Despite the unevenness of the autobiographies in terms of quantity and quality of reflection, it was nonetheless possible to collectively analyze the autobiographies. There was a core of common themes as students followed the suggestions on the handout (appendix A) and included details of their first exposure to a foreign language, information on their teachers, and other pertinent factors on their language learning history.

Only six students recalled having had exposure to a foreign language before beginning formal instruction at school. One other student referred, in passing, to picking up snatches of Spanish from the children's television program, *Sesame Street*. This student did not, however, attach much significance to the few vocabulary items she acquired naturalistically and discounted that experience as early exposure to a foreign language. Following her lead, I classified her in the category of classroom-only learners. It is possible, though, that other students would have acquired some isolated vocabulary items in the same way, but no one else included that information in their language learning history. Of the six students who documented prior exposure to a foreign language, two wrote of coming into contact with Spanish in a target language country: one on a visit to relatives in Venezuela, the other on a family holiday, also in Venezuela.

Four students first met a foreign language naturalistically in their homes. One student had this to say of her first foreign language exposure "My mother was a Venezuelan who as a child (sic), spoke to me partly in English, partly in Spanish." Another student wrote of having been taught Spanish by her mother, a Spanish teacher. Two students recalled hearing their grandparents or even great-grandparents speak a foreign language, patois in the case of one, Hindi[3] in the case of the other. But, whereas the Spanish-speaking mothers tried to teach their children the language, this was not the case for the *patois* or Hindi-speaking elders. According to the students' accounts, the use of these ancestral languages seemed to be a deliberate strategy to guard a private adult code that would not be understood by younger family members. This was certainly so in the case of the Hindi-speaking grandparents:

> My first exposure to a foreign language came as a young child when I heard my grandparents speaking Hindi. My response was immediate (according to my mother) - "Please teach me." Of course they didn't because Hindi was the language they used for private conversations.
>
> — PJB

Whether their first exposure to a foreign language was naturalistic or classroom-based, all the students, except two, had a positive introduction to foreign languages. They wrote of their curiosity and fascination at being ushered into what one student graphically described as "*un nouveau monde.*" In the students' own words:

> I was fascinated by it but unfortunately wasn't old enough to understand what they were talking about.
>
> — NOC
>
> I was totally mesmerized by this new way of speaking, as well as a little confused.
>
> — KS
>
> I distinctly remember that it was on my first day in Form 1 that I became fascinated with both Spanish and French.
>
> — VW
>
> J'étais fasciné par la culture différente, les môdes de vie étranges et une langue pleine de vie.
>
> — RR
>
> I found the idea of learning French new and fascinating.
>
> — NW
>
> I remember being excited at the idea that I was going to learn a foreign language.
>
> — MG
>
> I couldn't wait to begin learning French and Spanish for myself.
>
> — PJB

In the case of the classroom learners though, there was a very strong emotional reaction to the foreign language. While both naturalistic and classroom learners were fascinated by the new language, the impact of the new language was greater on classroom learners. Some of the students wrote that their fascination turned to love in the course of their studies:

> Little did I know that I would grow to love the language passionately.
>
> — MA
>
> J'ai fini par l'adorer ...
>
> — SM
>
> I grew to love the language even more.
>
> — NW

It was love at first *sound* for many. To hear them talk, they were swept off their feet, the first time they heard the language:

> My first contact with the French language began of course with my entrance into secondary school. It was then and there that I experienced a passion for this romantic language.
>
> — GA
>
> Avec le premier mot français j'étais amoureuse.
>
> — CM
>
> I instantly fell in love with the French language.
>
> — KN
>
> I really fell in love with French ...
>
> — ZW
>
> Pour moi c'était l'amour à première vue. J'ai tombé amoureux des langues tout à coup ...
>
> — LJ
>
> Je suis tombée en amour avec cette langue ...
>
> — RR
>
> I was introduced to French in Form One and I have never stopped loving the language ever since.
>
> — JR

The twenty-eight autobiographical accounts produced twenty-four instances of French described as an irresistible object of love. Many students seemed to have continued to see French in this way for much of their schooling. In some cases, there was almost an obsessive love, as for example:

> ... j'ai adoré cette langue ... Chaque jour j'étudiais même au manque des soins envers les autres matières ... C'était comme une obsession de la langue.
>
> — HJ

Sometimes though, there was hurt and disenchantment when things went wrong:

> I became briefly disillusioned with the language in Form 2 ...
>
> — KN
>
> Je me suis passioné pour le français ... Quel gaffe! A la fin de A Levels après avoir été la meilleur élève j'ai gagné le grade D. Vraiment, c'était la fin de ma vie. Après avoir sacrifié tout, c'est-à-dire les déjeuners de détentes, le temps avec mes amis/amies, et resté écouter, parler et apprendre le français j'ai gagnée le grade D. Quel horreur!
>
> — AH

The frequent use of the metaphor of falling in love, with the L2 being referred to as a lover or spouse is the most striking characteristic of the metaphors used by students to refer to their French language learning. What does the use of these metaphors imply? Cortazzi and Jin (1999, 150) posit that:

> A study of the conceptual metaphors produced by teachers and students should ... prove revealing, telling us something about their professional perceptions, their thinking and their learning.

However, the love metaphor was not the only metaphor that was spontaneously used by the students to convey their perception of the language. French was also a building (N=7).

> Something remains — a basic core around which you can begin to rebuild.
>
> — PJB
>
> I then had a good foundation
>
> — DJ
>
> I gained a solid foundation in the subject.
>
> — LR
>
> My foundation in French was extremely shaky ...
>
> — ZW
>
> ... the good foundation that had been laid in the three previous years.
>
> — PG
>
> and built upon the foundation which I had received ...
>
> — MH
>
> ... j'ai recu un bon fondement avec Mme H
>
> — RR

French was a tool (N=1), "un truc que l'on peut utiliser toute sa vie"; a key or passport to future endeavors (N =3); a life jacket (N=1); or unhappily, a deep pit (N=1) in the case of the student who had a bad first experience, "...the first time I had any dealings with French was when I was thrown into my 1st Form class..." - KS. French was very often described as something organic (N=9) that lived/breathed/flowed/grew/took root in learners:

En gros, le français est part de moi
— GM

Language learning, since secondary school, has been alive to me.
— VW

I nurtured this language ...
— MA

... she really made the language come alive for me.
— MA

20 years is a long time to have left it lying fallow ...
— PJB

The language flowed more easily ...
— PJB

C'est comme si le francais vive dedans moi. Je ne m'en débarasse pas.
— HJ

... voici quelque chose vivante.
— SM

Une germe avait été sémé.
— SM

However, the references to French as lover or spouse, the object of students' deepest passion and desires were quantitatively and qualitatively the dominant metaphors in the corpus.

J'ai détesté l'espagnol et j'adorais le français.
— NS

I still love the language with as much passion ...
— MA

Le français était ma vie.
— AH

L'amour du français a existé toujours.
— HJ

Oxford et al. (1998) cite work done by Bluestein (1995) and Ashton-Warner (quoted in Oxford et al. 1998) that supports the idea of a spousal relationship between teacher and student. Oxford et al. cite a respondent in Bluestein's (1995, 29) study of excellent teachers according to whom, "Teaching is a process of seduction: the teacher seduces the pupil toward himself or herself, and then redirects the seduced attention to the subject matter." Interestingly, in the present corpus, the use of the love metaphors was often accompanied by a reference to the French teacher as the one responsible for bringing the language to the students. Twenty-six of the twenty-eight diarists wrote of the role played by their teachers in awakening their interest in French language learning.

> I guess she did a good job because I instantly fell in love with the French language.
>
> — KN
>
> My liking for it grew and this was due in part to my teacher, Mrs. AS, she was kind and nice and enjoyed teaching the language.
>
> — NOC
>
> Il était facile à apprendre à cause de, à mon avis, mon professeur, Mme H.
>
> — RR
>
> J'ai détesté l'espagnol et j'adorais le français. Je crois c'était à cause du professeur.
>
> — NS
>
> Ms. MC who was my French teacher kept encouraging me because I had a keen interest in the language and with her help, I grew to love the language even more.
>
> — NW
>
> I think that the fact that my first French teacher came into the class speaking French very excitedly helped a lot.
>
> — PJB
>
> Both language teachers followed one specific approach—they entered, greet (sic) the new students, told them to sit down and introduced themselves all in the new language ... In the following months, both teaches demonstrated a particularly charismatic personality which I found easy to associate with the languages themselves.
>
> — VW

The teachers' impact on students' attitude to French is revealed very clearly in the following extract. The student, one of two who had had very negative first encounters with French, signals her change of attitude in the following words:

> It is at this point in time that my view of French completely transformed. I had always liked Spanish, but I really fell in love with French over my last four years at S, mainly thanks to my French teacher, Mr. C.
>
> — ZW

The teacher's role in facilitating language learning is thus an important theme in the autobiographical accounts. There was often an emphasis on the teacher's personality. Teachers were "wonderful", "fascinating", "charismatic", "kind" and "nice". The good teacher was sometimes described as a parent (N=3)

> elle faisait attention à chaque enfant dans sa classe toujours. Elle était là pour aider la plupart de temps.
>
> — AH
>
> Mme H était chouette! Elle nous a traité comme ses enfants.
>
> — RR

A good teacher was a kind, but firm parent:

Peut-être qu'il était la gentillesse mais manière stricte du prof quel que soit la raison, j'ai adoré cette langue.

— HJ

Another important quality that students seemed to appreciate in the mainly female teachers was their constancy and the sense of continuity that that gave to their language learning (N=13).

J'avais de la chance car j'ai gardé le même professeur de français jusqu'en terminal.

— NS

It was this teacher who became a staple in my life, teaching me French for the next seven years of my school career.

— VW

I had the same French teacher for five years. She was very thorough. She prepared us well for CXC.

— AA

However, in the final analysis, it was teacher knowledge and teacher efficacy that were the most commendable qualities (N=15). The ideal teacher was one who was "thorough" and "competent". Good teaching brought out the best, the shine in students:

Pendant les premières deux années de l'école secondaire, j'avais la même professeur. Son zèle pour la langue à mon avis m'avais transmis et depuis ces deux années j'ai brillé en français ...

— AL

Good teachers motivated students and helped them to reach their full potential:

In form 3 (I) encountered one of my favourite French teachers who I had straight up to fifth form, I was very confident for my CXC examination and I attained a distinction.

— KN

Good teachers/teaching also served as role models and the catalyst for students' eventual choice of a career in foreign languages:

At the end of Form III, I abandoned my plans to make law my profession and decided to do both French and Spanish.

— VW

... my school had an excellent Language Department, and this encouraged me even
more to pursue a career in the field of languages.

— DJ

The bad teacher/bad teaching was characterized by the absence of those
qualities which students valued. However, although there was an emphasis
on the personality of the teacher, a teacher's personality was not enough to
compensate for instructional deficiencies:

My Spanish teacher in Forms 4 and 5 was nice but she neglected to teach us some
grammar rules and I now realise that I was never taught the Spanish alphabet.

— AA

Bad teachers or teaching could ruin a student's chances of being
successful and undermine a student's confidence in her foreign language
aptitude (N=12) and her confidence in herself as a person (N=2). The
following extracts serve to illustrate the negative relationship between
teaching and learning for the students concerned.

I attained a grade C in French at A levels but that grade is not a credible testimony
of my capabilities as a French student. It is simply that I went into the exam without
any substantial knowledge of the three literature texts. My class and admittedly
myself included, spent most of our time wrangling with our French literature
teacher. We simply could not get along.

— JR

The following account is excerpted from an entry (the narration of the
student's relationship with her teachers occupies 270 of the 402 word
autobiographical account) by a student who loses a "good" teacher to illness,
only to have her replaced by a "bad" teacher. For this student and many
others, success or failure at language learning hinges primarily on teacher
effectiveness:

Le CXC, nous avions un autre prof. Elle n'avait jamais fait ce genre de travail.
J'étais très en colère avec l'école. Ici, nous préparions pour un examen majeur et il
nous donne un prof sans l'expérience d'apprendre à l'école ou même avec la façon
de CXC. Quand l'examen est arrivé, j'avais plus de la confiance en espagnol. J'ai
reçu la meilleure note en espagnol. Je n'étais pas surprenante.

— HJ

Only two students of the twelve who cited negative teacher-student
relationships seemed able to motivate themselves in the face of an
unsupportive learning environment. One student took it as a personal
challenge to succeed despite poor teaching and negative feedback:

I was determined to struggle with the subject and pass just out of sheer spite.

— KN

The overwhelming evidence coming out of the students' autobiographies suggests that many students conceptualized their learning in terms of the teaching. In the majority of autobiographies what emerged was a perspective on the student's role in the classroom and in foreign language learning vis-à-vis the teacher's role and teaching. Only two learners, both mature students, examined their foreign language learning independently of the role of teachers in their learning. The emphasis in the majority of accounts was on the teacher as facilitator of learning or obstacle to learning.

Wright (1990, 82) reminds us of the importance of the teacher in classroom-based acquisition:

Teaching can be seen as mediating between language and the learner within the formal context of the classroom.

He continues:

The teacher-learner role relationship lies at the very heart of the classroom process... An investigation of roles raises and addresses issues related to both classroom behavior and underlying value systems and attitudes held by individuals and groups. It also touches on issues that arise from a consideration of expectations of learning content and the ways in which teaching and learning take place. (83-84)

The autobiographies also contained a number of references to students' skill preferences: "J'ai toujours préféré l'oral à l'écrit sauf au moment des examens." NS, or to the skills which students found easier or more difficult (N= 13), for example, listening:

For me and I think for a lot of students learning a foreign language, the listening skill is always the hardest to develop.

— MG

and speaking,

I have to improve on my speaking skills in particular. I normally speak the language among my friends but when it is time for conversation of any kind in class, I get really nervous and can hardly speak intelligently.

— MA

Students also wrote about their learning environment, the material resources that were made available at school and the opportunities for interacting with French outside the classroom (N=11). Other students mentioned the role of their peers in learning (N=7). Three examples of peer support were cited, but four students thought their peers were a negative factor in their learning. Finally, some students commented on specific methodological approaches used by their teachers, which were particularly successful (N=3) or unsuccessful and detrimental to their learning (N=2).

Learning, *qua* learning, as distinct from learning as a product of teaching was mentioned in very few accounts. Three metaphors were chosen by a few learners to capture the essence of learning a language. Learning a foreign language was seen as a religious act requiring devotion (N=2), for example, "You must devote your time religiously to a language if you wish to succeed." JR. Learning a foreign language was conceptualized as a skill requiring constant practice (N=3): "C'est en forgeant qu'on devient forgeron." LM. And finally learning a foreign language was seen as a continuous, lifelong activity (N=4), "language learning for me is an ongoing experience." VW. These examples, which demonstrate a meta-awareness of learning were present in very few autobiographies. Moreover, in all instances except one, the diarist was not a recent secondary school graduate, but one who had worked for some time after her "A" levels.

The study of metaphors used in teaching and learning reveals how teachers and learners conceptualize and make sense of the process of teaching and learning. Cortazzi and Jin (1999, 150) contend that "the everyday talk of students and teachers is thoroughly imbued with metaphor and the proper locus of metaphor is the conceptual system." Thus, while questionnaires and other instruments that elicit information on students' beliefs present one insight into the students' belief systems, analyzing spontaneously produced metaphor is another way of understanding the beliefs that students hold.

Several studies have shown how teachers' conceptions of their role and responsibilities in the instructional process can be viewed through the lens of metaphor. Ellis (1999) also used metaphor to gain a better understanding of student beliefs. He points out that the kinds of beliefs revealed by a study of metaphor are seldom the kinds of beliefs collected when other more quantitative instruments are used. This point is underscored by Pajares (1992).

However, Pajares makes a point, often reiterated by those who work in a qualitative paradigm, when he says that the choice of a quantitative or a qualitative approach will depend on what the researcher wishes to know and how she wishes to gain that knowledge. This is a view which I share, for I feel that belief inventories and metaphor analysis are both valuable in cataloguing the beliefs that learners hold. Each approach supplies a different kind of data, but each contributes different pieces of the puzzle to add to a holistic understanding of how students see their own and the teacher's role and responsibility in second language acquisition. Thus, whereas the BALLI reveals more about students' beliefs, for example, about foreign language aptitude, the autobiographies provide valuable data on students' affective response to learning French.

In analyzing the beliefs that emerge in the student's autobiographies, it becomes evident that the most predominant metaphors are not those that relate to student's conceptions of language as an objective reality, but those that emphasize how students see themselves in relation to French. In looking back on their first encounter with French and on their continuing relationship with the language, the metaphor that best captures the essence of that relationship is falling in love with French. A comparison with Cortazzi and Jin's (1999) analysis of the metaphors teachers use to explain breakthroughs in learning is instructive.

According to Cortazzi and Jin (1999, 159), "the teachers' metaphors are clearly placed at the high point of the narrative. They are deeply evaluative of the recapitulated experience." They also posit that:

> The teachers often have no explanation for the learning (no theories of learning are cited in any of the narratives), or, as seems possible, the metaphor *is* the explanation or, at least, a striving to explain. (158)

Similarly, these students will probably be hard put to say how and why they approach the study of French as they do. The use of the conceptual metaphor of falling in love allows them to express the depth of their attachment, but the elusiveness of love, the difficulty of defining love, of making objective, rational decisions about the love object is also inherent in the use of this metaphor.

How do students' perception of French as a love object influence the attitudes, values, and beliefs they hold about learning French? If we extrapolate from the domain of language learning to the domain of love, we can be guided by Lakoff and Johnson's (1980) claim that the essence of metaphor is that it helps us to understand and experience something in terms of something else. Students who continue to conceptualize their language learning primarily as being in love with French may be focusing on those aspects of language that are unknown and mysterious and as a result acting in accordance with that conceptualization.

Interpreting metaphor and interpreting the salience of metaphor for the students in this research is, understandably, a subjective, tentative attempt to make sense of the data. Cortazzi and Jin suggest that the way to investigate whether or if metaphors are linked to learning, thinking, and behavior, whether metaphors are real, that is whether they have "cognitive and social validity for teachers and students" (1999, 152) or whether they are simply verbal devices, is to look at among other things, the frequency with which metaphors are used, the number of persons using the metaphors and the contexts of use. They conclude:

> The most convincing evidence would be to show clear relationships between teachers' metaphors (or those of students) and students' learning outcomes, or to relate particular sets of metaphors to different types of classroom behaviour and different approaches to learning. (152)

They add, though, that at present, it is premature to make causal relationships between learning outcomes and particular metaphors. If, however, as I have tried to show in this analysis, there is evidence that (a) the metaphors appear frequently in the data; (b) many speakers use those metaphors; and (c) the metaphors are used in significant learning contexts, it could be claimed that these metaphors are salient in the conceptual system of these learners of French.

Another point that is relevant to the basic research question of this study is how or where teachers fit in this conceptual system. At one level, it is evident that students think that their teachers' main role is to bring about learning, which in many cases is translated as bringing about examination success. From all the students' written accounts, this is the teacher's primary responsibility. But what other roles and responsibilities do students attach to teachers if conceptually they hold that teachers are center stage actors in making them fall in love with French? How does such thinking influence the nature of the interaction between student and teacher of French in other contexts?

In exploring the consequences of role definitions, Myers and Myers (1980) posit that once you figure out your own role and the role that the other person is likely to take, you possess a great amount of information, both on the kind of behavior that is expected of you and on the kind of behavior that can be expected from the other person. They contend further that when you first encounter someone there is a great degree of ambiguity, because role negotiation needs to start from scratch. If, however, students' socialization, or previous learning history, or conceptual system has provided them with a certain template of the expected behaviors of students of French and the expected behaviors of teachers of French, they may not see the need to re-negotiate teacher and student roles that are more appropriate to the new learning context.

While role negotiation is held to be problematic for most students as they make the transition from secondary to tertiary education, it is likely to be even more so, given the strong affective tenor of the students' relationship to French and their former French teachers. Furthermore, if students are expected to endorse a core function of their new role as university students as the assumption of responsibility for their learning, the lack of congruence between tertiary level teacher objectives and tertiary level student objectives is likely to be emphasized.

An analysis of the students' autobiographies and the predominant metaphors that emerge in them can serve to bridge the gap between student and teacher expectations, which upon further analysis may be closer than they initially appear. Turning to Oxford et al. (1998, 40) once again and their discussion of the metaphor of the teacher as lover or spouse, we see that this metaphor is just one of several included in the Learner-Centered Growth perspective: "In all of these metaphors, there [is] obvious concern for the welfare of every student, along with devoted sharing and facilitation."

Among the metaphors that are categorized as belonging to the Learner-Centered Growth perspective are the teacher as nurturer, the teacher as scaffolder and the teacher as delegator. Since both the teacher as lover or spouse and the teacher as nurturer/scaffolder/delegator are premised on the belief that teachers need to provide affective holding for students, as they help them to a greater maturity as language learners, there are shared assumptions about the end result of teaching. However, the external manifestations of the teacher as lover or spouse and the teacher as nurturer/scaffolder/delegator may be quite different. Indeed, it is the latter role, the teacher as delegator that is highly valued by proponents of learner autonomy. According to Oxford et al. (1998, 38-39):

> This metaphor suggests that the individual student has an innate potential for guiding his or her own learning—a potential that merely needs to be unlocked by the teacher. The *Teacher as Delegator* believes that it is in the students' best interest to delegate choices about learning to the students themselves ... The *Teacher as Delegator* is active in the sense of intentionally trying to create self-direction and self-expression in students and providing the needed resources. The *Teacher as Delegator* turns over significant control to the learner, who is assumed to be mature enough and to have the inner ability to determine objectives, decide on content, conduct learning activities and evaluate learning outcomes.

Oxford et al.'s conceptualization of the teacher as delegator describes fairly accurately the kind of facilitative role that I see as fundamental to helping students become more responsible for their learning. I do not, however, believe that upon their entry into university, the majority of post-A level students, in this context, are mature enough, nor have developed a high enough degree of metacognition to be self-directing. Very little in their past learning experience would have prepared them to adopt such a stance in their learning. I think that tertiary level language teachers who espouse the learner-centered growth perspective need to retain the diagnostician and planning role for some time. We need to create self-direction by integrating activities that will allow students to acquire learning autonomy, in addition to autonomy in the content area of instruction. We also need to maintain the affective holding attitude until students feel comfortable in their new role and can perform such a function for themselves.

4.3 Diary Studies of Three Students

> Inform the secondary school students that it is a big step from school life to university life in terms of work performance and relationships with lecturers. Receiving a high grade in A Level does not mean that you can easily pass your courses.

This opinion came from the personal information questionnaire of a second-year student (1996/7), in reply to the question, "If you had to suggest a change, what in your opinion, might improve the transition from secondary school to university life?" The implication in this student's statement is that, as I have suggested earlier, successful performance at the secondary level does not necessarily translate into successful performance at the tertiary level, if students are unable to manage their own learning. Bereft of the support of their secondary school teachers who have generally assumed the responsibility for planning, monitoring, and evaluating their learning, many students find themselves floundering, unable to be the kind of self-directed learners that their new learning environment demands.

The final set of data that I wish to examine allows us an insight into how three students in this study negotiated their new learning environment during the period of the intervention to promote learner autonomy. The data come from the diaries of three students who all entered university with a high level of proficiency, as revealed by their A Level grades: A in the case of one student and Bs in the case of two. I intend to show, through the exploration of the students' diaries, that what is likely to be a far greater predictor of success for these students is not so much their initial proficiency level, as the degree to which they are able to assume responsibility for their own learning. The diaries provide rich, qualitative, longitudinal data that enable us to see how the students' concept of themselves as tertiary level students and how the process of becoming autonomous is actualized in each case.

All three diarists documented significant factors in their language learning history, for example, their love of French, the role played by their teachers in their language learning, and their skill preferences. All three diarists could be considered successful language students based on their A level results. They were all full-time students who had been exposed mainly to traditional classroom-based teaching and, to a lesser degree, to varying amounts of instruction from L2 speakers. Michelle and Anne had been tutored by L2 speakers, while Nicole had spent one year in France. They were all between eighteen and twenty years old. As unemployed full-time students, all three lived at home while they pursued their degrees.

It is open to debate whether these apparent similarities concealed major differences in their outlook that would have affected their approach to language learning. The value of a diary study, however, is precisely that it affords the researcher the opportunity to examine personal variables that are likely to influence learners beyond some of the commonly researched variables, for example, the level of proficiency, classroom-based vs. naturalistic acquisition, age, and sex. In each case, the student's autobiographical account of her language learning will be presented first, then excerpts from her diary will illustrate significant factors that I identified in the autobiographies. The interpretation of the data will be interwoven throughout.

4.3.1 Michelle's Autobiography

I first became exposed to foreign languages (French and Spanish) when I entered secondary school in 1990, and it is now seven years since I have been studying the languages. It is my school experience with studying the languages which has nurtured my interest in and love for the languages (French in particular). I have been very fortunate to have had teachers who were committed to their vocation and did their jobs well. However, they lacked originality in terms of pedagogical methods applied. In my opinion they should have implemented activities which would have made learning French more interesting i.e. playing French games, playing French music, showing movies or video clips, teach about the culture of France (cuisine ...) etc.

I became a student at the Alliance Française in 1994 and had been until 1997 (when I wrote my G.C.E. 'A' Level exam). At the Alliance I attained a greater connaissance [sic] of the French culture and built upon the foundation which I had received in terms of my listening and conversational skills. Through the Alliance Française I have hosted students from Guadeloupe.

For the past year (or year and a half) I have been an ardent listening [sic] of *Rendez-Vous* a French radio programme co-ordinated by the cultural arm of the French embassy in Trinidad. I also view to [sic] the French news "France2" which is broadcast on the MEU Channel nightly. I also correspond with my penpal who is Guadeloupian but studying in Paris. She visited Trinidad this year and it was a wonderful experience. From time to time I read the French daily newspapers and magazines but I must admit that I don't do this as often as I would like.

I thoroughly enjoy studying French and I hope that my experience studying it at the University would [sic] be a rewarding one.

Analysis of Michelle. Although Michelle credits her secondary school teachers with fostering her interest in French, she does not include any details of her first exposure to French. We may assume that her introduction to French was a positive one, but there is no information on her early relationship with her French teacher, which allows us to verify this. Rather, what we have instead of a student's usual strong affective response to her teachers (and teaching) is a quite clear analysis of the strengths and weaknesses of her former teachers (and their teaching):

I have been very fortunate to have had teachers who ... (positive characteristics of teachers)
However, they ... (negative evaluation of teachers)

In my opinion they should have ... (ways in which the perceived deficiencies could have been improved)

Michelle's ability to monitor and evaluate her own learning, as she does her teachers' teaching, emerges in the data as one of her great strengths. Her admission, for example that she does not read French newspapers and magazines as often as she would like (or more likely, as often as she thinks she should) is the first of many examples that demonstrate her awareness of what is problematic in her language learning. But what is noteworthy about this student is that she is not content to simply identify her weaknesses, but once she has identified a deficiency, she sets her problem-solving skills to work to find the best way to correct her perceived deficiencies.

In her reflection on an oral examination, we see Michelle actively monitoring her performance. Her teacher's feedback helps her to determine how she can remedy what is problematic in her oral discourse.

October 13, 1997
This is the week of mid-term exams and today I had three. French Listening Comprehension, Orals and Written Expression.
Oral:This exam was not bad. My partner and I had to discuss a topic which I think is interesting: the advantages and disadvantages of the Internet in schools. While preparing for the exam in the 10 mins. allotted to us, I realised that I had some very good points, however I was unable to express the [sic] coherently in French due to lack of vocabulary. M. M pointed out our mistakes immediately after our discussions and this pleased me.

Writing on October 20, 1997, she stated:
Our exam scripts for grammar were returned and as predicted I did not do well ... I realise from this exam that I need to revise my grammar rules more thoroughly and

take the initiative to find and do extra grammar exercises which would allow me to practice and improve my grammar skills.

The point here is that, while many students are dependent on feedback from their teachers to improve their proficiency, Michelle welcomes such feedback when it is given, but can monitor and evaluate her own performance and adopt strategies which she sees as appropriate to the problem identified. Michelle's comment about not reading newspapers and magazines often enough is a good example of how she monitors and evaluates her learning. When I first read her autobiography, I did not attach much significance to this statement. However, as I read subsequent entries, it became clear that Michelle was very concerned about acquiring more vocabulary and very convinced that she needed to know more vocabulary to become a better language learner. She knew that reading newspapers and magazines was an effective strategy to increase her vocabulary, so that statement was in fact telegraphing:

> Reading newspapers and magazines is a good way to improve/increase my vocabulary.

> I do not do this as often as I would like.

> I need to do this more often to improve/increase my vocabulary (and become a better learner).

Extracts from her diary reveal the importance of vocabulary in Michelle's language learning:

October 13, 1997
Written expression: This was a very good exam (in terms of the exercise given). However, vocabulary was my problem.

January 26-30, 1998
Le dimanche j'ai écouté *Rendez-Vous* avec Christophe. Son invitée était sa femme ... Leur discours était très intéressant et j'ai gagné beaucoup de vocabulaire.

February 01-06, 1998
Mme C nous a donné une série d'exercices comme devoirs. J'ai apprécié cette feuille parce qu'elle aide avec la révision des expressions, on apprend vocabulaire ...

February 09-13, 1998
J'ai parlé beaucoup mais autrefois le vocabulaire et le grammaire (Les Français sont si précis!) posent les problèmes. J'ai un problème: j'étudie mon vocab mais quand je parle avec les autres ou je dois écrire une dissertation dans la classe j'oublie presque tous les mots. Ca m'énerve beaucoup.

In her autobiography, Michelle had been critical of her teachers for using few "pedagogical methods" and for failing to make learning French more interesting. It was therefore easy to interpret her references to the range of instructional approaches used by her university lecturers as positive evaluations, e.g:

> *la semaine de le 26-30 janvier*
> J'ai bien compris l'entrevue et je souhaite que M. M puisse utiliser les videos plus souvent dans ce cours ... Dans nos cours de grammaire nous avons étudié des expressions pour exprimer la cause. Mme C a utilisé un projecteur et c'était plus facile de prendre les notes.

What, however, was not immediately evident, was the extent to which Michelle evaluated activities based on whether they were interesting, that is promoting motivation in learning, or not interesting, i.e. lacking in originality and therefore un-motivating. In other words, in or out-of-class activities that were qualified as interesting often indicated a significant learning experience for Michelle, as the following extract indicates:

> *la semaine de 09-13 de février 1998*
> A l'Ambassade on prépare une exposition très interessant qui met sur scène certains écrivains antillaise. Parmi les ecrivains dans l'exposition est Aimé Césaire. Cette exposition m'intéresse beaucoup parce qu'il y a un peu d'histoire des îles francophone et il y a aussi le folklore de ces îles. Si ce que j'ai vu est un morceau de l'exposition, j'attends avec impatience le produit complet.

This reference to the exhibition on Franco-Caribbean writers is one of the rare occasions on which Michelle writes of her out-of-class exposure to French. The small number of references to what she did to heighten her exposure to French outside class times was somewhat surprising, given that Michelle had mentioned quite a variety of activities in her autobiography. However, in her weekly entries, apart from referring to *Rendez-Vous* on a few occasions, Michelle's primary focus was on her in-class learning, an indication perhaps of her focus on coming to terms with the demands of her first year at university.

In addition to focusing on building her vocabulary, another of Michelle's major concerns seems to be her listening and conversation skills. Once again, the reference to this concern was implicit rather than explicit in her autobiography. Michelle had stated that joining the Alliance Française had helped her to know more about French culture and build on her "listening and conversational skills". Her devotion to the weekly Embassy-sponsored radio program *Rendez-Vous* and the daily rebroadcast of the MEU news, can perhaps be explained in terms of her desire to improve her proficiency in those skill areas:

la semaine de 01-06 de février 1998
Dans notre cours de Listening Comprehension, M. M. a corrigé et nous a donné les notes de l'examen. A mon avis, l'examen était toujours difficile mais cette fois-ci j'ai mieux compris. Je dois écouter plus aux nouvelles de France mais mon problème est que je retourne trop tard à la maison. J'écoute les cassettes de RFI que j'ai emprunté à la bibliothèque et c'est pas mal parce que chaque cassette traite un sujet différent et on apprend beaucoup.

To improve conversation skills, Michelle joins a student-led conversation group called *Citron Vert.* She is not altogether happy with her initial efforts. She feels that her French sounded like a *patois,* but reassures herself that the important thing was that she talked.

Despite the obvious errors in her written French, Michelle does not seem to be as worried about her grammatical mastery as she is about her oral and aural skills. Yet, what distinguishes Michelle as an active learner is that, once she notices the gap between her actual performance and her ideal or the norm, she right away "takes the initiative" and adopts new strategies to meet her perceived needs. We saw this as Michelle's reaction after the results of the first grammar test. Similarly, as Michelle works on the grammar project in Semester II, she becomes aware of certain gaps in her grammar that had not been apparent before. She realizes, for example, that as far as she was concerned, "le conditionnel n'existe pas. Je ne l'utilise pas ni à l'orale ni à l'écrite!" The grammar project signals a breakthrough in her learning in another more crucial way. She makes the following revelation in her journal for the week of April 6-10, 1998:

J'ai décidé de continuer ce projet pendant mes grandes vacances parce qu'il est très intéressant et vraiment pousse l'idée de "autonomous learner". On est étudiant et prof. au même temps. Ce projet a changé la manière dans laquelle, je lis un texte. Dans ex. B de la première parite, les étudiants doivent rendez en francais quelques phrases ... J'ai eu de problèmes pour traduire les phrases en anglais ... Les Français et leur grammaire! J'ai beaucoup de travail à faire.

The full explication for what Cortazzi and Jin (1999) call the "click" (158), the point at which there is a breakthrough in learning, comes in the following entry. It seems that Michelle did not at first see the merit of using extracts from newspapers and magazines to create her grammar project. I believe that this is because, in the past, Michelle used authentic documents for vocabulary and comprehension, not for gaining a better understanding of how the language was structured. But, by having to scrutinize articles to find examples of the structures that she wished to illustrate, she developed an awareness of the fact that text comprehension depended not only on vocabulary but at a more fundamental level on the syntax, "nous pouvons vraiment comprendre ce qu'il y a dans un texte en reconnaissant les structures grammaticales."

It can be hypothesized that this awareness has led Michelle to move from a quantitative approach to learning, associated with surface approaches to learning, to a qualitative approach to learning associated with a deep-level approach. This breakthrough led her to reassess her own grammatical competence and notice certain gaps in her learning that she had been unaware of before. Thus, although she viewed the grammar project primarily as a teaching exercise, which would help other learners acquire certain grammatical structures, the learning she experiences in the course of the project changes her understanding of the teaching-learning dynamic.

Michelle's diary reveals that she enters the program as a learner who has a clear sense of her strengths and weaknesses in French. She is an active learner who monitors and evaluates her learning, and constantly strives to notice the gap between her performance and her ideal. As she progresses through her first year of tertiary level learning, Michelle develops more and more of the competencies of an autonomous learner. She determines her objectives; she defines the content and process of her learning within the limits allowed by the course; she selects her methods and techniques; and she becomes more adept at monitoring and evaluating her learning. Autonomy comes to represent for her a way of engaging in learning that enables her to be a teacher and student. This is important for Michelle, because when next she is faced with teachers who "lack originality in terms of pedagogical methods", her understanding of how to assume a teacher role to meet her own needs will empower her to be a better learner.

The one dimension of autonomy that seems missing from Michelle's account is a focus on interdependence with other students. Although Michelle mentions the benefit she derives from the conversation group run by the more advanced students, she does not speak in positive terms of the relationship with her peer during the grammar project. On the contrary, Michelle is so disappointed at what she sees as their unequal efforts on the grammar project that she adds, "J'ai décidé de ne travailler pas avec un partenaire dans un autre projet. Au début il n'avait pas des problèmes mais au fin, j'ai fait presque tout le travail." It is interesting to note how Michelle's perception is at odds with her partner's. Her partner, for her part, expresses her resentment at the way her efforts were undervalued by Michelle, "... je m'est senti comme si je n'ai rien fait pour le project parce que mon partenaire a essayé de faire la plupart du projet..."

I think that one factor that has contributed to the friction between them is Michelle's growing understanding of what it means to be an autonomous learner and how that awareness influences her attitude to the grammar project. Her partner, on the other hand, has not developed the same attitude to the grammar project and it is likely that she does not share Michelle's commitment to it. Thus, the usual disagreements that arise when students share responsibility for project work are perhaps being exacerbated by the fact that one student has attained a new level of "qualitative involvement" with her work. Even so, Michelle's own understanding of autonomy is still circumscribed by her inability to include the social dimension of autonomy in her frame of reference.

Finally, an analysis of Michelle's diary allows us to show how some of the beliefs she holds contribute to the approach she adopts in her learning and her willingness to assume responsibility for her learning. Thus, while she does probably believe it is important to speak French with an excellent accent (BALLI item 7), her desire to improve her proficiency overrides this belief, because she is more convinced of the need to practice a lot to become a fluent speaker of French (item 14). By extension, she does not believe that you should not say anything unless you can say it correctly (item 9). Although, initially she may have subscribed to the belief that the most important part of learning a foreign language is learning vocabulary (item 13), I think that by the end of the grammar project, she is aware that an understanding of how the language is structured is crucial to language proficiency.

In summary, the data from Michelle's diary enabled me to come to a better understanding of Michelle and some of the individual factors that affected her learning. I was able to follow Michelle's progress from a good language learner, who knew *when* and *where* to find resources to build on her learning to a good language learner who knew *how* to take charge of her learning.

4.3.2 Anne's Autobiography

My first exposure to languages was at primary school after Common entrance, those compulsory Spanish classes[4]. What we learned was pronunciation of vowels and basic vocabulary such as niño, niña, and phrases such as Cómo estás?

I then started French at Form 1. The languages at that level was fun. We learned songs and played games. One game that I remember in particular was BINGO in French which encouraged us to learn our numbers. The focus then was more on pronunciation and basic phrases as well. But from form 2, the languages got a little harder. The focus changed now to grammar which took all the fun out of learning the languages.

I had the same French teacher for five years. She was very thorough. She prepared us well for CXC. My Spanish teacher in Forms 4 and 5 was nice but she neglected to teach us some grammar rules and I now realise that I was never taught the Spanish alphabet.

I really enjoyed the Sixth form syllabus for languages. It exposed us to French and Spanish Literature. It feels great to know you can read a book in another language. My French teacher for A levels was horrendous. My class was totally frustrated. She did not know the syllabus. She did not know how to teach the Lit part of the course. The only thing she used to help with was pronunciation. The only thing that saved me was lessons with a teacher who was originally from France.

Spanish was good. The teacher was competent and very thorough.

My weak areas in the language are speaking and listening. With speaking, I tend to think in English and translate so my thoughts are not clearly expressed; and too, a case of nerves. In listening, at times I just do not understand what is being said or it is just insufficient vocabulary.

I like the French and Spanish courses at UWI especially comprehension orale where we are fine tuning our pronunciation. But I don't like analyse littéraire. I am doing a double major so French lit is compulsory. That means twice as much Lit. I really don't like literature.

Analysis of Anne. Anne seems to have very clear preferences about the activities that she enjoys and does not enjoy in language learning. Her memories of playing BINGO stand out, as this game encouraged her to learn numbers in an enjoyable way. The change of focus from language learning for enjoyment and to meet a real need—to be able to play the game, to language learning with an emphasis on grammatical mastery seemed to have been an important juncture in her language learning. Her Sixth Form experience seems to underscore Anne's preference for language learning activities that have personal meaning for her, "it feels great to know that you can read a book".

In one of her early (undated) entries in her diary, Anne documents her dislike of certain elements of the program:

post-October 13, 1997
Reflecting on the grammar test ... The major problem I had with that test was No. 2. Personally I found the instructions were a bit vague. I really did not like that specific exercise.

in another at the end of October, 1997
I don't like Reading Comprehension in both French and Spanish because I don't understand the questions and most times some isolated sentences in the passage ... As I have stated before, I don't like analyse littéraire and I think that it is having a

psychological effect on my performance in that subject. I just cannot seem to analyse as profoundly as the rest of the class.

09/02/98
Je ne participais pas dans la classe de conversation parce que je n'aime pas le sujet.

undated (late February, 1998)
Ma note pour l'expression oral a baissé parce que, je pense que je ne participais dans la classe de conversation. Je n'aimais pas le thême.
Occasionally, however, Anne expresses enthusiasm about certain activities in her courses:

06/10/97
Compréhension écrite
I really enjoy these classes because it teaches how to fully understand French documents. We also learn how to say the same thing using different words, thereby increasing our vocabulary.

end of October, 1997
I like the pronunciation classes in French, but the thing is that after the class I revert to my old pronunciation. I just don't remember what I learnt.

lundi 23 mars 1998
Dans ma classe d'espagnol pour compréhension oral, nous avons regardé un feuilleton. J'aime beaucoup cette manière d'écouter parce que si on ne comprend pas tous les mots, on peut deviner grâce à l'action sur la télé. ... Pour la classe de grammaire, j'aime l'idée de mélanger le grammaire avec ce que nous apprenons en production écrite. Je pense que je me souviens mieux avec ce méthode. Aussi, j'ai fait tous les exercies en ce qui concerne l'opposition. Les exercices sont autre manière où je peux me souvenir le grammaire.

In her diary Anne notes her reactions to class activities, her likes, her dislikes, what is easy, what is difficult, what has worked before and she is prepared to try again:

1/04/98
Pour les classes de A levels, mon professeur nous a enseigné comment les habitants prononcent. Je pense qu'on doit rétablir les classes de prononciation parce qu'on peut déchiffrer des mots.

what she is unsure of and rejects because it is new:

post- October 13, 1997
... Ex #3 where the past historic had to be used, hit me for six. When we were taught past historic in secondary school, we were only told that is a literary tense and not much emphasis was placed on it. Therefore that is the attitude I have towards the tense. I don't really take it on.

02/02/98
Ce semestre nous aprendons comment écrire une lettre adminstratif. Je ne peut pas écrire ce type de lettre très bien à cause du langue: c'est-à-dire, j'écris normalement dans un style familier et pour trouver les mots pour écrire dans un style formel est un problème.

My attempt to get Anne to monitor and evaluate her learning more closely, to become qualitatively engaged in her learning met with little success. My frustration is very palpable in the following comment I made in her diary:

What aspects of the course do you like? What motivated you to sign up as a double major Fr./Sp.? Was this your decision or did you do it because it seemed the right thing to do? I am trying to get at the reason for a certain diffidence, which I detect in your attitude. At this level, even though you may be unsure about your long-term career aspirations, you have to at least feel committed to you course of study otherwise it quickly becomes "insupportable".

This intervention did little to convince Anne about the need to become more active in her learning, as a subsequent extract shows:

27/10/97
Today in class I had to correct my own work on an assignment that I did. I am a bit undecided about this exercise. I think it is a good idea because it could be used as a gauge to see how much grammar you know; but then I thought it pointless because if I knew what my errors were, I would not have written them in the first place.

    When I read over my assignment, besides discovering a few absent accents and wrong articles, I thought my work was impeccable. But on checking the page with my errors it was anything but.

    Honestly I did not learn anything new from this exercise except that I must check over my work more carefully because I made some very stupid mistakes, I'll blame that on nerves.

While Anne does have some insight into what works,

undated early October, 1997
My orals in both languages are improving, mainly because of vocabulary and also I participate in class. I used to shy away from participation for fear of making mistakes; but I realise that that is part of learning.

and does not work for her (the relationship between non-participation in oral classes and her examination performance, the understanding that her lack of vocabulary hinders her listening), she seldom takes the initiative to meet her needs. The following extract shows that her attitude in Spanish is very much the same as in French:

lundi 23 mars 1998
Je ne suis pas très forte en compréhension écrite en espagnol. C'est à cause d'une manque des articles à lire. Oui, notre professeur nous fournit avec des articles mais ça n'est pas sufisant. Il n'y a pas des magazines espagnols pour lire.

The data suggest that Anne does not know how to manage her learning. She is not very adept at self-diagnosis and, even when she is, she seems unable to assume responsibility for meeting her needs. She uses few metacognitive strategies. She complains about a lack of reading material in Spanish, but makes no attempt to source magazines on her own. She looks at a low intermediate French course on television, "quand il n'y a pas de cricket" and expresses surprise that "je n'ai pas encore vu une amelioration."

She also seems to have a limited range of cognitive strategies for although she infers the meaning of a word based on on-screen action when looking at the news, she performs poorly at reading comprehension because she does not understand the questions and "most times some isolated sentences in the passage." She seems to favor rote learning as a cognitive strategy,

6/10/97
I have now fully realised how little I know in the use of ser and estar and past Tenses ... There are so many uses that I did not know before that it is taking a while for me to memorise.

end of February , 1998
Je comprends tous les aspects du grammaire. Le problème est d'apprendre par cœur tous les différents expressions.

1/04/98
J'ai commencé à mémoriser le grammaire. Il devient plus ou moins facile.

Although Anne enters the program with an adequate level of proficiency and continues to improve by virtue of exposure to the target language, she tends not to maximize learning opportunities and risks falling short of her potential. There is some ambivalence in the attitudes she holds to her language learning. This was evident from her personal information questionnaire, where, while on one hand she declared:

Ever since I started secondary school I have always had an affinity towards the languages and they came very naturally to me. Therefore I decided to enter a career in languages.

On the other, she said, "I could honestly say that I have not picked up a French book since I finished exams on 24th June, 1997." A similar ambivalence is revealed in her diary. It is difficult to state unequivocally the cause(s) of Anne's attitude to her foreign language learning. There are at least two references to the role of fear, "a case of nerves", as an obstacle to learning and the reason for non-performance. Another reason, I think, stems from the conceptions that Anne holds about teaching and learning. Anne equates successful foreign language learning with teaching that is "competent and very thorough":

> I had the same teacher for five years. She was very thorough. She prepared us well for CXC ... Spanish was good. The teacher was competent and very thorough.

Anne's autobiographical account of her language learning revealed that she sought teacher direction or, to borrow her words, "salvation", from a private tutor when her classroom teacher seemed unable to provide her with the kind of teaching that she desired. "The only thing that saved me was lessons with a teacher who was originally from France."

This student seems resistant to the idea of self-direction probably because of the way she conceptualizes teaching and learning, and teacher and student responsibility. Holec (1987) contends:

> Traditionally, a majority of teachers and learners alike have tended to think that the learner's responsibility should be limited to being the beneficiary, so to speak, of the [learning] process, its active manager being the teacher. (147)

Wenden (1991) cites work by Weinstein and Rogers (1985) that discuss the implications of the teacher's management of the process of learning. This research supports the view that while teacher management of the process of learning may result in effective teaching strategies, less successful students fail to develop active strategies and find themselves particularly at a disadvantage in tertiary level learning where the expectation of teachers is that students know how to learn.

Anne is a prime example of this kind of behavior. She has certain expectations about the role that teachers should assume in her learning and seems unable to negotiate a new role for herself, even when the context of teaching/learning changes. Her reluctance to find other sources of reading material in Spanish; her attitude to correcting her own work when she is called upon to do so; her preference for the known and familiar and her rejection of anything that is new; and finally the level of engagement in her learning, all suggest an external locus of control. Even her preference for ways of learning involving memorization, as opposed to ways of learning involving understanding, suggests according to Benson and Lor's (1999) typology that she is more inclined to see the teacher, and not the student, as the agent of learning.

Her positive memories about bingo and literature underscore how necessary it is for her to engage in tasks that she enjoys in order to improve her proficiency. Had she been an autonomous learner, Anne might have found more satisfaction in her language learning by choosing activities that she finds appealing and motivating, if her classroom learning does not provide such activities. She does select certain methods and techniques to improve her proficiency, but it is doubtful whether her choices are the most appropriate; her preference for rote learning as a cognitive strategy is a case in point. Finally, she shows little inclination to monitor and evaluate her performance.

Interestingly, in contrast to Michelle and Nicole, both of whom experience a learning epiphany through their work on the grammar project, Anne is not very forthcoming about her work on the grammar project. In her journal of 16/03/98, she explains why she has decided to work on certain grammatical structures:

> Je les ai choisi parce que je ne les comprend pas assez bien. A l'école, on ne m'a pas bien expliqué les pronoms possesifs... C'est seulement par ma curiosité que je sais ce qu'ils veulent dire. Les expressions de cause, conséquence et but sont quelque chose de nouveau et puisque j'ai reçu onze sur vingt dans mon test de grammaire, je pense que je dois les étudier bien pour ce projet.

But her most telling statement about her attitude to the grammar project is perhaps the following one:

> *1/04/98*
> ... Je ne suis pas très forte en grammaire et pour faire un petit livre de grammaire, c'est un peu ironique.

Although, Anne declares that the project will give her better scope for *understanding* certain grammatical structures in French, it is not clear that she has in fact transcended her conception of what it is to learn a language. Benson and Lor (1999) prove once again instructive in helping to clarify the issues. They distinguish between approaches to learning that seem more quantitative in orientation (focusing on storing in memory) and those that seem qualitative (focusing on understanding). Benson and Lor draw parallels between quantitative and surface approaches to learning and qualitative and deep approaches to learning. Anne's preference for memorizing seems more consonant with a quantitative approach to learning. Despite the intervention to promote learner autonomy, and despite my attempts to move students nearer to the experiential, transformative end of the continuum, Anne never really moved from her initial perspective of what it is to learn a language.

The final treatment to be carried out on Anne's diary is the comparison of spontaneous beliefs occurring in her diary and beliefs elicited by the BALLI. Anne probably believes in the importance of practicing to achieve fluency (item 14). She clearly believes in the importance of learning grammar rules (item 20). Her difficulty in comprehension which stems partly from the fact that she does not understand some isolated words probably means that she does not think "It is OK to guess if you don't know a word in French" (item 12).

Although she is aware that translation is not a very effective strategy (item 21), she nevertheless uses this strategy in her oral expression classes. Anne's inability to transfer strategies even from one foreign language to another, probably implies that she keeps her academic subjects in watertight compartments and thinks that learning a foreign language is quite different from learning other academic subjects (item 18). On the whole, Anne's diary reveals very limiting beliefs about the nature of language learning. These beliefs are perhaps manifestations of Anne's fundamental beliefs or conceptualizations about her role and responsibilities as a language learner.

4.3.3 Nicole's Autobiography

J'ai commencé à apprendre le français en sixième, l'espagnol aussi. J'ai détesté l'espagnol et j'adorais le français. Je crois que c'était à cause du professeur. J'avais de la chance car j'ai gardé le même professeur de français jusqu'en terminal. J'ai toujours préféré l'oral à l'écrit sauf au moment des examens. J'ai jamais trop hésité à parler en cours sauf si je ne savais pas le vocabulaire. Verbaliser pour moi était toujours plus expressif qu'écrire. Pour moi la grammaire ne me donnait pas trop de peine, cependant j'ai du mal à formuler des phrases bien "françaises".

Analysis of Nicole. Nicole's autobiography at ninety-eight words was one of the shortest submitted. By contrast, her diary entries were frequent and detailed, and quantitatively and qualitatively revealed one of the most comprehensive accounts of a student's learning process. Most of her diary entries reflect her efforts at trying to improve her proficiency. But perhaps the sentence that captures best Nicole's major preoccupation throughout her diary was the last sentence which expresses Nicole's anxiety about making her French sound really French, "j'ai du mal à formuler des phrases bien 'françaises'."

Nicole had spent a year in France, enrolled as a student in the English program of a French university. She was thus able to draw on her first hand experience of using the language for communicative and academic purposes. But, despite her very high level of proficiency, she was relentless in trying to improve her proficiency. Nicole was not a language major, but hoped to continue to improve her French and keep up her language skills while doing a major in another discipline.

As she stated in her diary, Nicole feels fairly confident about her oral proficiency because of her immersion experience:

1/10/97
After having spent 1 year in France I find that I have a much better grip on spoken French than before I left.

However, she understands the value of continuing to pay attention, to imitate, and pattern her French on that of native speakers.

6/10/97
The best way to improve my speech is by talking to native speakers. I will need not only to try to imitate how they speak but also to almost study their speech patterns, their pronunciation, their intonation, and accents in words and sentences. That would also help in understanding how the French speak and why they formulate their phrases the way they do.

14/11/97
J'aime beaucoup parler le français avec les autres, francophone ou pas. Je trouve pourtant que je suis beaucoup moins à l'aise lorsque je parle avec des francophones. Je fais plus attention avec eux parce que je sais qu'ils remarqueront toute suite mes fautes! Mais ça me fait du bien. Il faut analyser leur paroles et essayer de les imiter. Et les interjections et les pauses sont très importants. Les mois et les tois à la fin de phrase, les quois partout; des choses comme ça. Autant de les comprendre, il faut noter leur façon de s'exprimer et la construction des phrases.

Nicole's facility in the spoken language does not mean that she is always free from anxiety when her performance is being evaluated. On the contrary, in her autobiography, she admitted that although she preferred speaking the language to writing the language, this did not apply when it came to examinations. In the following extract from her second semester diary, Nicole demonstrates how even a competent speaker is affected by oral testing:

1/3/98
J'ai eu mon examen oral lundi après-midi. J'étais toute seule vue qu'il n'y avait personne sans partenaire. Je n'étais pas inquiète avant d'entrer dans la salle. Mais une fois que je m'y suis trouvée, j'ai commencé à pas vraiment paniquer mais ... Je n'avais pas compris le raisonnement pour un examen à deux. Je pensais que c'était pour finir plus vite. Mais maintenant je me rends compte que le fait d'être avec quelqu'un d'autre aide beaucoup. On ne se sent pas obligé à parler tout le temps pour remplir la silence (ce que me mettais d'autant moins à l'aise).

What this extract illustrates and what is clearly exemplified throughout her diary is that Nicole is a very active learner. She demonstrates both metalinguistic awareness and metacognitive awareness, as she devotes her time to planning, monitoring, and evaluating her learning, and interrogating the learning process, as she strives to improve her proficiency. She is very aware that the management of the learning process is a crucial issue, especially for the advanced language learner. The following extract demonstrates this awareness:

10/10/97
A Aix (où j'étais) on faisait la phonétique et beaucoup de cours sur la civilisation anglaise et américaine. A ce moment-là je croyais que la phonétique était nulle. Mais je dois avouer qu'entendre un Français parler l'Anglais comme s'il était né à Londres c'est étonnant et impressionant. Mais est-il nécessaire? Je ne sais pas. En ce qui concerne l'enseignement de la civilisation et l'histoire ça peut être utile. Mais est-ce que ça doit être la responsabilité des profs? Plutôt des étudiants je trouve. Le problème c'est que sans un cours spécifique pour, on n'est pas tellement motivé à le faire!

Nicole addresses her problem areas, writing, and literature, with the same determination to evaluate her performance and to try different strategies.

19/11/97
Je préfère écrire ce journal en français mais je ne sais pas trop pourquoi. Peut-être c'est parce que comme je parle *du* français c'est plus facile de parler en francais. Je trouve qu'en écrivant comme ça (n'importe quoi, les lettres etc.) je rencontre des problèmes que je retrouverai plus tard en expression écrite ou en conversation. Si je peux les résoudre ici (ou en brouillon) je sais comment faire mieux en examen.

Nicole's diary was the longest of all her peers. She wrote approximately ten lines about three times a week for the duration of the study. Although, she complained of sometimes being at a loss for things to write about, she became aware that writing both solved and created new problems which allowed her to notice the gap between her written production and that of the idealized native speaker. The following comment appears at the end of an entry where she discusses the theme for the semester, "Les Arts", and the role of the arts in society:

23/01/98
... (Ce n'était pas grande chose sur le français mais au moins j'ai pu m'exprimer sans trop de mal). Je dois rechercher la différence entre 'du moins' et 'au moins'!

Nicole's immersion experience has obviously given her an edge on her classmates when we compare her linguistic competence with that of her peers. She has developed an extreme sensitivity to the target language that it is difficult to acquire solely in the acquisition-poor environment of the classroom. Two examples of her awareness of the L2 are illustrated in the following extracts:

10/11/97
Comme je n'ai pas la télévision cablé je dois demander à mon cousin d'enregistrer les infos à la télé pour moi. Il est possible de parler très bien une langue sans savoir ce qui se passe dans le pays, mais il devient plus difficile à communiquer avec les gens de ce pays si on ne sais rien des actualités. Je trouve que les Français utilise beaucoup plus les évenements et les personnages dans la langue courante. Par exemple "un choix cornélien". Une connaissance de la culture et de la société est indispensable à la compréhension et la bonne usage de la langue.

23/3/98-13/4/98
En discutant avec P. je me suis rendu compte de l'importance de voyager dans un pays francophone si l'on est étudiant de la langue. Etant donné que dans une telle situation on apprend surtout en écoutant les paroles des francophones ceci engendre une sensibilité presque innée, ce qui pour moi est devenue sans prix.

Is Nicole an autonomous learner? Does she determine her objectives? Does she define the content and process of her learning? Does she select methods and techniques? Does she monitor and evaluate her progress and achievements? Nicole's diary shows many examples of the kinds of attitudes and behaviors associated with autonomous learners. Moreover, unlike many of her peers who upon entry possess a low level of metalinguistic awareness, Nicole is already a fairly sophisticated language learner.

By way of comparison, Michelle, the first learner reviewed, initially devoted much of her energies to increasing her vocabulary. The grammar project allowed her to put vocabulary in its proper perspective and to focus as well on how the L2 is structured. Anne, the second learner remained rule-bound, seeking chiefly to memorize grammatical components. Over-concern with declarative knowledge aiding, Anne never moved to a more sophisticated understanding of the way the target language works.

However, Nicole is never unduly constrained by vocabulary or grammar, in the sense of declarative knowledge. Her concern from the outset has been trying to make what she says sound French, trying to "formuler des phrases bien 'françaises'." Beyond the sentence level features of vocabulary and grammar Nicole has been more intent on mastering discourse features of the language and on gaining procedural knowledge. She tries to analyze and dissect and imitate ways of writing and speaking French, so that what she says and writes will be patterned on authentic samples of language. This preoccupation is again repeated in the following extract:

26/01/98
Je vous ai demandé de me dire qu'est-ce qu'il me faut travailler (moi personellement) des trucs avec lesquels je lutte tout le temps. Et vous m'avez répondu (comme vous le savez) qu'il faut que je fais attention au registre. Je suppose que c'est encore l'idée de garder une distance (tout à fait contre les américains) qui me pose le plus grand problème. Comme la plupart de mon "enseignement" en France, c'était très orale, j'ai gardé et assez bien maîtrisé ce ton. Je le trouve très difficile à m'exprimer clairement et pleinement dans un français très soutneu. (La même chose qu'avec vouvoyement et tutoiement). Il me faut apprendre ... LA LECTURE, encore je reviens à ça. Mais ça doit être une lecture analytique où je décompose la langue pour comprendre comment et pourquoi on a dit ces choses-là dans cet manière.

Although Nicole demonstrates many of the attitudes of an autonomous learner, there are still several areas where an intervention to promote autonomy can help her to become a better learner. In spite of being able to plan, monitor, and evaluate her learning, Nicole is not immune to the problems that beset many learners.

One of Nicole's concerns throughout her dairy is her ability to manage her time. This seems a problematic area for her in two ways: the difficulty of apportioning her time during examinations and on a larger scale the difficulty of finding the balance between competing interests in her studies. Earlier entries tend to reflect the difficulty in using her time:

12/10/97
... Pour les examens il me faut m'organiser pour que j'aie du temps pour bien relire et corriger ma copie ...

17/10/97
Encore l'usage de mon temps. J'ai pris trop de temps avant de commencer. J'ai hésité avec mon introduction et ainsi je devais me dépêcher vers la fin sans avoir fait une bonne conclusion.

31/10/97
... j'ai perdu beaucoup de temps avec mon introduction. Ainsi, comme avec ma lettre pour l'Expression Ecrite, je n'ai pas pu développer ma conclusion. Mon introduction était assez longue et ma conclusion très courte. La prof m'a écrit que ma dernière idée était très vague. J'ai été pressé.

Another area that causes Nicole concern is knowledge of her particular strengths and weaknesses as a learner. An intervention to promote autonomy gives Nicole the opportunity to introspect and helps to promote greater metacognitive awareness on her part.

Journal for the week of 23/02/98

J'ai remarqué que je comprends et j'accepte mieux les principes ou des règles de grammaire lorsque j'ai fait un exercise qui se concentre sur ce règle. Par exemple, je me sens d'autant plus à l'aise avec cette tournure de phrase que j'ai fait l'exercise la-dessus!

Journal for the week of 16/3/98

Avec l'opposition le seul problème qui m'affronte maintenant est d'apprendre toutes les expresions. Cependant comme avec la cause, la conséquence et le but je vais essayer de m'approprier quelques uns, ceux que je comprends le mieux et qui me semblent les plus utiles. Le reste je les apprendrai mais ils me seront plus difficile à les mettre en usage.

Journal for the week of 23/3/98-13/4/98

Après avoir lu les descriptions des méthodes de travail[5] j'étais toujours pas capable d'identifier le mien. Je savais déjà que je suis practicien mais je ne suis pas sûre en ce qui concerne être visuel ou auditif, si je suis nettement soit l'un soit l'autre. Je retiens bien les exemples mais parfois je retrouve l'image de la page du sujet. Pour synthétique et analytique je suis un peu confuse car je m'associe pas avec l'un ni l'autre. Je suppose que la distinction, pour quelques-uns, n'est pas toujours bien nette.

Despite the fact that Nicole cannot be said to have resolved the issue of her learning style by the end of the study, she has, nevertheless, grown in her understanding of how she learns best, as the following extract illustrates:

1/11/97

Je parle beaucoup avec les autres étudiants. Je trouve que ça me fait beaucoup de bien. Pour eux aussi bien sur. Mais quand j'essaie de leur expliquer une idée, je trouve que ça me l'explique aussi. Je comprends mieux après que je l'explique à quelqu'un d'autre.

Her work on the grammar project deepens this insight:

21/01/98

Je crois qu'en faisant ce projet on renforce bien tout ce qu'on travaille car on apprend mieux (soi-même) lorsqu'on enseigne quelque chose à quelqu'un d'autre.

The learning click or the trigger event for both Michelle and Nicole comes through the grammar project. Both Michelle and Nicole make an important discovery when they experience learning from a teacher's perspective, instead of from a student's perspective.

Candy shows how "re-placing" the teacher can lead students further along the path to transformative learning. Citing Ramsden (1985), he explores the importance of learners grappling with a subject as opposed to their being presented with pre-packaged ideas by their teachers. He (Candy 1988, 70) sees the process of "grappling with the complexities of a subject" as "an important part of deep-level transformational learning." By this reasoning then, the cognitive processes engaged when learners have to grapple with subjects, i.e. " 'sorting out' relevant from extraneous concepts and ideas" (70) confer an advantage on the autonomous/independent learner as opposed to the more dependent learner.

Candy further cites Farnes (1975) who argued that in the context of the Open University, an approach that required students to grapple with and sort out course material would engage them in a deeper level of learning. The conventional approach in which the course teams were the ones grappling and sorting out meant that it was the teachers not learners who perhaps had the richer learning experience. Farnes contends that if course leaders wish to have learners assume more responsibility for their learning then perhaps it is advisable that that learners control some of the tasks traditionally done by teachers. The conclusions drawn by these educators are similar to the hypotheses put forward by Dickinson (1995), who posits a strong link between motivation and the assumption of responsibility for learning.

Boud's (1988b) model of learner autonomy as a four-stage process implies, however, that an autonomous, independent learner, who assumes responsibility for her learning is only at the penultimate stage and not the final stage of her journey to autonomy. The autonomous learner who functions at the highest stage moves beyond *in*dependence, the assumption of individual responsibility, to *inter*dependence, the assumption of social responsibility. A careful inspection of Nicole's diary allows us to follow her trajectory from independence to interdependence. Nicole functions at the fourth stage, the point where the autonomous learner, understanding her interdependence, accepts social responsibility within the learning community.

Nicole's decision to form a study group comes on the heels of her understanding that the strength of an autonomous learner is her ability to function in dual roles as teacher-student. Three months earlier when she first made the comment on learning through teaching, cited in the extract above (1/11/97), "Je parle beaucoup ... quelqu'un d'autre," I had suggested to her that she participate in a study group which some students were thinking of forming. My comment at that time was the following:

> Qu'est-ce que ça vous dit d'aider ceux qui veulent monter un groupe de travail pour perfectionner la grammaire? Je ne veux pas qu'ils s'abdiquent en vous laissant tout faire, mais participer de temps à autre peut leur rendre (et vous aussi) service.

Several reasons can be advanced why Nicole did not respond to my earlier suggestion. It could be that it was not practical for her to do so before. Her difficulty with juggling the responsibilities of her major and her French courses could have made it impractical to consider forming a study group earlier. I think, however, that Nicole's decision to form a study group can be compared to her sudden awareness about the benefit of having a partner in the oral examination. Nicole needed a trigger event to give her a new insight on working as an autonomous learner, in collaboration with others, as the trigger event of the oral examination had helped her to see the value of having an oral partner. I think that Nicole's decision to move from an *in*dependent to an *inter*dependent mode signaled a new phase in her autonomy as a learner.

02/02/98
J'essaie d'établir un groupe de travail. J'espère que ça peut marcher parce que il peut faire du bien aux autres et moi aussi. Parfois j'ai du mal à trouver quelque chose de précis à écrire pour ce journal, un vrai problème ... peut-être c'est parce qu'il y a trop qui me reste à faire! Enfin. Je voudrais que ce groupe soit autonome et ca pourra se continuer dans les années à suivre.

This entry is a very important one. In many ways, it represents to me the high point of Nicole's growth as an autonomous learner. In a spontaneous, unsolicited way, this entry captures many of the issues of making autonomy a core value of the learning process:

- Autonomy does not negate collaboration; on the contrary, the accomplished autonomous learner understands the value of interdependence in learning;
- Autonomy frees teacher and learner to engage differently in the learning process when there is so much to do that the traditional focus on transmitting content information becomes inadequate;
- And, finally, autonomy has a role to play in a curriculum that envisages learning as a lifelong process, rather than an activity confined to the years of formal classroom instruction.

This analysis of Nicole's diary concludes by looking at whether there is any overlap between the beliefs reported in the diary and the beliefs in the BALLI. In her diary, Nicole makes several references to beliefs included in the BALLI. The beliefs contained in item 8 "It is necessary to know about France and francophone culture in order to speak French," and item 11 "It is better to learn French in a French-speaking country," both receive conditional support in her diary. Nicole agrees with the importance of practicing to achieve fluency (item 14) and guessing as a strategy (item 12). But, as I mentioned earlier, in the space of her diary entry, a student who chooses to has more scope for explaining her rationale than in a structured questionnaire. In the following extracts, Nicole does just this when she explains how and why she uses guessing:

> *21/11/97*
> Maintenant, en lisant un texte (surtout les textes litteraires) le vocabulaire que je ne connais pas me gêne pas trop ... Parfois je peux facilement deviner le sens d'un mot à cause du contexte et je me suis rendu compte que c'est dans cette façon-là, j'ai appris des mots en anglais: avec la lecture. Mais je les vérifie de temps en temps pour m'assurer que j'ai bien deviné.

This extract demonstrates that Nicole is an active learner and reader who adopts the cognitive strategy of guessing with a clear understanding of how guessing can help her to decipher the meaning of a text.

Another reference to an item in the beliefs inventory appears in Nicole's diary when she comments on translation as a cognitive strategy. The question of appropriate strategy use once again throws light on the limitations of a closed questionnaire when compared to the free response of a diary entry. Earlier, I described the belief that translation from L1 to L2 was the most important part of learning French as an idiosyncratic belief. Furthermore, I pointed it out as an obstacle to Anne's attempts to develop her oral proficiency. Nicole, however, refers to a very positive use of L2 to L1 translation in the following extract:

> *Journal for the week of 9/3/98*
> J'ai trouvé que pour les chiffres il est utile de traduire les numéros d'immatriculation. Pour les partiels de compréhension orale nous avions à trouver plusieurs chiffres (numéros de téléphone etc.) et les autres se plaignaient beaucoup. Je l'ai suggeré à quelques uns parce que moi je le trouve très utile et très facile. En plus il ne faut pas un grand effort. Qu'est-ce que vous en pensez?

Finally, while Nicole sees vocabulary as important to language learning (item 13), her preoccupation throughout her diary went further than simply acquiring vocabulary—a quantitative approach. Becoming a better learner, working to improve her proficiency, finding ways to continue learning are all intended to help her achieve her major objective, which she has defined as "formuler des phrases bien françaises."

4.3.4 Analyzing the Three Students

What can we learn about autonomy from these three students? No student set out to write a recipe of how to be (or not be) an autonomous learner. But, as we follow Michelle and Nicole's trajectory from the start to the end of the study, there are certain competencies that they both seem to share, competencies which, in contrast, Anne does not seem to have. Michelle and Nicole both seem to be active learners who plan, monitor, and evaluate their learning. The intervention to promote autonomy gives them the tools to deploy these metacognitive strategies more efficiently. Anne, on the other hand has not shown any real growth in metacognitive strategy use by the end of the year. She still seems very other-directed and there has been no noticeable shift in her thinking about the need to take charge of her learning.

Another point on which the three students differ is in their ability to transfer strategies from one task to another. Holec (1981) notes that the autonomous learner understands how knowledge of her mother tongue and her knowledge of other subjects can inform her learning of the target language. There are several instances that suggest that for Michelle and Nicole this is so. They both seem to conceive of their French language learning at two levels. There is, of course, a primary concern with learning French, i.e. components of the French language. But, it is evident that both Nicole and Michelle make linkages between their learning of French and their learning of other subjects.

Nicole, for example, is aware that the way she acquires vocabulary in French is similar to the way she acquired vocabulary in English. Michelle, on the other hand, sees the possibility of transferring skills acquired in French to a similar domain in English. The following is an excerpt from Michelle's diary:

> *Journal pour la semaine dele 26-30 janvier*
> ... nous avons commencé d'étudier les règles de la correspondence français. Nous avons travaillé sur les lettres Administratif et Commerciale. J'apprécie cette exercice parce qu'il existe deux avantages: on apprend comment on peut réussir une correspondance en français et on peut utiliser les mêmes idées en anglais.

In the case of Anne, there are quite a few references to her Spanish classes, but there is never any mention of transfer of successful strategies from one cognate subject to the other. Anne tends to compartmentalize her language learning into discrete entities and so seems not to apply successful strategies from one area to the next. At least, there is no evidence in her diary of her doing so.

A third area in which we see clear differences in the approach of these students is in how they manage their attitudes to language learning. Anne is aware of developing a "particular psychological attitude" to the parts of her instruction that she does not enjoy, however, she does not develop the skills to move beyond a purely affective reaction to the content of the syllabus. She judges activities mainly in terms of whether she likes them or not. She seems unable to manage her emotional reaction and replace her negative attitudes by more positive ones.

Nicole, more so than Michelle, expresses strong negative feelings about one aspect of the course. However, in her diary we see her engaging in deep introspection about her attitude and why she feels incompetent in this skill area. She is shown slowly coming to terms with her deficiencies and finally, finding a way, if not to like that part of the course, at least to manage her feelings to it. Anne, by contrast, seems unable to move beyond her psychological attitude to various aspects of the course. A learner training program to help Anne become autonomous will need to include a focus not only on cognitive and self-management strategies, but will need to address particularly the domains of person knowledge and attitudes toward personal responsibility and personal capability.

When I compare the depth of reflection found in Michelle and Nicole's diary as opposed to that found in Anne's, it is difficult to know what to make of the latter's sometimes very cryptic comments. Although she never states this, it is possible that Anne was not more forthcoming in her diary because she simply did not like the activity. Given her penchant for acting primarily in accordance with her likes and dislikes, one conclusion that can be drawn is that Anne did not disclose more of her thinking because she did not enjoy keeping a diary. Indeed, this is one of the difficulties with diary studies that some learners do not like the introspection that is required and that "good" diaries, in terms of the quantity and quality of data will only come from those students who are cognitively receptive to this methodology.

However, Anne has never been timid to express her likes and dislikes. The fact that she kept a diary in the second semester, when there was no penalty or reward attached to the task is perhaps an indication that she did not disagree with the principle of diary keeping. I interpret the paucity of information on her metacognitive growth as an indication there was no significant change in Anne's perspective during the course of the study. Her diary confirmed what the personal information questionnaire and autobiography had suggested, that Anne saw the control of the process and motivation in her foreign language as areas outside of her control. She exhibited neither the affective/motivational nor the metacognitive attributes of an autonomous learner. Her conceptions about her role in her language learning did not allow her to assume responsibility for managing her learning and improving her proficiency during the course of the study.

I do not feel that Anne became more autonomous by the end of the study. But I am hopeful that, at some stage of her tertiary level study, Anne will have a trigger event that will cause her to reexamine her assumptions about what it means to learn a foreign language. As she matures, Anne may find it less satisfactory to seek alternative tuition, when she finds herself in learning situations that do not meet her needs. If, however, she can develop control of the process and motivation in a manner similar to Michelle and Nicole, she may be able to meet her individual learning needs and enjoy a deeper engagement in the learning process.

4.3.5 Defining Autonomy: The Student Perspective

In the literature review of chapter 2, I cited several definitions of learner autonomy. Yet another view on what it is to be autonomous came out of the course evaluation questionnaires completed by students at the end of Semester II, April 1998. Students were asked, "How would you define an autonomous learner?" (appendix E). Twenty-five students (N=30) responded to the questionnaire. Some of the students gave the following definitions:

> A learner who takes an active role in his or her studies, that is one who assesses his strengths and weakness and through trial and error finds out which method of learning suits him.

> It is the ability to be able to learn for oneself through knowing what are the methods which work for you and acting on them to enhance one's ability.

> Someone who is able to take initiatives in his/her learning of a language. This way the student's understanding is deeper as he/she is able to learn in a way that suits their own study habits.

> An individual who can read a course without being "spoon-fed" by the lecturer (as is usually the case). This individual takes the initiative to do one's own research etc.

> An autonomous learner takes charge over his study of a language and is ready to take measures to ensure his success in language learning.

In Michelle and Nicole's diaries yet another perspective emerges on what it means to be an autonomous learner and develop a qualitative involvement in one's learning. Both students felt that the deepest engagement in their learning came when they became participants in the teaching act. For Michelle, being autonomous is described thus, "On est étudiant et prof. au même temps." (You are student and teacher at the same time). In Nicole's words the same perspective emerges, "Je crois qu'en faisant ce projet on renforce bien tout ce qu'on travaille car on apprend mieux (soi-même) lorsqu'on enseigne quelque chose à quelqu'un d'autre." (I think doing this project has reinforced what we've been studying, because you learn better when you teach something to someone else.) In both cases it was the journey to the other side of the teaching-learning frontier that gave

Michelle and Nicole access to a genuine learning experience and to deep-level or transformational learning. They were able to see learning in a different way and to some extent become someone else, "re-placing" the teacher in the process.

The new perspective on autonomy that emerges in Michelle and Nicole's accounts marks a radical departure from the way in which learning is often viewed in this educational context. One is often led to believe that, in the teacher-student dyad, the teacher is somehow in a hierarchical position, dominating (if not domineering) as the agent of teaching and learning. Instead, these students discover, in the course of an experiential approach to learning, that as autonomous learners their best learning takes place when *they* assume the responsibility for learning and teaching, when they become, in fact, capable of performing dual roles as student-teachers. In summary, another definition of autonomy that has emerged from this study is the one supplied by Michelle and Nicole, whereby autonomy is that conceptual space where the student becomes a teacher.

NOTES

1. This student's answer is reported as N/A in the graph.

2. It is not possible to state whether they felt that their differential success at foreign language learning was the result of a special ability. A decision, which in hindsight proved to be an unwise one, was made to omit this item from the questionnaire distributed in October 1997. The students were asked instead to reply to this question submitted in the form of a free response question at the end of the academic year. Unfortunately, the rate of response was too low to be statistically significant.

3. Bhojpuri, called Hindi in Trinidad, is different from, though related to, standard Hindi (Solomon 1993).

4. Many primary schools introduce students to Spanish and sometimes French, in the last term of their primary schooling, in the period following the 11+ examination.

5. (See appendix F).

Chapter Five

DRAWING CONCLUSIONS
AND LOOKING AHEAD

5.1 Summary

In this study, I looked at teacher/student responsibility in foreign language (French) learning. I argued that students had certain conceptions of their role and responsibility and their teachers' role and responsibility, based on their previous (language) learning experience. I underscored research findings that purport that autonomous learners assume responsibility for their learning and have a qualitative involvement in their learning. I suggested that if students were to become autonomous, they would see the learning alliance between themselves and their teachers differently.

Helping students to become autonomous meant helping them to acquire new conceptual tools to view differently (1) the process of language learning; (2) themselves as active participants; and (3) their teachers as partners in the learning alliance. A point of note was the fact that the three years in the undergraduate program represented the final phase of their formal language learning for many of the study's participants. Promoting autonomy among such a cohort of students meant helping them to optimize learning opportunities in the institutional setting, helping them to enjoy the benefits of a technology-enhanced learning environment and helping them to develop metacognitive and metalinguistc skills to continue to grow as lifelong language learners.

Data from the BALLI and the students' diaries confirmed that students had a number of intact beliefs about language learning. Some of these beliefs influenced the strategies that students deployed to improve their foreign language proficiency. At a higher level, though, students' beliefs could be subsumed into certain conceptions they held about the locus of control and responsibility for their foreign language learning. An analysis of the students' autobiographies revealed that although students spontaneously produced a number of metaphors to describe their language learning, the driving metaphor seemed to be linked to the target language as a love object and their teachers as necessary conduits to that object.

Students who remained captive to this vision of learning French filtered much of their subsequent language learning experience through this initial perspective. Other students seemed less constrained by their first reaction to French and less inclined to judge their language learning mainly in terms of affect. Moreover, while the former students remained predisposed to seeing their teachers as essential to their success as language learners, the latter students were more inclined to accept that their efforts could determine the outcome of their language learning. Their French language learning had become an affective and a cognitive undertaking and, hence, they seemed more capable of balancing both these perspectives when assessing their language learning.

In the second phase of the data analysis, an in-depth look at the diaries of three students allowed me to discover how each student configured her role as a language learner. I was also able to explore how each student reacted to the process of assuming more responsibility for her learning. Thus, it was possible to appreciate how Anne, the most teacher-directed student continued to have expectations of teacher management of her learning, while the two autonomous students, Michelle and Nicole, developed a new understanding of the learning alliance.

Michelle and Nicole's diaries revealed that the relationship between teacher and student in autonomy is not a hierarchical one, premised on teacher agency and student passivity. On the contrary, these students became most cognizant of what it means to be autonomous, when they assumed a very active role and engaged in tasks that are usually the preserve of the teacher. When they did this, the traditional dichotomy between teaching and learning and between the teacher and the learner dissolved, giving way to a student-teacher, a meta-cognitively more sophisticated learner, who is more aware of the process of her learning. When the autonomous students became student-teachers, it seems that they gained a new perspective on language learning and enjoyed richer learning experiences.

The findings of the study supported my original hypothesis that autonomous learners are prepared to accept more responsibility for their own learning. However, the study revealed a new dimension on learner autonomy. Judging from Michelle and Nicole's experience of autonomy, the teacher of autonomous students did not simply divest some of her responsibility to the learner. The autonomous learner was not the object of learning to be acted upon; instead she became subject, became teacher, albeit a student-teacher and, from her new vantage point, she was able to invest more fully in the learning process. In becoming a student-teacher, this transformed person was able to view learning from a perspective usually denied to her when she remained an object of learning.

It is precisely this capacity for viewing learning from multiple perspectives that is considered necessary for the learner who must take control of her learning in an era of technological change. Technology's promise of constant change requires learners to leave behind static and immutable ways of being and adopt multiple perspectives and multiple roles, if they are to be responsive to the changing paradigm of a technology-enhanced learning environment.

5.2 Significance of the Study

This qualitative study captured the attitudes, beliefs, and behaviors of a group of advanced French language learners in a particular institutional context. In a qualitative research methodology, the issue of generalizability is considered less germane than the in-depth understanding, which a qualitative approach facilitates. Yet, the significance of this study, which explores the hitherto un-researched area of tertiary level language learners in Trinidad and Tobago, compels us to consider some of the implications of this research, beyond the present group of learners.

The findings of the study underscore the need for more research on appropriate methodologies in this social context. Theories of language learning readily acknowledge the impact of environmental factors as well as learner-internal variables in classroom-based acquisition. Even so, the extent to which the students in this study are driven by their conceptions of language learning presents a compelling argument for more research on the factors that promote and hinder language learning in Trinidad and Tobago. The insights gained from this qualitative study reveal some of the deficiencies of current methodologies and suggest some orientations for future research in foreign language education.

In addition to pointing to a number of implications for the teaching and learning of foreign languages at the tertiary level and further upstream at the secondary level, this study draws attention to the need for a comprehensive language educational policy that addresses both societal needs and individual learner needs. If such a policy were in place and a climate more supportive of language learning cultivated, students of French would probably have a larger view of their language learning. They would be more inclined to see their French language proficiency both as a bridge to target language speakers and as a competency for life in the multicultural village of the 21st century. A well-conceptualized language education policy would provide the framework within which the issues of language education would be dealt with on a holistic basis.

Of prime significance, though, is the fact that this study has provided empirical evidence of the benefits of learner autonomy. These benefits are such that I think that all language learners should be exposed to an approach that seeks to develop a qualitative involvement in their learning. Career linguists, those students who are majors in French and Spanish, can be especially helped by an approach that transcends the singularity of each language and that seeks to promote greater metalinguistc awareness about language learning.

Adopting a discipline-wide approach to promote learning and linguistic autonomy will undoubtedly have a number of implications. Integrating learner autonomy into all language learning at the St. Augustine campus would imply taking into account, not only how autonomy may be promoted in the case of the more able entrant into the foreign language program, but also the promotion of autonomy in different populations, such as non-traditional entrants, less proficient language learners, and non-specialist language learners.

But, elaborating a modus operandi for autonomy for each of these populations is clearly beyond the scope of this conclusion. A more immediate concern must be elaborating the ways in which the participants in this study can be assisted in developing a more qualitative involvement in their learning. Consequently, I wish to present a number of recommendations for the promotion of autonomy based on the five areas of need that emerged from the data analysis reported in chapter 4.

5.3 Recommendations

The findings of this study suggest several ways in which current practice can be altered to be more responsive to the needs of entering foreign language students. I think that a major finding of this research has been the importance of supporting students' foreign language learning as they make the transition from secondary school language learners to university level language learners. Even the most autonomous learner in the study was seen to have clear learning needs which may not be met in the course of teaching which focuses solely on helping students acquire content knowledge.

5.3.1 Students need to have metacognitive support

The paradox of learner autonomy is that teachers need, at least, initially, to provide scaffolding and support for the nascent autonomous learner, until she is able to meet her own learning needs. Until students can recognize that learning is an internal process that may be aided by, but that is not dependent on teacher involvement, *teachers will need to guide and facilitate autonomy by providing students with metacognitive support.*

Language learners need to have opportunities to reflect and introspect on their language learning. Without a gradualist approach that helps them in their self-discovery, learners may remain convinced of their inability to self-diagnose their needs and determine the goals of their language learning. In the absence of a language adviser whose primary function would be to provide support of this kind for language students, I think the classroom teacher can use innovative ways to provide metacognitive support, in and out of the classroom.

Using technology to support language learning via web-based language advising is one way to support the metacognitive needs of language students. Providing metacognitive support must entail helping students to plan, monitor, and evaluate their learning. Importantly, students will need to be helped to see themselves as active agents of their own learning. Learners like Michelle and Nicole who are inclined to take the initiative must be encouraged in this. Whereas, learners like Anne, who are inclined to look to teachers for their salvation, must be encouraged to develop an internal locus of control.

Many of the areas that are traditionally addressed in academic advising programs will need to be integrated into the provision of metacognitive support for language students. Students will, for example, complete any of the well-known learning style inventories to arrive at an understanding of how they learn best. As students grow more familiar with the issues under discussion: issues of learning style, perceptual preferences, multiple intelligences and so on, more of this information could be offered to them in the target language, as was done in this study.

Students need to be encouraged to articulate their short-term and long-term language learning goals and subsequently to be helped to plan their language learning in keeping with these goals. Students need, moreover, to know how to balance their immediate and long-term language goals while coming to terms with the cognitive, social, and affective demands of higher education. Language advising for the advanced language learner must include both general metacognitive support and advice that is discipline specific. In this way, students can develop an awareness of the nature of the task of tertiary level language learning and an understanding of the skills and competencies that they need to become better managers of their own learning.

5.3.2 Students need to be provided with metalinguistic support

Students need to develop metalinguistic awareness of language learning. As I have shown through a very detailed analysis of the students' responses to the BALLI questionnaire, a fair number of their invalid beliefs spring from a lack of metacognitive knowledge. Advanced language learners need, however, to know more about language learning than "ordinary people" do. Second language acquisition research findings can be made available to learners at an appropriate level of sophistication to aid in the demystifying and the "demythifying" of language learning.

A beliefs inventory like the BALLI can be used to tease out students' beliefs on foreign language aptitude, the nature of language learning, learning and communication strategies, motivation and so on. This is, I think, an excellent starting point for engaging students in discussions about foreign language learning. However, this will need to be followed by learner training with an emphasis being placed on the provision of cognitive strategy training. This combination of metacognitive knowledge and explicit strategy training should ensure that advanced students approach their language learning more informed about the process in which they are engaged. The provision of metalinguistic support on a continuous basis will once again be facilitated if language advising were supported by new technologies.

One advantage of a web-based approach to language advising is that new technologies make possible multiple modes of interaction. Teachers and learners can engage in one-to-one exchange, or in one-to-many communication as may be necessary. Furthermore, web-based language advising need not be confined in time and space to the present student population. Incoming students will not need to wait until they are physically present at the university to begin to avail themselves of this information. Once they have registered for a language course, they should be able to access a site and start the process of reflecting on language learning.

A further advantage of this approach would be to initiate learners into the growing phenomenon of virtual learning communities. Listservs have become important for knowledge exchange and knowledge acquisition, both in academia and in other fields. Providing students with this kind of learning model will encourage them to develop a competency that will serve them in good stead for lifelong learning. Furthermore, any activity that puts students more in contact with the target language, especially one that focuses on using the language for authentic communication is likely to be beneficial to their language learning and promote linguistic autonomy. Above all, a virtual learning community would emphasize the availability of other human resources, in addition to the teacher, for language learning support.

5.3.3 Students need cooperative/collaborative modes of learning

The emphasis on cooperative and collaborative modes of learning must also be encouraged in regular classroom practice. The virtual learning community must be a reflection of the learning community in the classroom. Conceptualizing learning as a community engagement is likely to bring about radical changes, not only in the process of learning, but also in the assessment of learning. Given the students' previous learning background, the assessment of their learning would probably require special consideration.

Students are likely to attach little importance to group-based modes of assessment, if they know that the "real" assessment will be conducted on an individual basis. An alternative practice of assessment in a learning community will need to focus less on timed tests and other modes of assessment that promote competition and focus more on project work and methods that allow for cooperation and collaboration, thereby underscoring the social responsibility of autonomous learners. When the teacher has to assess learners on an individual basis, she can make greater use of portfolios and other types of assessment that still allow for an element of cooperation and peer learning support.

The promotion of cooperative and collaborative modes of learning does not minimize the importance of keeping the needs of the individual learner at the forefront of all instructional decisions. The students' diaries showed clearly the extent to which individual variables affected their language learning. Autonomous learners *can* find ways to meet their learning needs even in a very teacher-fronted classroom. But, a part of the teacher's responsibility must be to provide a range of learning experiences to cater for students with a variety of learning and perceptual styles. If a teacher has some prior knowledge of the learning preferences of her students, as she may, based on the information collected in her web-based language advising, she could draw on this knowledge to propose a variety of activities that would cater to a range of learning styles within the community of learners.

An important challenge for the teacher interested in promoting an autonomous approach with the participants of this study must be finding a way to meet students' affective individual needs within the community of learners. Students will need to feel that the teacher is open to providing affective support, in addition to metacognitive and metalinguistic support for their language learning. The challenge will lie in drawing on humanistic techniques in such a way that students can experience their language learning as an engagement of their affective and rational beings.

5.3.4 Students need to have access to experiential ways of learning

Foreign language learners need opportunities for experiential learning. One finding of this study was that students had their richest learning experience when they were engaged in the experiential learning activity of preparing a grammar workbook. Not only does experiential learning provide students with opportunities to learn by doing but, in its fullest expression, experiential learning allows students to become reflective practitioners and not passive consumers of language.

In a jointly negotiated curriculum, students can be given opportunities to choose from among a range of activities, those most in keeping with their personal preferences. But, in addition, they can also be expected to play a more proactive role, intervening in learning and teaching in some clearly defined ways. Peer teaching can assist students in becoming more active participants in the teaching and learning process. Teachers can share responsibility with students for presenting certain topics or organizing certain tasks. Authentic language work lends itself to this kind of manipulation but with some thought, so too does didactic work. An experiential learning activity that I find to be very successful is to have learners turn a newspaper or magazine article into a comprehension text, including questions and suggested answers. The opportunities to reflect on the process of comprehending and making meaning of texts are greater than when learners work with a prepared exercise. Such activities help learners to grapple with and sort out the meaning of texts.

5.3.5 Students need to have an immersion experience

Can students who have not had prolonged target language naturalistic exposure achieve a high level of linguistic autonomy? I think they can if they resolve to "live" the language as fully as possible in their L1 environment. Nevertheless, the weight of empirical and anecdotal evidence on the benefits of an immersion experience cannot be ignored. In this study, for example, Nicole was by far the most sophisticated language learner of the three students reviewed. She clearly possessed greater linguistic autonomy than her peers because of her year spent in the target language culture, though the study was inconclusive on whether this year abroad also explained her greater learning autonomy. But, there is little doubt in my mind that her year abroad allowed her to build on her already high level of proficiency (Advanced Level Grade A) and function with ease and competence in the target language.

Nicole was unique among her peers in having had the opportunity to spend a year in the target culture. At the time of this study, just six UWI St. Augustine students had spent a semester at l'Université des Antilles et de la Guyane (UAG), Martinique, over a three year period,[1] although a twenty year old reciprocal agreement to encourage student exchange between our universities had been revised and reactivated in 1994. The constraints which students face are mainly economic, although academic and administrative problems also hamper the free movement of Anglophone Caribbean students to the Francophone Caribbean and vice-versa. Yet, without a similar exposure, the advanced language student and especially, the potential linguist,[2] will be deprived of the benefits of a prolonged immersion experience. This leads me to the final recommendation of this study, which is the need to *include a study abroad component as part of the degree program for undergraduate language students*.

In the interim, in an attempt to afford students an immersion experience, greater recourse could be made to new technologies to give students an immersion experience *à distance*, until an immersion experience *en présentiel* becomes the norm for language undergraduates at St. Augustine. Even the use of low-level technology, like e-mail for tandem learning, can help students bridge the gap between the classroom and the target language and culture. Promoting the linguistic autonomy of the 21st century language learner would seem to imply a greater focus on study abroad experiences, during the period of formal learning.

5.4 Conclusion

In conclusion, I contend that learner autonomy will take root when priority is given to promoting greater learner engagement in the process of learning. An environment that encourages experiential learning, that sees a greater role for learner self-access and one that is premised on learner empowerment is likely to promote student responsibility in learning. Adopting an autonomous approach to language learning will imply rethinking the human and material resources that are currently offered to language learners. There will be need to monitor the innovation and keep it flexible to respond to changing learning and teaching objectives. Central to this will be ongoing research on the theory and practice of learner autonomy, so that the theory can be informed by practice and the practice grounded in a better theoretical understanding of the concept of learner autonomy.

NOTES

1. This imbalance continues. Between 1999 and 2004, for example, 14 UAG exchange students came to St. Augustine, but no St. Augustine exchange student went to UAG.

2. ESIT, for example, requires all applicants for its interpreting programmes to have lived for some time in a country where their L2 and L3 are spoken.

Appendix A

LEARNER AUTONOMY PROJECT IN FRENCH LANGUAGE LEARNING

In the following pages, you will find a brief description of a Learner Autonomy Project which will be conducted in the writing and grammar segments of the French language courses F14A/B during the academic year 1997/8. The overall aim of the project is to promote greater learner autonomy among students enrolled in the French language program at the University of the West Indies, St. Augustine.

Data from the project will be used, in the first instance, in a Ph.D. dissertation which I am preparing under the supervision of Dr. Ian Robertson, Senior Lecturer, Department of Liberal Arts. The general findings of the project will also be of interest to the wider research community engaged in the promotion of learner autonomy and, to this end, the project will be listed in the Learner Autonomy Project Inventory of the Scientific Commission on Learner Autonomy. As is customary in research projects of this nature, safeguards will be applied to ensure the anonymity of the participants.

Please feel free to contact me in person or by e-mail (bcarter@centre.uwi.tt; carters@carib-link.net; carters@trinidad.net) if you wish to know more about the project.

Thank you for your co-operation.

B. Carter
September, 1997

Are you an autonomous language learner?

Who is an "autonomous learner"?
- An autonomous learner is someone who has clear short term and long-term goals for his/her foreign language study.

- An autonomous learner participates in making decisions about the course in which s/he is a learner.
- An autonomous learner is someone who understands that his/her ultimate success as a language learner depends on him/herself.

Why is being an autonomous learner so important?
- By becoming an autonomous learner you take charge of your own learning. You set your own goals as distinct from the course goals - is your goal to be able to write French business letters? To understand a French film without subtitles? To live and work in a Francophone country?
- By becoming an autonomous learner you become more aware of your individual learning style; you get to know better what works for you. Do you learn better working in a small group or on your own? Are you a visual or an auditory learner?
- By becoming an autonomous learner, you learn about learning strategies: ways to improve different skills, for example techniques for vocabulary building.
- By becoming an autonomous learner, your make decisions that help to shape the course.
- In short, by becoming an autonomous learner, you enhance the quality of your French language learning: how to learn and keep on learning.

How will you become an autonomous learner?
- A number of small studies will be conducted this year, all designed to foster greater learner autonomy.
- In one study you will be asked to complete a questionnaire which seeks to explore your beliefs about foreign language learning.
- The major study will involve the keeping of a learner journal in which you will reflect on your language learning.
- Another study, using a system of learner contracts for grammar review, will also be carried out later this semester or early next semester.
- At the end of the academic year, the data obtained from all these studies will be analyzed to assess whether the project has been successful in promoting learner autonomy in F14A/B as a whole and among individual learners.

Using journals in language learning

A journal/diary is a written or an audio account used by teachers or learners to reflect on their teaching or learning of a foreign language.

Here are some guidelines for keeping your journal:

- If your journal is hand-written, keep it in a loose-leaf folder. If you use a computer, submit a printout or e-mail me your entries, if that is possible.
- There is no stipulated length for each entry, but aim to make each one at least five sentences long.
- Start by doing your autobiography as a language learner - your first exposure to foreign languages, your school experience, teachers, etc.
- Make entries on a regular basis. Spend about five minutes each day to record anything related to your classroom (an exercise which you enjoyed/did not enjoy and why; a better understanding of a rule, word etc.) or out of class (a reaction to a song, film, news item; a conversation with a native speaker) language learning.
- If you are unable to write something each day, try to write at least twice a week.
- Write in English or in French, whichever language feels more comfortable to express your thoughts at the time.
- Do not worry about the mechanics of your writing, punctuation etc. If you write in French, please do not expect to have your work 'corrected'. You may, however, use your entry to seek clarification on any aspect of language learning.
- I will write or e-mail a comment in response to what you have written.
- You will be awarded five marks (out of the Test 2 total) for completing this assignment. A completed assignment will consist of your learner autobiography, to be submitted on October 1 (or the nearest class) and entries for the period ending October 8; October 22; November 5; November 19 and December 1.
- If you feel at a loss about what to write at anytime, here are some areas that you might explore:
- Do you find that French is a difficult language to learn?
- Is writing French more difficult than speaking it?
- Do you feel that there is any benefit in having other students check your work?
- How do people learn a foreign language?
- Are you a good language learner?

Appendix B

PERSONAL INFORMATION QUESTIONNAIRE
F14A/B 1997/8

1. Name: _____ M [   ]   F [   ]
2. I.D. Number: 9_____
3. Age: _____
4. Address: (1)

    _____

    _____

    Address: (2)

    _____

    _____

5. Phone: (1) _____Phone: (2) _____
6. E-mail:

    _____

7. Are you a full-time student? Yes [   ]   No [   ]
    If not, please indicate how many hours a week you work:

    _____

8. Advanced Level Grade _____ Year of examination_____
9. How have you maintained your French language skills since your
    'A' level examination?

    _____

    _____

    _____

    _____

10. What is your major?   French [   ] Spanish [   ]
    French/Linguistics [   ] French/Spanish [   ] Other (please specify)

    _____

    _____

11. What other courses are you taking? Please list.

    _____

12.   Please state the reason(s) for your choice of major/double major?

_____

13.   Why did you decide to continue your higher education at this time?

_____
_____
_____
_____
_____

14.   What are your expectations about university life?

_____
_____
_____
_____

15.   What do you expect your life to be in 10 or 15 years from now?

_____
_____
_____
_____
_____

       Please feel free to add any other comments

_____
_____
_____
_____

Appendix C

BELIEFS ABOUT LANGUAGE LEARNING INVENTORY

This survey is part of an ongoing study about student beliefs and foreign language learning. Kindly complete the form with the information requested. Thank you for your cooperation.

Below are beliefs that some people have about foreign language learning. Read each statement and then decide if you (1) strongly agree; (2) agree; (3) neither agree nor disagree; (4) disagree; (5) strongly disagree.

Please circle the choice that best reflects your opinion. There are no right or wrong answers. We are simply interested in your opinions.

Course:_____
Date:_____

1. It is easier for children than it is for adults to learn a foreign language.

1   2   3   4   5

2. Some people are born with a special ability which helps them to learn a foreign language.

1   2   3   4   5

3. Some languages are easier to learn than others.

1   2   3   4   5

4. Give an example of a language that you think is difficult to learn.

_____

5. Give an example of a language that is easy to learn.

_____

6. French is: a) a very difficult language
                 b) a difficult language
                 c) a language of medium difficulty
                 d) an easy language
                 e) a very easy language

7. It is important to speak French with an excellent accent.

              1   2   3   4   5

8. It is necessary to know about France and Francophone culture in order to speak French.

              1   2   3   4   5

9. You shouldn't say anything in French unless you can say it correctly.

              1   2   3   4   5

10. It is easier for someone who already speaks a foreign language to learn another one.

              1   2   3   4   5

11. It is better to learn French in a French-speaking country.

              1   2   3   4   5

12. It is OK to guess if you don't know a word in French

1   2   3   4   5

13. The most important part of learning a foreign language is learning vocabulary.

1   2   3   4   5

14. It is important to practise a lot in order to become a fluent speaker of French.

1   2   3   4   5

15. If you are allowed to get away with mistakes at the early stages, it will be hard to get rid of them later.

1   2   3   4   5

16. Women learn a language more easily than men.

1   2   3   4   5

17. It is easier to speak than to understand a foreign language.

1   2   3   4   5

18. Learning a foreign language is different from learning other academic subjects.

1   2   3   4   5

19. If students learn to speak French very well, it will help them get a job.

1   2   3   4   5

20. Learning another language is mostly a matter of learning grammar rules.

1   2   3   4   5

21. The most important part of learning French is learning how to translate from English.

1   2   3   4   5

22. It is easier to develop reading skills than writing skills in a foreign language.

1   2   3   4   5

23. People who are good in mathematics or science are not good in foreign languages.

1   2   3   4   5

24. People in Trinidad and Tobago place a lot of importance on learning foreign languages.

1   2   3   4   5

25. People who speak more than one language are very intelligent.

1   2   3   4   5

26. People in Trinidad and Tobago are good at learning foreign languages.

1   2   3   4   5

27. Everyone can learn a foreign language.

        1   2   3   4   5

28. It is necessary to speak their language in order to communicate
successfully with French speakers.

        1   2   3   4   5

29. If someone spent one hour a day learning a language, how long would it
take him/her to speak the language very well?
a) less than a year
b) 1-2 years
c) 3-5 years
d) 5-10 years
e) it depends on the language and the person

30. I believe that I will ultimately learn to speak French very well.

        1   2   3   4   5

Adapted from Horwitz, "The beliefs about language learning of beginning
university foreign language students" (283-94)

Appendix D

COURSE EVALUATION QUESTIONNAIRES

November 1997 – F14A 1997/8

Please complete the following questionnaire and return it by December 05, 1997. Thank you for your time and your cooperation. **B. Carter**

1. What, in your opinion, were the objectives of the first semester programme in French language?

_____
_____
_____

2. Do you feel that the objectives of the course were met?

[   ] Yes   [   ] No   [   ] Unsure

3. Given your reasons for enrolling in this course, were your objectives met?

_____
_____
_____

4. What do you know now, that might have been helpful at the start of the semester?

_____
_____
_____

5. How do you rate the course?

[ ] not challenging enough   [ ] a little challenging
[ ] fairly challenging   [ ] challenging
[ ] very challenging

6. What aspect of the course did you most enjoy? (You may choose several)

[ ] class discussion   [ ] in-class assignments
[ ] out of class assignments   [ ] general content
[ ] multi-media   [ ] student participation
[ ] native speaker interaction   [ ] student/student interaction
[ ] student/teacher interaction   [ ] other (please specify)

7. What aspect of the course did you least enjoy? (You may choose several)

[ ] class discussion   [ ] in-class assignments
[ ] out of class assignments   [ ] general content
[ ] multi-media   [ ] student participation
[ ] native speaker interaction   [ ] student/student interaction
[ ] student/teacher interaction   [ ] other (please specify)

8. How do you rate your performance in each of the course components
   during the semester?

oral expression

_____

written expression

_____

listening comprehension

_____

reading comprehension

_____

grammar

_____

analyse littéraire

_____

9. What would you like to learn that you did not learn in this course?

_____
_____
_____

10. What changes would you suggest to help you improve your language skills?

_____
_____
_____

11 a. Do you consider yourself to have been successful in the course?

[ ] Yes   [ ] No

   b. How would you define success in this course? Please explain.

_____
_____
_____

12. How has the course affected your short-term and long-term goals as a learner of French?

_____
_____
_____

13. Any further comments?

_____
_____
_____

April 1998 – F14B 1997/8

Please complete the following questionnaire. Thank you for your time and your cooperation. **B. Carter**

1. Please list the objectives of this course.

_____
_____

2. Do you feel that the objectives of the course were met?

[   ] Yes   [   ] No   [   ] Unsure

3. Given your reasons for enrolling in this course, were your objectives met?

[   ] Yes   [   ] No   [   ] Unsure

4. One of the objectives of the course was to help you become an autonomous learner. Has that objective been met?

[   ] Yes   [   ] No   [   ] Unsure

5. How would you define an autonomous learner?

_____

_____

_____

6. Were you challenged in this course?

[   ] Yes   [   ] No   [   ] Unsure

7. Have you been successful in this course?

[   ] Yes   [   ] No   [   ] Unsure

8. The most helpful/interesting aspect of this course was?

_____

_____

_____

9. The least helpful/interesting aspect of this course was?

_____

_____

_____

10. Any further comments?

_____

_____

_____

Appendix E

F14A 1997/8

1ère semaine en classe
Ecrivez un article a l'intention des lecteurs du Petit Francofeel (le journal estudiantin) pour expliquer votre décision d'entrer en faculté cette année.

2e semaine: devoir a la maison
Lisez le dossier 9 «L'Ecole et après» (Espaces 3). Ecrivez une lettre au « Courrier des Lecteurs » de France-Antilles ou vous donnez votre avis sur l'enseignement secondaire en France.

3e semaine en classe
Avoir des diplômes est la clé de la réussite---Discutez

4e semaine: devoir a la maison
Lors d'un séjour linguistique en Guadeloupe, on vous demande de faire une intervention a la télé sur la reforme de l'enseignement secondaire/un sujet polémique dans l'éducation dans votre pays. Pour mieux présenter le sujet, rédigez votre texte.

5e, 7e, 8e semaines en classe
Préparez un guide d'une dizaine de pages pour des bacheliers antillais qui veulent s'inscrire en anglais langue étrangère a UWI. Pour bien renseigner ces étudiants, votre guide devrait parler :
- Du programme de la Faculté des Lettres
- Du logement dans les résidences du campus ou chez des particuliers
- De la bibliothèque, de la restauration, du service de santé etc.
- Du transport et des loisirs a St.Augustine et éventuellement en ville.

N 'oubliez pas de leur donner des renseignements pratiques pour le voyage et pour leur séjour a Trinidad. N.B. Le guide remplacera Test 2.

6e semaine
Test 1

9e semaine
Corrigé du Test 1 & rédaction du guide

10e semaine
Dernière séance pour la rédaction du guide

11e semaine
Présentation des guides pendant le cours d'expression écrite

Consignes générales
Essayez de varier le vocabulaire et la syntaxe pour chaque devoir. Pour les devoirs faits a la maison, consultez le dictionnaire et un livre de grammaire. Essayez de vous auto-corriger, c'est- à-dire, vérifiez le temps et les modes des verbes ; l'accord en genre et nombre ; vérifiez le vocabulaire et l'orthographe ; n'oubliez pas la ponctuation

Evaluation
Chaque devoir sera juge sur le contenu et la correction de la langue et note sur 20(barème universitaire).
   1.   Contenu = cohérence, richesse de vocabulaire et de syntaxe etc.
   2.   correction de la langue = accords, verbes, orthographe etc.
   3.   Ne dépassez pas les 400 mots, s.v.p.

F14B 1997/8: Projet de langue française
La grammaire autrement

A la fin de ce projet la classe aura élaboré une banque de données sur la grammaire de niveaux intermédiare et avancé dans l'enseignement supérieur.

Méthodes de travail
A partir des textes pris dans la presse écrite - publicités, faits divers, éditoriaux etc, proposer des exercices pour faciliter la compréhension de cinq des structures choisies.* (voir liste à la page 3).
Le travail final doit être sous forme d'exercices de langue et leur corrigé conçus à partir des documents authentiques de la presse française ou

francophone, et des explications en français de la grammaire qui est à la base des structures choisies.

Ces exercices figureront dans un dossier de grammaire fait sur ordinateur pour les besoins des étudiants de cette année et des années à venir.

Tout en faisant votre recherche, discutez dans votre journal les problèmes, les difficultés survenus au cours du projet. Le projet peut se faire seul ou avec un partenaire.

Consignes

Le travail à remettre doit être le vôtre. Il ne doit pas être pris dans un livre de grammaire.

A cette fin, chaque exercice proposé doit être accompagné de l'article etc., qui est à l'origine du travail.

Le projet sera noté sur dix, comme résultat le deuxième test de grammaire et le deuxième test d'expression écrite seront notés chacun sur 15 au lieu de 20. Si votre projet est un travail de groupe les partenaires auront tous la même note.

Le projet est à rendre au plus tard le lundi 20 avril.

Objectifs linguistiques du français, langue étrangère niveaux avancé
- imparfait/passé composé
- concordance des temps:imparfait – imparfai; imparfait - passé composé
- imparfait dans le récit
- conditionnel présent
- concordance des temps: si plus imparfait plus conditionnel
- conditionnel de désir, de souhait, de demande, de suggestion plus infinitif ou subjonctif
- si plus imparfait plus conditionnel
- si plus-que-parfait plus conditionnel passé
- hypothèse sans si
- semi-auxiliaire:faire plus infinitif/laisser plus infinitif/se faire plus infinitif/se laisser plus infinitif
- subjonctif d'obligation,de nécessité, d'ordre, de volonté, de défense, de désir, de souhait, d'opinion, d'émotion
- subjonctif passé avec avoir et être
- expressions qui amènent les différents subjonctifs
- locutions conjonctives demandant le subjonctif
- expressions de quantité
- pronoms relatifs
- ce ... qui, ce ... que, ce ... dont, ce ... quoi

- simultanéité dans le passé
- style indirect/discours indirect au passé
- plus-que-parfait
- les relations: but, cause, conséquence, opposition, temps
- expression demandant ces relations
- prépositions et articles
- les indéfinis
- pronoms possessifs

Appendix F

Pour Mieux Comprendre vos Methodes de Travail

Découvrez vos points FORTS et vos points FAIBLES.

QUI ÊTES VOUS?	VOS POINTS FORTS	VOS POINTS FAIBLES
Théoricien	Vous avez besoin de connaître *la règle* pour comprendre. Si les cours sont présentés de façon déductive (règle→ exemple), vous en sortez sans difficulté.	Vous avez du mal à appliquer les règles aux exemples, doncà faire des exercices. CONSIGNE : Obligez-vous à donner d'autres exemples que ceux donnés en cours.
Practicien	Vous retenez *les exemples.* Vous comprenez la règle si on vous donne d'abord des exemples concrets. A partir des exemples, vous retrouvez facilement la règle.	CONSIGNE : Quand vous apprenez vos cours, entraînez-vous à retrouver la règle à partir des exemples que vous avez retenus en faisant l'exercice à l'envers.
Visuel	Vous travaillez à partir des images, de l'espace et des formes. Vous faites des schémas, des tableaux. Vous surlignez et vous soulignez avec des couleurs différentes	Si vos professeurs parlent beaucoup sans utiliser le tableau, vous perdez le fil du cours.

Continued on next page

Continued

QUI ÊTES VOUS?	VOS POINTS FORTS	VOS POINTS FAIBLES
Auditif	Le langage est très important pour vous. En cours vous retenez très bien les explications verbales.	Vous êtes en difficulté avec les messages visuels.
Plutôt synthétique	Vous voyez d'abord l'ensemble des choses. Vous avez une vue d'ensemble du raisonnement à conduire, de la dissertation à mener.	Vous perdez le fil dans les longues explications.
Plutôt analytique	Vous travaillez plutôt pas à pas. Vous privilégiez les détails et décomposez les étapes pour atteindre votre but.	Ne vous noyez pas dans les détails! Et ne vous en tenez pas non plus aux grandes lignes quand vous apprenez un cours : lisez les textes entièrement.

Quelques abréviations courantes

Pour prendre des notes en français, il est utile de connaître un certain nombre d'abréviations qui permettent d'écrire rapidement les mots les plus usuels.

MOTS	ABBREVIATIONS
avant	av
beaucoup	bp
c'est-à-dire	cad
cependant	cpd
combien	cb
comme	c
dans	ds
grand	gd
heure	h
jour	j
longtemps	lps
mais	ms
même	m
minute	mn
nombre	nb
nombreux	nbx
nous	ns
pendant	pdt
petit	pt

Continued on next page

Continued

MOTS	ABBREVIATIONS
plusieurs	Pls
point	pt
pour	pr
problème	pb
quand	qu
quelque	qq
quelque chose	qqc
quelqu'un	qqu
quelquefois	qqf
qu'est-ce que	qcq
sans	ss
sauf	sf
sont	st
suivant	sv
temps	tps
toujours	tjr
tous	ts
tout	tt
toute	tte
vous	vs

Appendix G

DIARY EXTRACTS

Page 104

- J'étais fasciné par la culture différente, les môdes de vie étranges et une langue pleine de vie. RR
- I was fascinated by the different culture, by the different cultural practices and by a language that was full of life.

Page 105

- Avec le premier mot français j'étais amoureuse. — CM
- From the very first French word, I fell in love.
- Pour moi c'était l'amour à première vue. J'ai tombé amoureux des langues tout à coup — LJ
- It was love at first sight. I fell in love with these languages right away.
- Je suis tombée en amour avec cette langue — RR
- I fell in love with this language.
- Les autres matières C'était comme une obsession de la langue — HJ
- It was though I was obsessed with the language.

Page 106

- Je me suis passioné pour le français! Quel gaffe! A la fin de A Levels après avoir été la meilleur élève j'ai gagné le grade D. Vraiment, c'était la fin de ma vie. Après avoir sacrifié tout, c'est-à-dire les déjeuners de détentes, le temps avec mes amis/amies, et resté écouter, parler et apprendre le français j'ai gagnée le grade D. Quel horreur! — AH

- I fell in love with French. What an error. After A levels, after having been the best student I received a D. Really, it was the end of my life. After giving up every thing—carefree lunchtimes, time with my friends, just spending all my spare times peaking and listening to French. I received a D. What a disaster.

- j'ai recu un bon fondement avec Mme H. — RR
- I received a good foundation with Mrs. H.

Page 107

- En gros, le français est part de moi. — GM
- French is just a part of my life.
- C'est comme si le francais vive dedans moi. Je ne m'en débarasse pas. — HJ
- It is as though French lives inside of me. I can't get rid of it.
- Voici quelque chose vivante. — SM
- Here's something that's alive.
- Une germe avait été sémé
- A seed had been planted.
- J'ai détesté l'espagnol et j'adorais le français. — NS
- I hated Spanish and loved French.
- Le français était ma vie. — AH
- French was my life.
- L'amour du français a existé toujours. — HJ
- That love for French still existed.

Page 108

- Il était facile à apprendre à cause de, à mon avis, mon professeur, Mme H. — RR
- It was easy to learn, I think, because of my teacher, Mrs. H.
- J'ai détesté l'espagnol et j'adorais le français. Je crois c'était à cause du profeseur. — NS
- I hated Spanish and loved French. I think it was because of the teacher.
- Elle faisait attention à chaque enfant dans sa classe toujours. Elle était là pour aider la plupart de temps." — AH

- She always paid attention to each child in her class. She was there to help most of the time.
- Mme H était chouette! Elle nous a traité comme ses enfants. — RR
- Mrs. H was really very kind. She treated each one of us as though we were her children.

Page 109

- Peut-être qu'il était la gentillesse mais manière stricte du prof quel que soit la raison, j'ai adoré cette langue. — HJ
- Perhaps it was the kind but firm manner of the teacher, whatever the reason, I loved this language.
- J'avais de la chance car j'ai gardé le même professeur de français jusqu'en terminal . — NS
- I was lucky, for I kept the same teacher up to the end of Sixth Form.
- Pendant les premières deux années de l'école secondaire, j'avais la même professeur. Son zèle pour la langue à mon avis m'avais transmis et depuis ces deux années j'ai brillé en français... — AL
- During the first 2 years of secondary school, I had the same teacher. She communicated her zeal for the language to me and during those 2 years, I shone in French.

Page 110

- Le CXC, nous avions un autre prof. Elle n'avait jamais fait ce genre de travail. J'étais très en colère avec l'école. Ici, nous préparions pour un examen majeur et il nous donne un prof sans l'expérience d'apprendre à l'école ou même avec la façon de CXC. Quand l'examen est arrivé, j'avais plus de la confiance en espagnol. J'ai reçu la meilleure note en espagnol. Je n'étais pas surprenante. — HJ
- For the CXC examination, we had another teacher. She had never done this kind of work before. I was very angry with the school. Here we were preparing for a major examination and they gave us a teacher who had nor prior teaching experience nor even any knowledge of the CXC syllabus. When the exam came around, I was far more confident about my Spanish. I received a better mark in Spanish. I was not at all surprised.

Page 111

- J'ai toujours préféré l'oral à l'écrit sauf au moment des examens.
                                                                    — NS
- I've always preferred oral to written French, except when it comes to exams.

Page 119

January 26-30, 1998 :
- Le dimanche j'ai écouté <<Rendez-Vous>> avec Christophe. Son invitée était sa femme☐Leur discours était très intéressant et j'ai gagné beaucoup de vocabulaire.
- On Sunday, I listened to "Rendez-vous" with Christophe. His wife was his guest that day. Their exchange was very interesting, I gained a lot of vocabulary.

February 01-06, 1998
- Mme C nous a donné une série d'exercices comme devoirs. J'ai apprécié cette feuille parce qu'elle aide avec la révision des expressions, on apprend vocabulaire.
- Mrs. C gave us s number of exercises to do for home-work. I was glad to have this worksheet because it helped me with the revision of expressions, and I learned some vocabulary.

February 09-13, 1998
- J'ai parlé beaucoup mais autrefois le vocabulaire et le grammaire (Les Français sont si précis !) posent les problèmes. J'ai un problème : j'étudie mon vocab mais quand je parle avec les autres ou je dois écrire une dissertation dans la classe j'oublie presque tous les mots. Ca m'énerve beaucoup.
- I talked a lot, but once again vocabulary and grammar (The French are so precise!) gave me a number of headaches. I have a problem: I study my vocabulary, but when I speak with people or have to write an essay in class, I forget almost all the words. That really irritates me.

Page 120

La semaine de le 26-30 janvier (the week of 26-30 January).
- J'ai bien compris l'entrevue et je souhaite que M. M puisse utiliser les videos plus souvent dans ce cours. Dans nos cours de grammaire

nous avons étudié des expressions pour exprimer la cause. Mme C a utilisé un projecteur et c'était plus facile de prendre les notes.
- I understood the interview very well and I wish that Mr. M would use videos in class more often. In our grammar classes, we studied ways to express cause. Mrs. C used a projector and that made it easier to take notes.

La semaine de 09-13 de février 1998 (the week of 9-13 February, 1998)
- A l'Ambassade on prépare une exposition très interessant qui met sur scène certains écrivains antillaise. Parmi les ecrivains dans l'exposition est Aimé Césaire. Cette exposition m'intéresse beaucoup parce qu'il y a un peu d'histoire des îles francophone et il y a aussi le folklore de ces îles. Si ce que j'ai vu est un morceau de l'exposition, j'attends avec impatience le produit complet.
- At the Embassy, they are preparing a very interesting exhibition on a number of French West Indian writers. Aimé Césaire is one of the authors being featured. I am very interested in this exhibition which gives some of the history and folklore of these islands. If what I've seen is a peek of the exhibition, I can hardly wait to see the whole thing.

Page 121

La semaine de 01-06 de février 1998 (the week of 01-06 February, 1998)
- Dans notre cours de Listening Comprehension, M. M a corrigé et nous a donné les notes de l'examen. A mon avis, l'examen était toujours difficile mais cette fois-ci j'ai mieux compris. Je dois écouter plus aux nouvelles de France mais mon problème est que je retourne trop tard à la maison. J'écoute les cassettes de RFI que j'ai emprunté à la bibliothèque et c'est pas mal parce que chaque cassette traite un sujet différent et on apprend beaucoup.
- In our listening comprehension class, M. M corrected and gave us our exam mark. I still think that the exam was difficult, but this time I understood better. I must listen to the French news, but my problem is that I get home too late. I listen to the RFI cassettes that I borrow at the [BCLE] library and it's not too bad because each cassette looks at it different topic and you learn a lot.

- J'ai décidé de continuer ce projet pendant mes grandes vacances parce qu'il est très intéressant et vraiment pousse l'idée de "autonomous learner". On est étudiant et prof. au même temps. Ce projet a changé la manière dans laquelle, je lis un texte. Dans ex. B de la première partie, les étudiants doivent rendez en francais quelques phrases J'ai eu de problèmes pour traduire les phrases en anglais Les Français et leur grammaire! J'ai beaucoup de travail à faire.

- I've decided to continue this project during the long holidays because it is very interesting and really helps me to explore the idea of being an autonomous learner. You are student and teacher at the same time. This project has changed how I read a text. In ex. B of the first part, student will have to put a few sentences into French. I had a difficult time trying to put these sentences into English. The French and their grammar! I have a lot of work to do.

Page 124

09/02/98
- Je ne participais pas dans la classe de conversation parce que je n'aime pas le sujet.
- I did not take part in the conversation class because I do not like the topic.

Page 125

Undated (late February, 1998)
- Ma note pour l'expression oral a baissé parce que, je pense que je ne participais dans la classe de conversation. Je n'aimais pas le thème.
- My mark in oral expression went down. I think it was because I did not participate much in the conversation classes, because I did not like the theme.

lundi 23 mars 1998
- Dans ma classe d'espagnol pour compréhension oral, nous avons regardé un feuilleton. J'aime beaucoup cette manière d'écouter parce que si on ne comprend pas tous les mots, on peut deviner grâce à l'action sur la télé. .Pour la classe de grammaire, j'aime l'idée de mélanger le grammaire avec ce que nous apprenons en production écrite. Je pense que je me souviens mieux avec ce méthode. Aussi, j'ai fait tous les exercies en ce qui concerne l'opposition. Les exercices sont autre manière où je peux me souvenir le grammaire.

- In my Spanish listening comprehension class, we looked at a TV serial. I like this way of practising our listening, because even though we don't understand all the words, we can guess (and follow the story) from what is taking place on the screen. I like the idea of integrating our grammar with our written expression. I think that I remember better this way. I did all the assignments on opposition. These exercises are another way to remember the grammar,

1/04/98

- Pour les classes de A levels, mon professeur nous a enseigné comment les habitants prononcent. Je pense qu'on doit rétablir les classes de prononciation parce qu'on peut déchiffrer des mots.
- Our A level teacher taught us pronunciation. I think that we should have pronunciation classes again, because we will be able to figure out the words better if we do.

02/02/98

- Ce semestre nous aprendons comment écrire une lettre adminstratif. Je ne peut pas écrire ce type de lettre très bien à cause du langue: c'est-à-dire, j'écris normalement dans un style familier et pour trouver les mots pour écrire dans un style formel est un problème
- This semester, we are learning how to write a formal letter. I cannot write this type of letter very well, because of the language required. I normally write in a very informal register and it is difficult to find the right words to write very formally.

Page 126

lundi 23 mars 1998 (Monday 23 March, 1998)

- Je ne suis pas très forte en compréhension écrite en espagnol. C'est à cause d'une manque des articles à lire. Oui, notre professeur nous fournit avec des articles mais ça n'est pas sufisant. Il n'y a pas des magazines espagnols pour lire.
- I am not very good at reading comprehension in Spanish. I think it is because there are not enough articles to read. Yes, our teacher does give us articles to read, but not enough. There are no Spanish magazines that we can read.

Page 127

End of February, 1998
- Je comprends tous les aspects du grammaire. Le problème est d'apprendre par cœur tous les différents expressions.
- I understand all the grammar. The problem is to learn the different expressions by heart.

1/04/98
- J'ai commencé à mémoriser le grammaire. Il devient plus ou moins facile.
- I have begun to memorise the grammar. It is becoming more or less easier.

Page 129

- Je les ai choisi parce que je ne les comprend pas assez bien. A l'école, on ne m'a pas bien expliqué les pronoms possesifs □ C'est seulement par ma curiosité que je sais ce qu'ils veulent dire. Les expressions de cause, conséquence et but sont quelque chose de nouveau et puisque j'ai reçu onze sur vingt dans mon test de grammaire, je pense que je dois les étudier bien pour ce projet.
- I decided to work on these (structures) because I do not understand them so well. At school, no one ever really explained possessive pronouns. It is only through my own curiousity that I know what they mean. The expressions showing cause, consequence and purpose are something new and since I received 11 out of 20 in my grammar test, I think that I should study them well for this project.

1/04/98
- Je ne suis pas très forte en grammaire et pour faire un petit livre de grammaire, c'est un peu ironique.
- I am not very good at grammar and it's therefore rather ironic having to produce a booklet on grammar.

Page 130

- I began learning French in form I, Spanish as well. I hated Spanish but loved French. I think it was because of the teacher. I was lucky. I had the same teacher right up to Sixth form. I've always preferred the oral aspect of the language, rather than the written part, except at exam time. I've never hesitated too much to talk in class, except if I didn't know the vocabulary. I have always been able to express myself far more effectively, far more fully in speaking rather than in writing. Grammar isn't too problematic, but I have difficulty expressing myself in a truly French way.

Page 131

14/11/97

- J'aime beaucoup parler le français avec les autres, francophone ou pas. Je trouve pourtant que je suis beaucoup moins à l'aise lorsque je parle avec des francophones. Je fais plus attention avec eux parce que je sais qu'ils remarqueront toute suite mes fautes! Mais ça me fait du bien. Il faut analyser leur paroles et essayer de les imiter. Et les interjections et les pauses sont très importants. Les mois et les tois à la fin de phrase, les quois partout; des choses comme ça. Autant de les comprendre, il faut noter leur façon de s'exprimer et la construction des phrases.

- I enjoy talking French with other people, whether or not they are native speakers. I find, however, that I am much less at ease with native speakers. I am much more careful with them because I know that they will notice my mistakes right away. But that's good for me. I have to analyse their words and try to imitate them. The interjections and pauses are very important. The 'mois' and 'tois' at the end of sentences, the 'quois' everywhere, things like that. More than just understanding what they are saying, you have to pay close attention to how they express themselves and the way the construct their sentences.

1/3/98

- J'ai eu mon examen oral lundi après-midi. J'étais toute seule vue qu'il n'y avait personne sans partenaire. Je n'étais pas inquiète avant d'entrer dans la salle. Mais une fois que je m'y suis trouvée, j'ai commencé à pas vraiment paniquer mais☐Je n'avais pas compris le raisonnement pour un examen à deux. Je pensais que c'était pour finir plus vite. Mais maintenant je me rends compte que le fait d'être avec quelqu'un d'autre aide beaucoup. On ne se sent pas obligé à parler tout le temps pour remplir la silence (ce que me mettais d'autant moins à l'aise).

- I had my oral exam on Monday afternoon. I was all alone since I was the only person without a partner. I wasn't really worried before going into the exam. But once I got into the room, I began not exactly to panic, but Before this I'd never really understood why we were examined in pairs. I simply thought it was to finish faster. Now I understand that being with someone else is very helpful. You do not feel obliged to talk all the time to fill the silence (which made me feel even less at ease and confident).

Page 132

10/10/97
- A Aix (où j'étais) on faisait la phonétique et beaucoup de cours sur la civilisation anglaise et américaine. A ce moment-là je croyais que la phonétique était nulle. Mais je dois avouer qu'entendre un Français parler l'Anglais comme s'il était né à Londres c'est étonnant et impressionant. Mais est-il nécessaire? Je ne sais pas. En ce qui concerne l'enseignement de la civilisation et l'histoire ça peut être utilie. Mais est-ce que ça doit être la responsabilité des profs? Plutôt des étudiants je trouve. Le problème c'est que sans un cours spécifique pour, on n'est pas tellement motivé à le faire!
- At Aix, where I studied, we did phonetics and many classes on British and American civilisation. Back then I used to think that phonetics was a waste of time. But I must admit that it is surprising and very impressive to hear a Frenchman speak as though he were London-born. But is it necessary? I don't know. It is perhaps necessary and useful to teach civilisation and history. But should that be the lecturer's responsibility. More like the students', I think. The problem is that unless one has a course where that is one of the objectives, one isn't really motivated to do it one's own.

19/11/97
- Je préfère écrire ce journal en français mais je ne sais pas trop pourquoi. Peut-être c'est parce que comme je parle du français c'est plus facile de parler en francais. Je trouve qu'en écrivant comme ça (n'importe quoi, les lettres etc.) je rencontre des problèmes que je retrouverai plus tard en expression écrite ou en conversation. Si je peux les résoudre ici (ou en brouillon) je sais comment faire mieux en examen.
- I prefer to write this diary in French, but I am not quite sure why. Perhaps it is because I am speaking about French, I find it easier to

speak in French. I find that when I write like that (it doesn't matter what, letters etc.) I meet problems that I am likely to run into once again later in written expression or conversation. If I can find a solution to these problems here (in rough copy) I'll be better able to handle them in an exam.

23/01/98

- (Ce n'était pas grande chose sur le français mais au moins j'ai pu m'exprimer sans trop de mal). Je dois rechercher la différence entre 'du moins' et 'au moins'!
- (It's not that much about French, but at least I was able to express myself without too much difficulty). I must look up the difference between 'du moins' and 'au moins'!

Page 133

10/11/97

- Comme je n'ai pas la télévision cablé je dois demander à mon cousin d'enregistrer les infos à la télé pour moi. Il est possible de parler très bien une langue sans savoir ce qui se passe dans le pays, mais il devient plus difficile à communiquer avec les gens de ce pays si on ne sais rien des actualités. Je trouve que les Français utilise beaucoup plus les évenements et les personnages dans la langue courante. Par exemple "un choix cornélien". Une connaissance de la culture et de la société est indispensable à la compréhension et la bonne usage de la langue.
- I do not have cable TV, so I must have my cousin tape the TV news for me. It is possible to speak a language very well without knowing what is going on inside a country, but it becomes more difficult to communicate with people from this country if you are not abreast of current events. I find that the French make frequent reference to events and personalities in their everyday language. Take for example the expression 'a Cornelian choice'. You must know the culture and the society to truly understand and use the language effectively.

23/3/98-13/4/98

- En discutant avec P. je me suis rendu compte de l'importance de voyager dans un pays francophone si l'on est étudiant de la langue. Etant donné que dans une telle situation on apprend surtout en écoutant les paroles des francophones ceci engendre une sensibilité presque innée, ce qui pour moi est devenue sans prix.

- In talking with P. I came to realise the importance of visiting a French-speaking country if you are studying the language. Given that in such a situation you learn from hearing native speakers speak, you develop an almost innate sensitivity to the language, something which I have come to value immensely.

Page 133-34

26/01/98

- Je vous ai demandé de me dire qu'est-ce qu'il me faut travailler (moi personellement) des trucs avec lesquels je lutte tout le temps. Et vous m'avez répondu (comme vous le savez) qu'il faut que je fais attention au registre. Je suppose que c'est encore l'idée de garder une distance (tout à fait contre les américains) qui me pose le plus grand problème. Comme la plupart de mon "enseignement" en France, c'était très orale, j'ai gardé et assez bien maîtrisé ce ton. Je le trouve très difficile à m'exprimer clairement et pleinement dans un français très soutenu. (La même chose qu'avec vouvoyement et tutoiement). Il me faut apprendre LA LECTURE, encore je reviens à ça. Mais ça doit être une lecture analytique où je décompose la langue pour comprendre comment et pourquoi on a dit ces choses-là dans cet manière.

- I asked you to tell me what I need to do (me, personally) the sort of things that I struggle against all the time. And you told me (as you know) that I must be careful with the register that I use. I suppose that once again it is this question of keeping one's distance (quite unlike the Americans) which is the most difficult thing for me. As the greater part of my 'education' in France was very oral, I have kept and mastered that tone fairly well. I have a lot of difficulty in expressing myself fully and clearly in very formal French. (I suppose it is like using 'tu' and 'vous'.) This therefore is something that I need to learn. READING, once again I come back to that. But that has to be a very analytical type of reading where I dissect the language to understand how and why things are said in the way that they are.

12/10/97

- Pour les examens il me faut m'organiser pour que j'aie du temps pour bien relire et corriger ma copie.

- I have to be careful to give myself sufficient time to re-read and correct my paper during my exams.

17/10/97
- Encore l'usage de mon temps. J'ai pris trop de temps avant de commencer. J'ai hésité avec mon introduction et ainsi je devais me dépêcher vers la fin sans avoir fait une bonne conclusion.
- Once again my time. I took too long to get started. I hesitated with my introduction and so I had to hurry towards the end and couldn't conclude properly.

31/10/97
- j'ai perdu beaucoup de temps avec mon introduction. Ainsi, comme avec ma lettre pour l'Expression Ecrite, je n'ai pas pu développer ma conclusion. Mon introduction était assez longue et ma conclusion très courte. La prof m'a écrit que ma dernière idée était très vague. J'ai été pressé.
- I lost a lot of time with my introduction. I was not able to develop my conclusion, a repeat of the situation in written expression. My introduction was rather long and my conclusion was very short. The lecturer wrote that my last idea lacked precision. I was short on time.

Journal for the week of 23/02/98
- J'ai remarqué que je comprends et j'accepte mieux les principes ou des règles de grammaire lorsque j'ai fait un exercise qui se concentre sur ce règle. Par exemple, je me sens d'autant plus à l'aise avec cette tournure de phrase que j'ai fait l'exercise la-dessus!
- I noticed that I understand and appreciate grammar rules better when I do an exercise to practise the rule. For example, I feel 'all the more' at ease using this expression, because I did the exercise on 'all the more'.

Page 135

Journal for the week of 16/3/98
- Avec l'opposition le seul problème qui m'affronte maintenant est d'apprendre toutes les expresions. Cependant comme avec la cause, la conséquence et le but je vais essayer de m'approprier quelques uns, ceux que je comprends le mieux et qui me semblent les plus

utiles. Le reste je les apprendrai mais ils me seront plus difficile à les mettre en usage.

- The only problem that I face when doing expressions of contrast is to learn all these new expressions. However, I plan to do exactly like I did when we met the expressions of cause, consequence and purpose and that is to try to appropriate those that I understand best and which I find the most useful.

Journal for the week of 23/3/98-13/4/98

- Après avoir lu les descriptions des méthodes de travail j'étais toujours pas capable d'identifier le mien. Je savais déjà que je suis practicien mais je ne suis pas sûre en ce qui concerne être visuel ou auditif, si je suis nettement soit l'un soit l'autre. Je retiens bien les exemples mais parfois je retrouve l'image de la page du sujet. Pour synthétique et analytique je suis un peu confuse car je m'associe pas avec l'un ni l'autre. Je suppose que la distinction, pour quelques-uns, n'est pas toujours bien nette.

- After reading the descriptions of different learning styles, I am still incapable of identifying mine. I already knew that I was a pragmatist, but I am not sure whether I am visual or auditory, or if I am clearly one more than the other. I retain examples fairly well, but sometimes I can bring to mind the page of the text. I am not very clear whether I am a globalist or a serialist because I do not see myself as either one or the other. I suppose for some people, there is no clear style preference.

1/11/97

- Je parle beaucoup avec les autres étudiants. Je trouve que ça me fait beaucoup de bien. Pour eux aussi bien sur. Mais quand j'essaie de leur expliquer une idée, je trouve que ça me l'explique aussi. Je comprends mieux après que je l'explique à quelqu'un d'autre.

- I talk a lot with the other students. I find that doing that does me a lot of good. Does them good too, I'm sure. But when I try to explain an idea to them, I find that I too benefit from the explanation. I understand better after explaining something to someone else.

21/01/98

- Je crois qu'en faisant ce projet on renforce bien tout ce qu'on travaille car on apprend mieux (soi-même) lorsqu'on enseigne quelque chose à quelqu'un d'autre.

- I think that doing this project helps to reinforce what we are working on, because one learns better when one tries to teach something to someone else.

- "Qu'est-ce que ça vous dit d'aider ceux qui veulent monter un groupe de travail pour perfectionner la grammaire? Je ne veux pas qu'ils s'abdiquent en vous laissant tout faire, mais participer de temps à autre peut leur rendre (et vous aussi) service."
- "What do you say about lending a hand to those who want to form a study group to improve their grammar? I don't want them to leave it all up to you, but joining in from time to time can help them (and help you too)."

Page 137

02/02/98

J'essaie d'établir un groupe de travail. J'espère que ça peut marcher parce que il peut faire du bien aux autres et moi aussi. Parfois j'ai du mal à trouver quelque chose de précis à écrire pour ce journal, un vrai problème peut-être c'est parce qu'il y a trop qui me reste à faire! Enfin. Je voudrais que ce groupe soit autonome et ca pourra se continuer dans les années à suivre.

I am trying to set up a study group. I hope that it will work, because it will help others and help me also. Sometimes I have a hard time trying to find something to write in this diary, it's a real problem perhaps that is because I have some much still to do! Anyway. I would like this group to be autonomous and continue for the rest of our programme.

Page 138

21/11/97

Maintenant, en lisant un texte (surtout les textes litteraires) le vocabulaire que je ne connais pas me gêne pas trop! Parfois je peux facilement deviner le sens d'un mot à cause du contexte et je me suis rendu compte que c'est dans cette façon-là, j'ai appris des mots en anglais: avec la lecture. Mais je les vérifie de temps en temps pour m'assurer que j'ai bien deviné.

Now, whenever I read a text (especially literary texts), I'm not too bothered by the words that I do not know. Sometimes, I find it easy to guess the meaning of a word from the context and I realise that was how I learned words in English: from reading. But, I still check from time to time to make sure that I guessed right.

Journal for the week of 9/3/98
J'ai trouvé que pour les chiffres il est utile de traduire les numéros d'immatriculation. Pour les partiels de compréhension orale nous avions à trouver plusieurs chiffres (numéros de téléphone etc.) et les autres se plaignaient beaucoup. Je l'ai suggeré à quelques uns parce que moi je le trouve très utile et très facile. En plus il ne faut pas un grand effort. Qu'est-ce que vous en pensez?

I find it helpful to translate the numbers of the number plates when we have a test on numbers. For our mid-semester listening comprehension test, we had to find several numbers (phone numbers etc.) and the others complained a lot. I suggested that they do the same, because I find it a very useful and rather easy way to proceed. It really does not require much effort when you approach it that way. What do you think?

Page 139

Journal pour la semaine dele 26-30 janvier (diary for the week of 26-30 January)
nous avons commencé d'étudier les règles de la correspondence français. Nous avons travaillé sur les lettres Administratif et Commerciale. J'apprécie cette exercise parce qu'il existe deux avantages: on apprend comment on peut réussir une correspondance en français et on peut utiliser les mêmes idées en anglais.

we have begun to study the rules on formal letter writing in French. We have worked on business and other types of formal correspondence. I like this exercise because there are 2 advantages: we learn how it works in French and we can apply that knowledge to our English letter writing.

References

Abraham, R. G., and R. J. Vann. 1987. Strategies of two learners: A case study. In *Learner strategies in language learning*, eds. A. Wenden, and J. Rubin, 85-102. London: Prentice Hall.

Allwright, D., and K. M. Bailey. 1991. *Focus on the language classroom: An introduction to classroom research for language teachers*. Cambridge: Cambridge University Press.

Altman, H. B. 1970-1971. Individualized foreign language instruction: What does it mean? *Foreign Language Annals* 4:421-22.

———. 1972-1973. The three R's of individualization: Reeducation, responsibility, and relevance. *Foreign Language Annals* 6:206-13.

Aoki, N. 1999. Affect and the role of teachers in the development of learner autonomy. In *Affect in language learning*, ed. J. Arnold, 142-54. Cambridge: Cambridge University Press.

Aoki, N. and R. C. Smith. 1999. Learner autonomy in cultural context: The case of Japan. In *Learner autonomy in language learning: Defining the field and effecting change*, eds. S. Cotterall, and D. Crabbe, 19-27. Bayreuth Contributions to Glottodidactics, Vol 8. Frankfurt am Main: Peter Lang.

Arnold, J., ed. 1999. *Affect in language learning*. Cambridge: Cambridge University Press.

Arnold, J. and H. D. Brown. 1999. Introduction. A map of the terrain. In *Affect in language learning*, ed. J. Arnold, 1-24. Cambridge: Cambridge University Press.

Bacon, S. M., and M. D. Finnemann. 1990. A study of the attitudes, motives, and strategies of university foreign language students and their disposition to authentic oral and written input. *Modern Language Journal* 74:459-73.

———. 1992. Sex differences in self-reported beliefs about foreign language learning and authentic oral and written input. *Language Learning* 42:471-95

Bailey, K. M. 1983. Competitiveness and anxiety in adult second language learning: Looking at and through the diary studies. In *Classroom oriented research in second language acquisition*, eds. H. W. Seliger, and M. H. Long, 67-103. Rowley, MA: Newbury House.

———. 1990. The use of diary studies in teacher education programs. In *Second language teacher education*, eds. J. C. Richards, and D. Nunan, 215-26. Cambridge: Cambridge University Press.

Bailey, K. M., and D. Nunan, eds. 1996. *Voices from the language classroom: Qualitative research in second language education*. Cambridge: Cambridge University Press.

Bailey, K. M., and R. Oschner. 1983. A methodological review of the diary studies: Windmill tilting or social science? In *Studies in second language acquisition: Series on issues in second language research*, eds. K. M. Bailey, M. H. Long, and S. Peck, 188-98. Rowley, MA: Newbury House.

Bailly, S. 1993. La formation de conseiller. *Mélanges Pédagogiques* 22:63-83.

Barbot, M.-J. 1997. Cap sur l'autoformation: Multimédias, des outils à s'approprier. *Le Français dans le Monde,* July 1997, 54-63. Paris: Hachette.

Bauer, L., and P. Trudgill, eds. 1998. *Language Myths*. Harmondsworth: Penguin.

Beauvois, M. H. 1992. Computer-assisted classroom discussion in the foreign language classroom: Conversation in slow motion. *Foreign Language Annals* 25:455-64.

Benson, P. 1996. Concepts of autonomy in language learning. In *Taking control: Autonomy in language learning*, eds. R. Pemberton, et al., 27-34. Hong Kong: Hong Kong University Press.

———. 1997. The philosophy and politics of learner autonomy. In *Autonomy and independence in language learning*, eds. P. Benson, and P. Voller, 18-34. London: Longman.

———. 2001. *Teaching and researching autonomy in language learning*. Harlow: Longman.

———. 2002. Autonomy and communication. In *Learner autonomy 7: Challenges to research and practice,* eds. P. Benson, and S. Toogood, 10-28. Dublin: Authentik.

Benson, P., A. Chik, and H-Y. Lim. 2003. Becoming autonomous in an Asian context. Autonomy as a sociocultural process. In *Learner autonomy across cultures*, eds. D. Palfreyman, and R. C. Smith, 23-40. Basingstoke: Palgrave Macmillan.

Benson, P., and W. Lor. 1999. Conceptions of language and language learning. *System* 27:459-72.

Benson, P., and P. Voller, eds. 1997. *Autonomy and independence in language learning*. London: Longman.

————. 1997. Introduction: Autonomy and independence in language learning. In *Autonomy and independence in language learning*, eds. P. Benson, and P. Voller, 1-12. London: Longman.

Birchwood, K. 1982. Martinique, je t'aime. *St Joseph's Convent San Fernando, School Magazine* 1982, 14.

Bloomfield, L. 1933. *Language*. New York: McGraw-Hill.

Bogdan, R., and S. K. Biklen. 1998. *Qualitative research for education: An introduction to theory and methods*. 3rd ed. Needham Heights, MA: Allyn and Bacon.

Boud, D., ed. 1988. *Developing student autonomy in learning*. 2nd ed. London: Kogan Page.

————. 1988. Moving towards autonomy. In *Developing student autonomy in learning*. 2nd ed. Ed. D. Boud, 17-39. London: Kogan Page.

Bourne, C. 1993. Education for development: The challenge of the 21st century. *Caribbean Curriculum* 3 (2): 1-12.

Broady, E. 1996. Learner attitudes towards self-direction. In *Promoting learner autonomy in university language teaching*, eds. E. Broady, and M.-M. Kenning, 215-35. London: AFLS/CILT.

Broady, E., and M.-M. Kenning, eds. 1996a. *Promoting learner autonomy in university language teaching*. London: AFLS/CILT.

————. 1996b. Learner autonomy: An introduction to the issues. In *Promoting learner autonomy in university language teaching*, eds. E. Broady, and M.-M. Kenning, 9-21. London: AFLS/CILT.

Brown, A. 1994. Processes to support the use of information technology to enhance learning. *Computers and Education* 22:145-53.

Brown, H. D. 1987. *Principles of language learning and teaching*. 2nd ed. Englewood Cliffs, NJ: Prentice Hall.

Bushell, A. 1995. Language learning and the 'weak' advanced student. *Language Learning Journal* 12:38-39.

Cameron, L. 1990. Staying within the script: Personality and self-directed learning. *System* 18:65-75.

Cameron, L., and G. Low, eds. 1999. *Researching and applying metaphor*. Cambridge: Cambridge University Press.

Canale, M., and M. Swain. 1980. Theoretical bases of communicative approaches to second language teaching and testing. *Applied Linguistics* 1:1-47.

Candlin, C. N. 1991. General Editor's Preface. In *Learning strategies for learner autonomy*, by A. Wenden, xi-xii. Englewood Cliffs: Prentice Hall.

Candy, P. 1988. On the attainment of subject-matter autonomy. In *Developing student autonomy in learning.* 2nd ed. Ed. D. Boud, 59-76. London: Kogan Page.

Caribbean Examinations Council. 1995. Report on candidates' work in the secondary education certificate examination. St. Michael, Barbados: Caribbean Examinations Council.

————. 1999. Report on candidates' work in the secondary education certificate examination. St. Michael, Barbados: Caribbean Examinations Council.

Carrington, L. D., C. B. Borely, and H. E. Knight. 1974. Linguistic exposure of Trinidadian children. *Caribbean Journal of Education* 1:12-24.

Carroll, J. B. 1967-1968. Foreign language proficiency levels attained by language majors near graduation from college. *Foreign Language Annals* 1:131-51.

Carter, B. 1998. Fostering learner autonomy among mature language learners. *Caribbean Journal of Education* 20:102-16.

Carter, B. 2004. A call to action: Will French survive this time in the school curriculum in Trinidad and Tobago? *Caribbean Curriculum* 11:71-84.

Child, D. 1994. *Psychology and the teacher.* 5th ed. London: Cassell.

Chomsky, N. 1982. *Some concepts and consequences of the theory of government and binding.* Massachusetts: MIT Press.

Cohen, A., and C. Hosenfeld. 1981. Some uses of mentalistic data in second language research. *Language Learning* 31:285-313.

Cook, V. 1993. *Linguistics and second language acquisition.* London: Macmillan.

Corder, S. P. 1973. *Introducing applied linguistics.* Harmondsworth: Penguin.

Cornwall, M. 1988. Putting it into practice: Promoting independent learning in a traditional institution. In *Developing student autonomy in learning.* 2nd ed. Ed. David Boud, 242-57. London: Kogan Page.

Cortazzi, M., and L. Jin. 1999. Bridges to learning: Metaphors of teaching, learning and language. In *Researching and applying metaphor*, eds. L. Cameron, and G. Low, 149-76. Cambridge: Cambridge University Press.

Cotterall, S. 1995. Readiness for autonomy: Investigating learner beliefs. *System* 23:195-205.

————. 1999. Key variables in language learning: What do learners believe about them? *System* 27:493-513.

Cotterall, S., and D. Crabbe. 1999. *Learner autonomy in language learning: Defining the field and effecting change*. Bayreuth Contributions to Glottodidactics, Vol 8. Frankfurt am Main: Peter Lang.

Crabbe, D., A. Hoffmann, and S. Cotterall. 2001. Examining the discourse of learner advisory sessions. *AILA Review* 15:2-15.

Crandall, J. A. 1999. Cooperative language learning and affective factors. In *Affect in language learning*, ed. J. Arnold, 226-45. Cambridge: Cambridge University Press.

Cranton, P. 1994. *Understanding and promoting transformative learning: A guide for educators of adults*. The Jossey-Bass Higher and Adult Education Series. San Francisco: Jossey-Bass Publishers.

Creswell, J. W. 1994. *Research design: Qualitative and quantitative approaches*. Thousand Oaks, CA: Sage Publications.

Dam, L. 1995. *Learner autonomy 3: From theory to classroom practice*. Dublin: Authentik.

———. 2003. Developing learner autonomy: The teacher's responsibility. In *Learner autonomy in the foreign language classroom: Teacher, learner, curriculum and assessment*, eds. D. Little, J. Ridley, and E. Ushioda, 135-46. Dublin: Authentik.

Dam, L., and L. Legenhausen. 1996. The acquisition of vocabulary in an autonomous learning environment - The first months of beginning English. In *Taking control: Autonomy in language learning*, eds. R. Pemberton, et al., 265-80. Hong Kong: Hong Kong University Press.

Davis, K. A. 1995. Qualitative theory and methods in applied linguistic research. *TESOL Quarterly* 29:427-53.

Deci, E. L., and R. M. Ryan. 1985. *Intrinsic motivation and self-determination in human behaviour*. New York: Plenum Press.

Dickinson, L. 1995. Autonomy and motivation: A literature review. Special Issue. *System* 23:165-74.

———. 1997. Telling people to be autonomous (or directing them to be self-directed). AUTO-L@ycvax.york.cuny.edu. November 7, 1997.

———. 1999. E-Colloquium on self-access language learning (SALL). AUTO-L@ycvax.york.cuny.edu. June 16, 1999.

Dickinson, L., and D. Carver. 1980. Learning how to learn: Steps towards self-direction in foreign language learning in schools. *ELT Journal* 35:1-7.

Dickson, M. 1996. Promoting autonomy through a listening curriculum. In *Promoting learner autonomy in university language teaching*, eds. E. Broady, and M. -M. Kenning, 61-80. London: AFLS/CILT.

Disick, R. S. 1973. Individualized instruction: Promise versus reality. *Modern Language Journal* 57:248-50.

Dörnyei, Z., and A. Malderez. 1999. The role of group dynamics in foreign language learning and teaching. In *Affect in language learning*, ed. J. Arnold, 155-69. Cambridge: Cambridge University Press.

Doughty, C., and J. Williams, eds. 1998. *Focus on form in classroom second language acquisition*. Cambridge: Cambridge University Press.

Ehrman, M. 1998. The learning alliance: Conscious and unconscious aspects of the second language teacher's role. *System* 26:93-106.

Ehrman, M., and R. L. Oxford. 1989. Effects of sex differences, career choice, and psychological type on adult language learning strategies. *Modern Language Journal* 73:1-13.

Ellis, G., and B. Sinclair. 1989. *Learning to learn English: A course in learner training*. Cambridge: Cambridge University Press.

Ellis, R. 1999. A metaphorical analysis of learner beliefs. Paper presented at the symposium on learner beliefs about language learning, 12th World Congress of Applied Linguistics, AILA 99: Waseda University, Tokyo, Japan, August 1-6, 1999.

Erickson, F. 1986. Qualitative methods in research on teaching. In *Handbook of research on teaching*. 3rd ed. Ed. M. C. Wittrock, 119-61. New York: Macmillan.

Esch, E. 1996. Promoting learner autonomy: Criteria for the selection of appropriate methods. In *Taking control: Autonomy in language learning*, eds. R. Pemberton, et al., 35-48. Hong Kong: Hong Kong University Press.

———. 1997. Learner training for autonomous language learning. In *Autonomy and independence in language learning*, eds. P. Benson, and P. Voller, 164-76. London: Longman.

Farnes, N. 1975. Student-centred learning. *Teaching at a Distance* 3:2-6.

Fernández-Toro, M., and F. R. Jones. 1996. Going solo: Learners' experiences of self-instruction and self-instruction training. In *Promoting learner autonomy in university language teaching*, eds. E. Broady, and M. -M. Kenning, 185-214. London: AFLS/CILT.

Flavell, J. H. 1979. Metacognition and cognitive monitoring: A new area of cognitive-developmental inquiry. *American Psychologist* 34:906-11.

Freed, B., ed. 1991. *Foreign language acquisition research and the classroom*. Lexington, MA: D. C. Heath and Co.

Freire, P. 1972. *Pedagogy of the oppressed.* Harmondsworth: Penguin.

Fry, J. 1988. Diary studies in classroom SLA research: Problems and prospects. *JALT Journal* 9:158-67.

Gall, M. D., W. R. Borg, and J. P. Gall. 1996. *Educational research: An introduction.* 6th ed. White Plains, NY: Longman.

Gamble, W. H. 1866. Trinidad: Historical and descriptive. London: Yates and Alexander. Quoted in L. D. Carrington, C. B. Borely, and H. E. Knight. 1974. Linguistic exposure of Trinidadian children. *Caribbean Journal of Education* 1:12-24.

Gardner, H. 1993. *Multiple intelligences: The theory in practice.* New York: Basic Books.

Gaspar, C. 1998. Situating French language teaching and learning in the age of the Internet. *The French Review* 72:69-80.

Gass, S. M. and S. S. Magnan. 1993. Second-language production: SLA research in speaking and writing. In *Research in language learning principles, processes, and prospects*, ed. A. Omaggio Hadley, 156-97. Lincolnwood: National Textbook Co.

Grabe, W. 1991. Current developments in second language reading research. *TESOL Quarterly* 25:375-406.

Greaney, V., and T. Kellaghan. 1995. Equity issues in public examinations in developing countries. World Bank technical Paper 272. Asia Technical Series. Washington, D C: The World Bank.

Gremmo, M.-J. 1993. Conseiller n'est pas enseigner: Le rôle du conseiller dans l'entretien de conseil. *Mélanges Pédagogiques* 22:33-61.

Gremmo, M.-J., and P. Riley. 1995. Autonomy, self-direction and self-access in language teaching and learning: The history of an idea. *System* 23:151-64.

Grotjahn, R. 1991. The research programme subjective theories. A new approach in second language research. *Studies in Second Language Acquisition* 13:187-214.

Hammond, N., N. Gardner, S. Heath, M. Kibby, T. Mayes, R. McAleese, C. Mullings, A Trapp. 1992. Blocks to the effective use of information technology in higher education. *Computers and Education* 18:155-62.

Hanzeli, V. E., and F. W. D. Love. 1971-1972. From individualized instruction to individualized learning. *Foreign Language Annals* 5:321-30.

Henner-Stanchina, C. 1986-1987. Autonomy as metacognitive awareness: Suggestions for training self-monitoring of listening comprehension. *Mélanges Pédagogiques* 1986-1987, 69-102.

Higgs, J. 1988. Planning learning experiences to promote autonomous learning. In *Developing student autonomy in learning.* 2nd ed. Ed. D. Boud, 40-58. London: Kogan Page.

Hilleson, M. 1996. I want to talk with them, but I don't want them to hear: An introspective study of second language anxiety in an English-medium school. In *Voices from the language classroom*, eds. K. M. Bailey, and D. Nunan, 248-75. Cambridge: Cambridge University Press.

Hoffmann, A. 1999. Discourse surrounding goals in an undergraduate ESL writing course. In *Learner autonomy in language learning: Defining the field and effecting change*, eds. S. Cotterall, and D. Crabbe, 127-38. Bayreuth Contributions to Glottodidactics, Vol 8. Frankfurt am Main: Peter Lang.

Holec, H. 1981. *Autonomy and foreign language learning.* Oxford: Pergamon Press. (First published 1979, Strasbourg: Council of Europe.)

————. 1987. The learner as manager: Managing learning or managing to learn? In *Learner strategies in language learning*, eds. A. Wenden, and J. Rubin, 145-56. London: Prentice Hall.

————. 1990. Qu'est-ce qu'apprendre à apprendre. *Mélanges Pédagogiques* 1990, 75-87.

————. 1996. Self-directed learning: An alternative form of training. *Language Teaching* 29:89-93.

————. 1997. Main features of the educational approach adopted. In *Learner autonomy in modern languages: Research and development*, eds. H. Holec, and I. Huttunen, 23-32. Strasbourg: Council of Europe.

Holec, H., and I. Huttunen, eds. 1997. *Learner autonomy in modern languages: Research and development.* Strasbourg: Council of Europe.

Holliday, A. 1994. *Appropriate methodology and social context.* Cambridge: Cambridge University Press.

————. 2003. Social autonomy: Addressing the dangers of culturism in TESOL. In *Learner autonomy across cultures*, eds. D. Palfreyman, and R. C. Smith, 110-26. Basingstoke: Palgrave Macmillan.

Hornberger, N. H. 1994. Ethnography. In Alternatives in TESOL research: Descriptive, interpretive, and ideological orientations, ed. A. Cumming, 688-90. *TESOL Quarterly* 28: 673-703.

Horwitz, E. K. 1987. Surveying student beliefs about language learning. In *Learner strategies in language learning*, eds. A. Wenden, and J. Rubin, 119-29. London: Prentice Hall.

————. 1988. The beliefs about language learning of beginning university foreign language students. *Modern Language Journal* 72: 283-94.
————. 1999. Cultural and situational influences on foreign language learners' beliefs about language learning: A review of BALLI studies. *System* 27:557-76.

Hoven, D. 1992. CALL in a language learning environment. *CÆLL Journal* 3.2: 19-27.

Huttunen, I. 1996. Learning to learn: An overview. *Language Teaching* 29:86-89.

Jehng, J-C. J., S. C. Johnson, and R. C. Anderson. 1993. Schooling and students' epistemological beliefs about learning. *Contemporary Educational Psychology* 18:23-35.

John, D. G. 1990. Language isn't enough: Language students and careers. *Canadian Modern Language Review* 46:514-26.

Johnson, D. M., and M. Saville-Troike. 1992. Validity and reliability in qualitative research on second language acquisition and teaching: Two researchers comment...*TESOL Quarterly* 26:602-05.

Katz, A. 1996. Teaching style: A way to understand instruction in language classrooms. In *Voices from the language classroom: Qualitative research in second language education*, eds. K. M. Bailey, and D. Nunan, 57-87. Cambridge: Cambridge University Press.

Kelly, R. 1996. Language counselling for learner autonomy: The skilled helper in self-access language learning. In *Taking control: Autonomy in language learning*, eds. R. Pemberton, et al., 93-113. Hong Kong: Hong Kong University Press.

Kenny, B. 1993. For more autonomy. *System* 21:431-42.

Kern, R. G. 1995. Students' and teachers' beliefs about language learning. *Foreign Language Annals* 28:71-92.

Knapper, C. 1988. Technology and lifelong learning. In *Developing student autonomy in learning.* 2nd ed. Ed., D. Boud, 91-106. London: Kogan Page.

Knapper, C., and A. J. Cropley. 1991. *Lifelong learning in higher education.* London: Kogan Page.

Knowles, M. 1988. Preface. In *Developing student autonomy in learning.* 2nd ed. Ed., D. Boud, 4-6. London: Kogan Page.

Koenig, E. L., E. Chia, and J. Povey.1983. *A sociolinguistic profile of urban centers in Cameroon.* Kinsey Hall, University of California Los Angeles: Crossroads Press.

Kohonen, V. 1992. Experiential language learning: Second language learning as cooperative learner education. In *Collaborative language learning and teaching*, ed. D. Nunan, 14-39. Cambridge: Cambridge University Press.

———. 1999. Authentic assessment in affective foreign language education. In *Affect in language learning*, ed. J. Arnold, 279-94. Cambridge: Cambridge University Press.

Krashen, S. D. 1981. *Second language acquisition and second language learning.* Oxford: Pergamon Press.

————. 1982. *Principles and practice in second language acquisition.* Oxford: Pergamon Press.

Lakoff, G., and M. Johnson. 1980. *Metaphors we live by.* Chicago, IL: Chicago University Press.

Lambert, N. M., and B. L. McCombs. 1998. Introduction: Learner-centered schools and classrooms as a direction for school reform. In *How students learn: Reforming schools through learner-centered education,* eds. N. M. Lambert, and B. L. McCombs, 1-22. Washington, DC: American Psychological Association.

LeCompte, M. D., J. Preissle, and R. Tesch. 1993. *Ethnography and qualitative design in educational research.* 2nd ed. San Diego, CA: Academic Press.

Lincoln, Y. S., and E. G. Guba. 1985. *Naturalistic inquiry.* Beverly Hills, CA: Sage.

Little, D. 1991. *Learner autonomy 1: Definitions, issues and problems.* Dublin: Authentik.

————. 1996. Freedom to learn and compulsion to interact: Promoting learner autonomy through the use of information systems and information technologies. In *Taking control: Autonomy in language learning,* eds. R. Pemberton, et al., 203-18. Hong Kong: Hong Kong University Press.

————. 1999. Learner autonomy is more than a Western cultural construct. In *Learner autonomy in language learning: Defining the field and effecting change,* eds. S. Cotterall, and D. Crabbe, 11-18. Bayreuth Contributions to Glottodidactics, Vol 8. Frankfurt am Main: Peter Lang.

Littlewood, W. T. 1999. Defining and developing autonomy in East Asian contexts. *Applied Linguistics* 20:71-94.

Lodge, A. 2000. Higher education. In *New perspectives on teaching and learning modern languages,* ed. S. Green, 105-23. Clevedon: Multilingual Matters.

Long, M. H. 1980. Inside the "black box": Methodological issues in classroom research on language learning. *Language Learning* 30:1-42.

Maley, A. 1984. I've got religion: Evangelism in language teaching. In *Initiatives in communicative language teaching: A book of readings,* eds. S. J. Savignon, and M. S. Berns, 79-86. New York: Addison-Wesley.

Marsh, D. 1997. Computer conferencing: Taking the loneliness out of independent learning. *Language Learning Journal* 15:21-25.

Matsumoto, K. 1987. Diary studies of second language acquisition: A critical overview. *JALT Journal* 9:17-34.

————. 1994. Introspection, verbal reports and second language learning strategy research. *Canadian Modern Language Review* 50:363-86.

———. 1996. Helping L2 learners reflect on classroom learning. *ELT Journal* 50:143-49.

McIntyre, A. 1995. Feature address. Foreign language education in a changing economy. In *Proceedings of the third Caribbean language conference. towards the global economy: Challenges and options for foreign language educators in the hemisphere.* Port of Spain, Trinidad and Tobago: NIHERST.11-15.

McLaren, P. 1999. A pedagogy of possibility: Reflecting upon Paulo Freire's politics of education. *Educational Researcher* 28.2: 49-56.

Merriam, S. B. 1988. Case study research in education: A qualitative approach. San Francisco: Jossey-Bass.

Miller, E. 1998. Education for all in the Caribbean: A mid-decade review of issues. *Caribbean Journal of Education* 19:1-35.

Miller, L. and R. B. Ginsberg. 1995. Folklinguistic theories of language learning. In *Second language acquisition in a study abroad context*, ed. B. F. Freed, 293-315. Amsterdam: John Benjamins.

Morgan, C. 1993. Attitude change and foreign language culture learning. *Language Teaching* 26:63-75.

Morrison, B. 2002. The troubling process of mapping and evaluating a self-access language learning centre. In *Learner autonomy 7: Challenges to research and practice*, eds. P. Benson, and S. Toogood, 71-85. Dublin: Authentik.

Moskowitz, G. 1978. *Caring and sharing in the foreign language class: A sourcebook on humanistic techniques.* Boston, MA: Heinle & Heinle.

———. 1999. Enhancing personal development: Humanistic activities at work. In *Affect in language learning*, ed. J. Arnold, 177-93. Cambridge: Cambridge University Press.

Moulden, H. 1980. Extending SDL in an engineering college: Experiment year two. *Mélanges Pédagogiques* 1980, 81-116.

———. 1990. Assessing the self-directedness of foreign language learners. *Mélanges Pédagogiques* 1990, 107-19.

———. 1993. The learner trainer's labours lost? *Mélanges Pédagogiques* 21:111-20.

Mozzon-McPherson, M. 2001. Language advising: Towards a new discursive world? In *Beyond language teaching towards language advising*, eds. M. Mozzon-McPherson, and R. Vismans, 2-17. London: Centre for Information on Language Teaching and Research.

Mozzon-McPherson, M., and R. Vismans, eds. 2001. *Beyond language teaching towards language advising.* London: Centre for Information on Language Teaching and Research.

Myers, G. E., and M. T. Myers. 1980. *The dynamics of human communication: A laboratory approach.* 3rd ed. New York: McGraw Hill.

Naiman, N., M. Fröhlich, H.H. Stern, and A. Todesco. 1978. *The good language learner.* Toronto: Ontario Institute for Studies in Education.

Nunan, D. 1988. *The learner-centred curriculum: A study in second language teaching.* Cambridge: Cambridge University Press.

———. 1996. Towards autonomous learning: Some theoretical, empirical and practical issues. In *Taking control: Autonomy in language learning,* eds. R. Pemberton, et al., 13-26. Hong Kong: Hong Kong University Press.

O'Malley, J. M., and A. U. Chamot. 1990. *Learning strategies in second language acquisition.* Cambridge: Cambridge University Press.

Omaggio Hadley, A. 1993. *Teaching language in context.* 2nd ed. Boston: Heinle & Heinle.

Oxford, R. L. 1990. *Language learning strategies: What every teacher should know.* New York: Newbury House.

———. 2003. Toward a more systematic model of L2 learner autonomy. In *Learner autonomy across cultures,* eds. D. Palfreyman, and R. C. Smith, 75-91. Basingstoke: Palgrave Macmillan.

Oxford, R. L., S. Tomlinson, A. Barcelos, C. Harrington, R. Z. Lavine, A. Saleh, A. Longhini. 1998. Clashing metaphors about classroom teachers: Toward a systematic typology for the language teaching field. *System* 26:3-50.

Pajares, M. F. 1992. Teachers' beliefs and educational research: Cleaning up a messy construct. *Review of Educational Research* 62:307-32.

Palfreyman, D. 2003. Introduction: Culture and learner autonomy. In *Learner autonomy across cultures,* eds. D. Palfreyman, and R. C. Smith, 1-19. Basingstoke: Palgrave Macmillan.

Palfreyman, D., and R. C. Smith, eds. 2003. *Learner autonomy across cultures.* Basingstoke: Palgrave Macmillan.

Palmer, C. H. 1992. Diaries for self-assessment and INSET evaluation. *European Journal of Teacher Education* 15:227-38.

Park, G. P. 1995. Language learning strategies and beliefs about language learning of university students learning English in Korea. PhD diss., The University of Texas at Austin.

Parris, S. G. 1998. Why learner-centered assessment is better than high-stakes testing. In *How students learn: Reforming schools through learner-centered education,* eds. N. M. Lambert, and B. L. McCombs, 189-209. Washington, DC: American Psychological Association.

Pemberton, R., E. S. L. Li , W. W. F. Or, and H. D. Pierson, eds. 1996. *Taking control: Autonomy in language learning*. Hong Kong: Hong Kong University Press.

Pemberton, R., S. Toogood, S. Ho, and J. Lam. 2001.Approaches to advising for self-directed learning. *AILA Review* 15:16-25.

Pennycook, A. 1990. Critical pedagogy and second language education. *System* 18:303-14.

———. 1997. Cultural alternatives and autonomy. In *Autonomy and independence in language learning*, eds. P. Benson, and P. Voller, 35-53. London: Longman.

Peshkin, A. 1993. The goodness of qualitative research. *Educational Researcher* 22.2: 23-29.

Phillips, D., and V. Stencel. 1983. *The second foreign language. Past development, current trends, future prospects*. London: Hodder and Stoughton.

Phillips, J. 1976. Review article: Individualization. *Foreign Language Annals* 9:17-21.

Pierson, H. D. 1996. Learner culture and learner autonomy in the Hong Kong Chinese context. In *Taking Control: Autonomy in language learning*, eds. R. Pemberton, et al., 49-58. Hong Kong: Hong Kong University Press.

Porter, P. A., L. M. Goldstein, J. Leatherman, and S. Conrad. 1990. An ongoing dialogue: Learning logs for teaching preparation. In *Second language teacher education*, eds. J. C. Richards, and D. Nunan, 227-40. Cambridge: Cambridge University Press.

Press, M. -C. 1996. Ethnicity and the autonomous language learner: Different beliefs and learning strategies? In *Promoting learner autonomy in university language teaching*, eds. E. Broady, and M. -M. Kenning, 237-59. London: AFLS/CILT.

Ramsden, P. 1979. Student learning and perceptions of the academic environment. *Higher Education* 8:411-27.

Rees-Miller, J. 1993. A critical appraisal of learner training: Theoretical bases and teaching implications. *TESOL Quarterly* 27:679-89.

Rézeau, J. 1999. Re: learner beliefs. Online posting. AUTO-L@ycvax.york.cuny.edu. November 21, 1999.

Richards, J. C., and C. Lockhart. 1994. *Reflective teaching in second language classrooms*. Cambridge: Cambridge University Press.

Richards, J. C., and D. Nunan, eds. 1990. *Second language teacher education*. Cambridge: Cambridge University Press.

Riley, P. 1989. Learner's representations of language and language learning. *Mélanges Pédagogiques* 1989, 65-72.

————. 1997a. "'Bats' and 'balls': Beliefs about talk and beliefs about language learning. *Mélanges Pédagogiques* 23:125-53.

————. 1997b. The guru and the conjurer: Aspects of counselling for self-access. In *Autonomy and independence in language learning*, eds. P. Benson, and P. Voller, 114-31. London: Longman.

————.2003. Self-access as access to 'self': Cultural variation in the notions of self and personhood. In *Learner autonomy across cultures*, eds. D. Palfreyman, and R. C. Smith, 92-109. Basingstoke: Palgrave Macmillan.

Robertson, I. 1996. Language education policy: Towards a rational approach for Caribbean states. In *Caribbean language issues old and new*, ed. P. Christie, 112-19. Kingston, Jamaica: The University of the West Indies Press.

Rubin, J. 1994. A review of second language listening comprehension research. *Modern Language Journal* 78:199-221.

Sakui, K., and S. J. Gaies. 1999. Investigating Japanese learners' beliefs about language learning. *System* 27:473-92.

Saussure, F. de. 1965. *Cours de linguistique générale*. eds. C. Bally, A. Sechehaye, and A. Riedlinger. 3rd ed. Paris: Payot.

Schaefer Fu, G. 1999. Guidelines for productive language counseling-tools for implementing autonomy. In *Learner autonomy in language learning: Defining the field and effecting change*, eds. S. Cotterall, D. Crabbe, 105-10. Bayreuth Contributions to Glottodidactics, Vol 8. Frankfurt am Main: Peter Lang.

Scharle, Á., and A. Szabó. 2000. Learner autonomy: *A guide to developing learner responsibility*. Cambridge: Cambridge University Press.

Schumann, F. M. 1980. Diary of a language learner: A further analysis. In *Research in second language acquisition: Selected papers of the Los Angeles second language research forum*, eds. R. C. Scarcella and S. D. Krashen, 51-57. Rowley, MA: Newbury House.

Schumann, F. M., and J. H. Schumann. 1977. Diary of a language learner: An introspective study of second language learning. In *On TESOL '77: Teaching and learning English as a second language: Trends in research and practice*, eds. H. D. Brown, C. A. Yorio, and R. H. Crymes, 241-48. Washington, DC: TESOL.

Scovel, T. 1978. The effect of affect on foreign language learning: A review of the anxiety research. *Language Learning* 28:129-42.

Sealey, W. 1983. *A sociolinguistic profile of Trinidad*. Mimeo. Caribbean Lexicography Project, Port of Spain, Trinidad and Tobago.

Seelye, H. N. 1984. *Teaching culture: Strategies for intercultural communication*. Lincolnwood, IL: National Textbook Company.

Serra, O. 2000. Integrating a self-access system in a language learning institution: A model for implementation. *Links & Letters* 7:95-109.

Seliger, H. W., and E. Shohamy. 1989. Second language research methods. Oxford: Oxford University Press.

Sheerin, S. 1997. An exploration of the relationship between self-access and independent learning. In *Autonomy and independence in language learning*, eds. P. Benson, and P. Voller, 54-65. London: Longman.

Sinclair, B. 1996. Materials design for the promotion of learner autonomy: How explicit is 'explicit'? In *Taking control: Autonomy in language learning*, eds. R. Pemberton, et al., 149-65. Hong Kong: Hong Kong University Press.

———. 1999. E-Roundtable on beliefs/knowledge. Online posting. AUTO-L@ycvax.york.cuny.edu. November 5, 1999.

Sinclair, B., and G. Ellis. 1992. Survey review: Learner training in EFL course books. *ELT Journal* 46:209-25.

Skehan, P. 1989. *Individual differences in second language learning*. London: Arnold.

———. 1991. Individual differences in second language learning. *Studies in Second Language Acquisition* 13:275-98.

Skinner, B. F. 1957. *Verbal behavior*. New York: Appleton-Century-Crofts.

Smith, R. C. 2003. Pedagogy for autonomy as (becoming-) appropriate methodology. In *Learner autonomy across cultures*, eds. D. Palfreyman, and R. C. Smith, 129-46. Basingstoke: Palgrave Macmillan.

Snow, C. E and Hoefnagel-Höhle, M. 1978. Age differences in second language acquisition. In *Second language acquisition: A book of readings*, ed. E. Hatch, 333-44. Rowley, MA: Newbury.

Solomon, D. 1993. *The speech of Trinidad*. St. Augustine, Trinidad and Tobago: School of Continuing Studies, University of the West Indies.

Spack, R., and C. Sadow. 1983. Student-teacher working journals in ESL freshman composition. *TESOL Quarterly* 17:575-93.

Sridhar, S. N. 1994. A reality check for SLA theories. *TESOL Quarterly* 28:800-05.

Stern, H. H. 1983. *Fundamental concepts of language teaching*. Oxford: Oxford University Press.

Stevick, E. W. 1990. *Humanism in language teaching: A critical perspective*. Oxford: Oxford University Press.

Swaffar, J. and S. Bacon. 1993. Reading and listening comprehension: Perspectives on research and implications for practice. In *Research in language learning principles, processes, and prospects*, ed. A. Omaggio Hadley, 124-55. Lincolnwood, IL: National Textbook Co.

Swain, Merrill. Mediating second language learning through collaborative dialogue. Plenary address at 12th World Congress of Applied Linguistics, AILA 99: Waseda University, Tokyo, Japan, August 1-6, 1999.

Thomson, C. K. 1992. Learner-centered tasks in the foreign language classroom. *Foreign Language Annals* 25:523-31.

———. 1996. Self-assessment in self-directed learning: Issues of learner diversity. In *Taking control: Autonomy in language learning*, eds. R. Pemberton, et al., 77-91. Hong Kong: Hong Kong University Press.

Toogood, S., and R. Pemberton. 2002. Integrating self-directed learning into the curriculum: A case study. In *Learner autonomy 7: Challenges to research and practice*, eds. P. Benson, and S. Toogood, 86-110. Dublin: Authentik.

Trim, J. 1996. Modern languages in the Council of Europe. *Language Teaching* 29:81-85.

Trim, J. L. M. 1997. Preface. In *Learner autonomy in modern languages. Research and development*, eds. H. Holec, and I. Huttunen, v-vi. Strasbourg: Council of Europe.

Trinidad and Tobago Central Statistical Office 1993. Annual statistical digest. Vol. 1992. Port of Spain, Trinidad and Tobago: Government Printery.

Trinidad and Tobago Central Statistical Office 1989. Examination results for secondary and tertiary 1986-1988. Port of Spain, Trinidad and Tobago: Government Printery.

Tudor, I. 1996. *Learner-centredness as language education*. Cambridge: Cambridge University Press.

Underhill, A. 1999. Facilitation in language teaching. In *Affect in language learning*, ed. J. Arnold, 125-41. Cambridge: Cambridge University Press.

Van Ek, J. A. 1975. *The threshold level*. Strasbourg: Council of Europe.

Van Lier, Leo. 1996. *Interaction in the language curriculum*. New York: Longman.

Victori, M. 1999. An analysis of writing knowledge in EFL composing: A case study of two effective and two less effective writers. *System* 27:537-55.

———. 1999. Methodological issues in research on learners' beliefs about language learning. Paper presented at the symposium on learner beliefs about language learning. 12th World Congress of Applied Linguistics, AILA 99: Waseda University, Tokyo, Japan, August 1-6, 1999.

————. 2002. Views on self-access language learning: A talk with Leslie Dickinson, Lindsay Miller, Gill Sturtridge and Radha Ravindran. *Links & Letters* 7:165-80.

Victori, M, and W. Lockhart. 1995. Enhancing metacognition in self-directed language learning. *System* 23:223-34.

Voller, P. 1997. Does the teacher have a role in autonomous language learning? In *Autonomy and independence in language learning*, eds. P. Benson, and P. Voller, 98-113. London: Longman.

Voller, P., E. Martyn, and V. Pickard. 1999. One-to-one counseling for autonomous learning in a self-access centre: Final report on an action learning project. In *Learner autonomy in language learning: Defining the field and effecting change*, eds. S. Cotterall, and D. Crabbe, 111-26. Bayreuth Contributions to Glottodidactics, Vol 8. Frankfurt am Main: Peter Lang.

Wang, M.C., and A.S. Palincsar. 1989. Teaching students to assume an active role in their learning. In Knowledge base for the beginning teacher. Oxford: Pergamon Press. Quoted in L. Dickinson. 1995. Autonomy and motivation: A literature review. Special Issue. *System* 23:165-74.

Warschauer, M. 1997. Computer-mediated collaborative learning: Theory and practice. *Modern Language Journal* 81:470-81.

Watkins, D. 1996. Learning theories and approaches to research: A cross-cultural perspective. In *The Chinese learner: Cultural, psychological and contextual influences*, eds. D. A Watkins, and J. B. Biggs, 3-24. Melbourne: Comparative Education Research Centre. Hong Kong/Australian Council for Educational Research.

Wenden, A. 1986. What do second-language learners know about their language learning? A second look at retrospective accounts. *Applied Linguistics* 7:186-201.

————. 1991. *Learner strategies for learner autonomy*. London: Prentice Hall.

————. 1998. Metacognitive knowledge and language learning. *Applied Linguistics* 19:515-37.

————. 1999. Learner autonomy in language learning: Retrospect and prospect. Plenary address at 12th World Congress of Applied Linguistics, AILA 99: Waseda University, Tokyo, Japan, August 1-6, 1999.

————. 1999. E-Roundtable on beliefs/knowledge. Online posting. AUTO-L@ycvax.york.cuny.edu. November 9,1999.

Wenden, A., and J. Rubin, eds. 1987. *Learner strategies in language learning*. London: Prentice Hall.

Whalen, K., M. de Bie, L. Morrison, and D. Beausoleil. 1994. Peer-pairing: The first steps of an enquiry into the processes of teaching and learning in the second language classroom. *Canadian Modern Language Review* 50:558-82.

White, C. 1999. Expectations and emergent beliefs of self-instructed language learners. *System* 27:443-57.

Wilkins, D. A. 1974. *Second language learning and teaching.* London: Edward Arnold.

Wittrock, M. C. 1986. Students' thought processes. In *Handbook of research on teaching.* 3rd ed. Ed., M. C. Wittrock, 297-314. New York: Macmillan.

Wolfe, D. 1993. Reflections on the use of technology in my language career. *Canadian Modern Language Review* 50:178-83.

Wright, T. 1987. *Roles of teachers and learners.* Oxford: Oxford University Press.

———. 1990. Understanding classroom role relationships. In *Second language teacher education,* eds. J. C. Richards, and D. Nunan, 82-97. Cambridge: Cambridge University Press.

Yang, N. -D. 1992. Second language learners' beliefs about language learning and their use of learning strategies: A study of college students of English in Taiwan. PhD diss., The University of Texas at Austin.

———. 1999. The relationship between EFL learners' beliefs and learning strategy use. *System* 27:515-35.

Yetming, G. 1995. Closing address. The business of language: A banker's view. Proceedings of the third Caribbean language conference. Towards the global economy:Cchallenges and options for foreign language educators in the hemisphere. Port of Spain, Trinidad and Tobago: NIHERST. 167-72.

Index